KU-307-358

6/08

THE WORKS OF
WILLIAM
SHAKESPEARE

VOLUME THREE

THE SHAKESPEARE MEMORIAL THEATRE

Stratford-on-Avon

THE WORKS OF WILLIAM SHAKESPEARE

VOLUME THREE

King Henry IV: First Part
King Henry IV: Second Part
The Life of King Henry V
King Henry VI: First Part

THE PEEBLES CLASSIC LIBRARY

SANDY LESBERG, *Editor*

All Rights Reserved
ISBN 0-85690-041-9

Published by Peebles Press International
U.S.A.: 10 Columbus Circle, New York, NY 10019
U.K.: 12 Thayer Street, London W1M 5LD

Distributed by WHS Distributors

PRINTED AND BOUND IN THE U.S.A.

CONTENTS

KING HENRY THE FOURTH
FIRST PART

DRAMATIS PERSONÆ

KING HENRY THE FOURTH
HENRY, *Prince of Wales*
PRINCE JOHN OF LANCASTER } *sons to the King*
EARL OF WESTMORELAND
SIR WALTER BLUNT
THOMAS PERCY, *Earl of Worcester*
HENRY PERCY, *Earl of Northumberland*
HENRY PERCY, *surnamed* HOTSPUR, *his son*
EDMUND MORTIMER, *Earl of March*
SCROOP, *Archbishop of York*
ARCHIBALD, *Earl of Douglas*
OWEN GLENDOWER
SIR RICHARD VERNON
SIR JOHN FALSTAFF
SIR MICHAEL, *a friend to the Archbishop of York*
POINS
GADSHILL
PETO
BARDOLPH

LADY PERCY, *wife to Hotspur, and sister to Mortimer*
LADY MORTIMER, *daughter to Glendower, and wife to Mortimer*
MISTRESS QUICKLY, *hostess of a tavern in Eastcheap*

Lords, Officers, Sheriff, Vintner, Chamberlain, Drawers, Carriers, Travellers, and Attendants

SCENE—*England*

THE FIRST PART OF

KING HENRY IV

ACT ONE

Scene I.—London. A Room in the Palace

Enter King Henry, Westmoreland, Sir Walter Blunt, *and others*

K. Hen. So shaken as we are, so wan with care,
Find we a time for frighted peace to pant,
And breathe short-winded accents of new broils
To be commenced in strands afar remote.
No more the thirsty entrance of this soil
Shall daub her lips with her own children's blood;
No more shall trenching war channel her fields,
Nor bruise her flowerets with the arméd hoofs
Of hostile paces: those opposéd eyes,
Which, like the meteors of a troubled heaven,
All of one nature, of one substance bred,
Did lately meet in the intestine shock
And furious close of civil butchery,
Shall now, in mutual well-beseeming ranks,
March all one way, and be no more opposed
Against acquaintance, kindred, and allies:
The edge of war, like an ill-sheathed knife,
No more shall cut his master.   Therefore, friends,
As far as to the sepulchre of Christ,—
Whose soldier now, under whose blesséd cross
We are impressed and engaged to fight,—
Forthwith a power of English shall we levy;
Whose arms were moulded in their mothers' wombs
To chase these pagans in those holy fields
Over whose acres walked those blesséd feet
Which, fourteen hundred years ago were nailed
For our advantage on the bitter cross.
But this our purpose is a twelvemonth old,
And bootless 'tis to tell you we will go:
Therefore we meet not now —Then, let me hear
Of you, my gentle cousin Westmoreland,

15

What yesternight our council did decree,
In forwarding this dear expedience.
    West.   My liege, this haste was hot in question,
And many limits of the charge set down
But yesternight: when, all athwart, there came
A post from Wales loaden with heavy news;
Whose worst was,—that the noble Mortimer,
Leading the men of Herefordshire to fight
Against the irregular and wild Glendower,
Was by the rude hands of that Welshman taken,
A thousand of his people butcheréd;
Upon whose dead corpse there was such misuse,
Such beastly, shameless transformation,
By those Welshwomen done, as may not be
Without much shame re-told or spoken of.
    K. Hen.   It seems, then, that the tidings of this broil
Brake off our business for the Holy Land.
    West.   This, matched with other, did, my gracious lord;
For more uneven and unwelcome news
Came from the north, and thus it did import:
On Holy-rood day, the gallant Hotspur there,
Young Harry Percy, and brave Archibald,
That ever-valiant and appovéd Scot
At Holmedon met,
Where they did spend a sad and bloody hour,
As by discharge of their artillery,
And shape of likelihood, the news was told;
For he that brought them, in the very heat
And pride of their contention did take horse,
Uncertain of the issue any way.
    K. Hen.   Here is a dear and true-industrious friend,
Sir Walter Blunt, new lighted from his horse,
Stained with the variation of each soil
Betwixt that Holmedon and this seat of ours;
And he hath brought us smooth and welcome news.
The Earl of Douglas is discomfited;
Ten thousand bold Scots, two-and-twenty knights,
Balked in their own blood, did Sir Walter see
On Holmedon's plains: of prisoners, Hotspur took
Mordake the Earl of Fife, and eldest son
To beaten Douglas, and the Earls of Athol,
Of Murray, Angus, and Menteith.
And is not this an honourable spoil?
A gallant prize? ha, cousin, is it not?
    West.   In faith,
It is a conquest for a prince to boast of.
    K. Hen.   Yea, there thou mak'st me sad, and mak'st me
       sin
In envy that my Lord Northumberland
Should be the father of so blest a son,—

A son, who is the theme of honour's tongue;
Amongst a grove, the very straightest plant;
Who is sweet Fortune's minion and her pride:
Whilst I, by looking on the praise of him,
See riot and dishonour stain the brow
Of my young Harry. O that it could be proved,
That some night-tripping fairy had exchanged
In cradle-clothes our children where they lay,
And called mine Percy, his Plantagenet!
Then would I have his Harry, and he mine.
But let him from my thoughts.—What think you, coz,
Of this young Percy's pride? the prisoners
Which he in this adventure hath surprised
To his own use he keeps, and sends me word,
I shall have none but Mordake Earl of Fife.
    West.   This is his uncle's teaching, this is Worcester,
Malevolent to you in all aspécts;
Which makes him prune himself, and bristle up
The crest of youth against your dignity.
    K. Hen.   But I have sent for him to answer this;
And, for this cause, awhile we must neglect
Our holy purpose to Jerusalem.
Cousin, on Wednesday next our council we
Will hold at Windsor,—so inform the lords:
But come yourself with speed to us again;
For more is to be said and to be done
Than out of anger can be utteréd.
    West.   I will, my liege.   [*Exeunt*

SCENE II.—London.   Before a Tavern

Enter PRINCE HENRY *and* FALSTAFF

    Fal.   Now, Hal, what time of day is it, lad?
    P. Hen.   Thou art so fat-witted, with drinking of old
sack, and unbuttoning thee after supper, and sleeping upon
benches after noon, that thou hast forgotten to demand
that truly which thou wouldst truly know.   What a devil
hast thou to do with the time of the day? unless hours
were cups of sack, and minutes capons, and clocks the
tongues of bawds, and dials the signs of leaping-houses,
and the blessed sun himself a fair hot wench in flame-
coloured taffeta,—I see no reason why thou shouldst be so
superfluous to demand the time of the day.
    Fal.   Indeed, you come near me now, Hal, for we, that
take purses go by the moon and the seven stars, and not
by Phœbus,—he, 'that wandering knight so fair.'   And, I
pr'ythee, sweet wag, when thou art king,—as, God save
thy grace—majesty, I should say, for grace thou wilt have
none,—

17

P. Hen. What, none?

Fal. No, by my troth,—not so much as will serve to be prologue to an egg and butter.

P. Hen. Well, how then? come roundly, roundly.

Fal. Marry, then, sweet wag, when thou art king, let not us that are squires of the night's body be called thieves of the day's beauty: let us be Diana's foresters, gentlemen of the shade, minions of the moon; and let men say we be men of good government, being governed, as the sea is, by our noble and chaste mistress the moon, under whose countenance we steal.

P. Hen. Thou sayest well, and it holds well too; for the fortune of us that are the moon's men doth ebb and flow like the sea, being governed as the sea is, by the moon. As for proof now: a purse of gold most resolutely snatched on Monday night, and most dissolutely spent on Tuesday morning; got with swearing 'lay by;' and spent with crying 'bring in;' now in as low an ebb as the foot of the ladder, and by-and-by in as high a flow as the ridge of the gallows.

Fal. By the Lord, thou sayest true, lad. And is not my hostess of the tavern a most sweet wench?

P. Hen. As the honey of Hybla, my old lad of the castle. And is not a buff jerkin a most sweet robe of durance?

Fal. How now, how now, mad wag! what, in thy quips, and thy quiddities? what a plague have I to do with a buff jerkin?

P. Hen. Why, what a pox have I to do with my hostess of the tavern?

Fal. Well, thou hast called her to a reckoning many a time and oft.

P. Hen. Did I ever call for thee to pay thy part?

Fal. No; I'll give thee thy due, thou hast paid all there.

P. Hen. Yea, and elsewhere, so far as my coin would stretch; and, where it would not, I have used my credit.

Fal. Yea, and so used it, that were it not here apparent that thou art heir-apparent—But, I pr'ythee, sweet wag, shall there be gallows standing in England when thou art king? and resolution thus fobbed as it is with the rusty curb of old father Antick the law? Do not thou, when thou art king, hang a thief.

P. Hen. No; thou shalt.

Fal. Shall I? O rare! By the Lord, I'll be a brave judge.

P. Hen. Thou judgest false already: I mean, thou shalt have the hanging of the thieves, and so become a rare hangman.

Fal. Well, Hal, well; and in some sort it jumps with

my humour as well as waiting in the court, I can tell you.

P. Hen. For obtaining of suits?

Fal. Yea, for obtaining of suits, whereof the hangman hath no lean wardrobe. 'Sblood, I am as melancholy as a gib cat, or a lugged bear.

P. Hen. Or an old lion, or a lover's lute.

Fal. Yea, or the drone of a Lincolnshire bag-pipe.

P. Hen. What sayest thou to a hare, or the melancholy of Moor-ditch?

Fal. Thou hast the most unsavoury similes, and art, indeed, the most comparative, rascalliest,—sweet young prince.—But, Hal, I pr'ythee, trouble me no more with vanity. I would to God thou and I knew where a commodity of good names were to be bought. An old lord of the council rated me the other day in the street about you, sir,—but I marked him not; and yet he talked very wisely, —but I regarded him not; and yet he talked wisely, and in the street too.

P. Hen. Thou didst well; for wisdom cries out in the streets, and no man regards it.

Fal. O, thou hast damnable iteration, and art, indeed, able to corrupt a saint. Thou hast done much harm upon me, Hal,—God forgive thee for it. Before I knew thee, Hal, I knew nothing; and now am I, if a man should speak truly, little better than one of the wicked. I must give over this life, and I will give it over; by the Lord, an I do not, I am a villain: I'll be damned for never a king's son in Christendom.

P. Hen. Where shall we take a purse to-morrow, Jack?

Fal. 'Zounds, where thou wilt, lad, I'll make one; an I do not, call me villain, and baffle me.

P. Hen. I see a good amendment of life in thee,—from praying to purse-taking.

Enter POINS, *at a distance*

Fal. Why, Hal, 't is my vocation, Hal; 't is no sin for a man to labour in his vocation.—Poins!—Now shall we know if Gadshill have set a match.—O, if men were to be saved by merit, what hole in hell were hot enough for him? This is the most omnipotent villain, that ever cried, 'Stand!' to a true man.

P. Hen. Good morrow, Ned.

Poins. Good morrow, sweet Hal.—What says Monsieur Remorse? What says Sir John Sack-and-Sugar? Jack, how agrees the devil and thee about thy soul that thou soldest him on Good Friday last for a cup of Madeira and a cold capon's leg?

P. Hen. Sir John stands to his word —the devil shall have his bargain; for he was never yet a breaker of proverbs,—he will give the devil his due.

Poins. Then art thou damned for keeping thy word with the devil.

P. Hen. Else he had been damned for cozening the devil.

Poins. But, my lads, my lads, to-morrow morning, by four o'clock, early at Gadshill. There are pilgrims going to Canterbury with rich offerings, and traders riding to London with fat purses: I have visors for you all; you have horses for yourselves. Gadshill lies to-night in Rochester: I have bespoke supper to-morrow night in Eastcheap: we may do it as secure as sleep. If you will go, I will stuff your purses full of crowns; if you will not, tarry at home and be hanged.

Fal. Hear ye, Yedward; if I tarry at home and go not, I'll hang you for going.

Poins. You will, chops?

Fal. Hal, wilt thou make one?"

P. Hen. Who, I rob? I a thief? not I, by my faith.

Fal. There's neither honesty, manhood, nor good fellowship in thee, nor thou camest not of the blood royal, if thou darest not stand for ten shillings.

P. Hen. Well then, once in my days, I'll be a madcap.

Fal. Why, that's well said.

P. Hen. Well, come what will, I'll tarry at home.

Fal. By the Lord, I'll be a traitor, then, when thou art king.

P. Hen. I care not.

Poins. Sir John, I pr'ythee, leave the prince and me alone: I will lay him down such reasons for this adventure, that he shall go.

Fal. Well, God give thee the spirit of persuasion, and him the ears of profiting, that what thou speakest may move, and what he hears may be believed, that the true prince may, for recreation sake, prove a false thief; for the poor abuses of the time want countenance. Farewell: you shall find me in Eastcheap.

P. Hen. Farewell, the latter spring! Farewell, All-hallown summer!   [*Exit Falstaff*

Poins. Now, my good sweet honey lord, ride with us to-morrow: I have a jest to execute that I cannot manage alone. Falstaff, Bardolph, Peto, and Gadshill, shall rob those men that we have already waylaid; yourself and I will not be there; and when they have the booty, if you and I do not rob them, cut this head off from my shoulders.

P. Hen. But how shall we part with them in setting forth?

Poins. Why, we will set forth before or after them, and appoint them a place of meeting, wherein it is at our pleasure to fail; and then will they adventure upon the exploit themselves; which they shall have no sooner achieved, but we'll set upon them.

P. Hen. Yea, but 't is like that they will know us by our horses, by our habits, and by every other appointment, to be ourselves.

Poins. Tut! our horses they shall not see, I'll tie them in the wood; our visors we will change, after we leave them; and, sirrah, I have cases of buckram for the nonce, to inmask our noted outward garments.

P. Hen. Yea, but I doubt they will be too hard for us.

Poins. Well, for two of them, I know them to be as true-bred cowards as ever turned back; and for the third, if he fight longer than he sees reason, I'll forswear arms. The virtue of this jest will be, the incomprehensible lies that this same fat rogue will tell us when we meet at supper: how thirty, at least, he fought with; what wards, what blows, what extremities he endured; and in the reproof of this lies the jest.

P. Hen. Well, I'll go with thee: provide us all things necessary, and meet me to-morrow night in Eastcheap, there I'll sup.   Farewell.

Poins. Farewell, my lord.   [*Exit*

P. Hen. I know you all, and will awhile uphold
The unyoked humour of your idleness.
Yet herein will I imitate the sun,
Who doth permit the base contagious clouds
To smother up his beauty from the world,
That when he please again to be himself,
Being wanted, he may be more wondered at
By breaking through the foul and ugly mists
Of vapours that did seem to strangle him.
If all the year were playing holidays,
To sport would be as tedious as to work;
But when they seldom come, they wished-for come
And nothing pleaseth but rare accidents.
So, when this loose behaviour I throw off,
And pay the debt I never promiséd,
By how much better than my word I am,
By so much shall I falsify men's hopes;
And, like bright metal on a sullen ground,
My reformation, glittering o'er my fault,
Shall show more goodly and attract more eyes
Than that which hath no foil to set it off.
I'll so offend, to make offence a skill;
Redeeming time, when men think least I will.   [*Exit*

Scene III.—London. A Room in the Palace

Enter King Henry, Northumberland, Worcester,
Hotspur, Sir Walter Blunt, *and others*

K. Hen. My blood hath been too cold and temperate,
Unapt to stir at these indignities;
And you have found me, for accordingly
You tread upon my patience: but be sure
I will from henceforth rather be myself,—
Mighty, and to be feared,—than my condition,
Which hath been smooth as oil, soft as young down,
And therefore lost that title of respect
Which the proud soul ne'er pays but to the proud.
Wor. Our house, my sovereign liege, little deserves
The scourge of greatness to be used on it;
And that same greatness to which our own hands
Have holp to make so portly.
North. My lord,—
K. Hen. Worcester, get thee gone; for I do see
Danger and disobedience in thine eye.
O, sir,
Your presence is too bold and peremptory,
And majesty might never yet endure
The moody frontier of a servant brow.
You have good leave to leave us; when we need
Your use and counsel, we shall send for you.—

                                        [*Exit Worcester*
[*To Northumberland*] You were about to speak.
North.   Yea, my good lord.
Those prisoners in your highness' name demanded,
Which Harry Percy here at Holmedon took,
Were, as he says, not with such strength denied
As was delivered to your majesty:
Either envy, therefore, or misprision
Is guilty of this fault, and not my son.
Hot. My liege, I did deny no prisoners.
But I remember, when the fight was done,
When I was dry with rage and extreme toil,
Breathless and faint, leaning upon my sword,
Came there a certain lord, neat, trimly dressed,
Fresh as a bridegroom; and his chin, new reaped,
Showed like a stubble-land at harvest home;
He was perfuméd like a milliner,
And 'twixt his finger and his thumb he held
A pouncet-box, which ever and anon
He gave his nose, and took 't away again;
Who, therewith angry, when it next came there,
Took it in snuff:—and still he smiled and talked;

And, as the soldiers bore dead bodies by,
He called them untaught knaves, unmannerly,
To bring a slovenly unhandsome corse
Betwixt the wind and his nobility.
With many holiday and lady terms
He questioned me; among the rest, demanded
My prisoners in your majesty's behalf.
I then, all smarting with my wounds being cold
To be so pestered with a popinjay,
Out of my grief and my impatience
Answered neglectingly, I know not what,—
He should, or should not;—for he made me mad
To see him shine so brisk, and smell so sweet,
And talk so like a waiting-gentlewoman
Of guns and drums and wounds,—God save the mark!—
And telling me the sovereign'st thing on earth
Was parmacity for an inward bruise;
And that it was great pity, so it was,
That villainous saltpetre should be digged
Out of the bowels of the harmless earth,
Which many a good tall fellow had destroyed
So cowardly; and, but for these vile guns,
He would himself have been a soldier.
This bald unjointed chat of his, my lord,
I answered indirectly, as I said;
And, I beseech you, let not his report
Come current for an accusation
Betwixt my love and your high majesty.
    Blunt. The circumstance considered, good my lord,
Whatever Harry Percy then had said
To such a person, and in such a place,
At such a time, with all the rest re-told,
May reasonably die, and never rise
To do him wrong, or any way impeach
What then he said, so he unsay it now.
    K. Hen. Why, yet he doth deny his prisoners,
But with proviso, and exception,—
That we, at our own charge, shall ransom straight
His brother-in-law, the foolish Mortimer;
Who, on my soul, hath wilfully betrayed
The lives of those that he did lead to fight
Against the great magician, damned Glendower,
Whose daughter, as we hear, the Earl of March
Hath lately married. Shall our coffers, then,
Be emptied to redeem a traitor home?
Shall we buy treason?—and indent with fears
When they have lost and forfeited themselves?
No, on the barren mountains let him starve;
For I shall never hold that man my friend,
Whose tongue shall ask me for one penny cost

To ransom home revolted Mortimer.
    Hot.   Revolted Mortimer!
He never did fall off, my sovereign liege,
But by the chance of war: to prove that true
Needs no more but one tongue for all those wounds,
The mouthéd wounds, which valiantly he took,
When on the gentle Severn's sedgy bank,
In single opposition, hand to hand,
He did confound the best part of an hour
In changing hardiment with great Glendower.
Three times they breathed, and three times did they drink,
Upon agreement, of swift Severn's flood;
Who then, affrighted with their bloody looks,
Ran fearfully among the trembling reeds,
And hid his crisp head in the hollow bank
Blood-stainéd with these valiant combatants.
Never did base and rotten policy
Colour her working with such deadly wounds;
Nor never could the noble Mortimer
Receive so many, and all willingly:
Then let him not be slandered with revolt.
    K. Hen.   Thou dost belie him, Percy, thou dost belie
          him;
He never did encounter with Glendower.
I tell thee,
He durst as well have met the devil alone
As Owen Glendower for an enemy.
Art thou not ashamed?   But, sirrah, henceforth
Let me not hear you speak of Mortimer.
Send me your prisoners with the speediest means,
Or you shall hear in such a kind from me
As will displease you.—My Lord Northumberland,
We license your departure with your son.—
Send us your prisoners, or you'll hear of it.
               [*Exeunt King Henry, Blunt, and Train*
    Hot.   And if the devil come and roar for them,
I will not send them.—I will after straight,
And tell him so: for I will ease my heart,
Although it be with hazard of my head.
    North.   What, drunk with choler? stay, and pause
          awhile:
Here comes your uncle.

Re-enter WORCESTER

    Hot.   Speak of Mortimer!
'Zounds! I will speak of him; and let my soul
Want mercy, if I do not join with him:
Yea, on his part, I'll empty all these veins,
And shed my dear blood drop by drop i' the dust,

But I will lift the down-trod Mortimer
As high i' the air as this unthankful king,
As this ingrate and cankered Bolingbroke.
    North. [*To Worcester*] Brother, the king hath made
        your nephew mad.
    Wor. Who struck this heat up after I was gone?
    Hot. He will, forsooth, have all my prisoners;
And when I urged the ransom once again
Of my wife's brother, then his cheek looked pale,
And on my face he turned an eye of death,
Trembling even at the name of Mortimer.
    Wor. I cannot blame him. Was he not proclaimed,
By Richard that is dead, the next of blood?
    North. He was; I heard the proclamation:
And then it was when the unhappy king—
Whose wrongs in us God pardon!—did set forth
Upon his Irish expedition;
From whence he, intercepted, did return
To be deposed and shortly murderéd.
    Wor. And for whose death we in the world's wide
        mouth
Live scandalised and foully spoken of.
    Hot. But, soft, I pray you, did King Richard then
Proclaim my brother Edmund Mortimer
Heir to the crown?
    North.   He did; myself did hear it.
    Hot. Nay, then I cannot blame his cousin king,
That wished him on the barren mountains starve.
But shall it be that you, that set the crown
Upon the head of this forgetful man,
And for his sake wear the detested blot
Or murderous subornation,—shall it be,
That you a world of curses undergo,
Being the agents, or base second means,
The cords, the ladder, or the hangman rather?—
O, pardon me, that I descend so low,
To show the line and the predicament,
Wherein you range under this subtle king:—
Shall it, for shame, be spoken in these days,
Or fill up chronicles in time to come,
That men of your nobility and power
Did gage them both in an unjust behalf—
As both of you, God pardon it! have done—
To put down Richard, that sweet lovely rose,
And plant this thorn, this canker, Bolingbroke?
And shall it, in more shame, be further spoken,
That you are fooled, discarded, and shook off
By him for whom these shames ye underwent?
No! yet time serves wherein you may redeem
Your banished honours, and restore yourselves

Into the good thoughts of the world again;
Revenge the jeering and disdained contempt
Of this proud king, who studies day and night
To answer all the debt he owes to you
Even with the bloody payment of your deaths.
Therefore, I say,—
    Wor.   Peace, cousin, say no more.
And now I will unclasp a secret book,
And to your quick-conceiving discontents
I'll read you matter deep and dangerous,
As full of peril and adventurous spirit
As to o'er-walk a current, roaring loud,
On the unsteadfast footing of a spear.
    Hot.   If he fall in, good-night!—or sink or swim:—
Send danger from the east unto the west,
So honour cross it from the north to south,
And let them grapple:—O, the blood more stirs
To rouse a lion than to start a hare!
    North.   Imagination of some great exploit
Drives him beyond the bounds of patience.
    Hot.   By Heaven, methinks, it were an easy leap
To pluck bright honour from the pale-faced moon;
Or dive into the bottom of the deep,
Where fathom-line could never touch the ground,
And pluck up drownéd honour by the locks,
So he that doth redeem her thence might wear
Without corrival all her dignities:
But out upon this half-faced fellowship!
    Wor.   He apprehends a world of figures here,
But not the form of what he should attend.—
Good cousin, give me audience for a while.
    Hot.   I cry you mercy.
    Wor.   Those same noble Scots,
That are your prisoners,—
    Hot.   I'll keep them all.
By God, he shall not have a Scot of them;
No, if a Scot would save his soul, he shall not.
I'll keep them, by this hand.
    Wor.   You start away,
And lend no ear unto my purposes.—
Those prisoners you shall keep.
    Hot.   Nay, I will: that's flat.
He said, he would not ransom Mortimer;
Forbad my tongue to speak of Mortimer;
But I will find him when he lies asleep,
And in his ear I'll holla—'Mortimer!'
Nay,
I'll have a starling shall be taught to speak
Nothing but 'Mortimer,' and give it him,
To keep his anger still in motion.

Wor.   Hear you, cousin; a word.
Hot.   All studies here I solemnly defy,
Save how to gall and pinch this Bolingbroke:
And that same sword-and-buckler Prince of Wales,
But that I think his father loves him not,
And would be glad he met with some mischance,
I'd have him poisoned with a pot of ale.
Wor.   Farewell, kinsman: I will talk to you
When you are better tempered to attend.
North.   Why, what a wasp-stung and impatient fool
Art thou, to break into this woman's mood,
Tying thine ear to no tongue but thine own!
Hot.   Why, look you, I am whipped and scourged with
              rods,
Nettled, and stung with pismires, when I hear
Of this vile politician, Bolingbroke.
In Richard's time,—what do ye call the place?—
A plague upon 't—it is in Glostershire;—
'T was where the madcap duke his uncle kept,—
His uncle York,—where I first bowed my knee
Unto this king of smiles, this Bolingbroke,
'Sblood!
When you and he came back from Ravenspurg.
North.   At Berkley Castle.
Hot.   You say true:—
Why, what a candy deal of courtesy
This fawning greyhound then did proffer me!
Look,—'when his infant fortune came to age,'
And,—'gentle Harry Percy,'—and,—'kind cousin,'—
O, the devil take such cozeners!—God forgive me!—
Good uncle, tell your tale; for I have done.
Wor.   Nay, if you have not, to 't again;
We'll stay your leisure.
Hot.   I have done, i' faith.
Wor.   Then once more to your Scottish prisoners.
Deliver them up without their ransom straight,
And make the Douglas' son your only mean
For powers in Scotland; which, for divers reasons
Which I shall send you written, be assured,
Will easily be granted.—[*To Northumberland*]—You, my
              lord,
Your son in Scotland being thus employed,
Shall secretly into the bosom creep
Of that same noble prelate well-beloved,
The archbishop.
Hot.   Of York, is't not?
Wor.   True; who bears hard
His brother's death at Bristol, the Lord Scroop.
I speak not this in estimation,
As what I think might be, but what I know

27

Is ruminated, plotted, and set down,
And only stays but to behold the face
Of that occasion that shall bring it on.
   Hot. I smell 't: upon my life, it will do well.
   North. Before the game's afoot, thou still lett'st slip.
   Hot. Why, it cannot choose but be a noble plot:—
And then the power of Scotland and of York,—
To join with Mortimer, ha?
   Wor.   And so they shall.
   Hot. In faith, it is exceedingly well aimed.
   Wor. And 't is no little reason bids us speed,
To save our heads by raising of a head;
For, bear ourselves as even as we can,
The king will always think him in our debt,
And think we think ourselves unsatisfied,
Till he hath found a time to pay us home.
And see already how he doth begin
To make us strangers to his looks of love.
   Hot. He does, he does: we'll be revenged on him.
   Wor. Cousin, farewell:—No further go in this
Than I by letters shall direct your course.
When time is ripe,—which will be suddenly,—
I'll steal to Glendower, and Lord Mortimer;
Where you and Douglas, and our powers at once,
As I will fashion it, shall happily meet,
To bear our fortunes in our own strong arms,
Which now we hold at much uncertainty.
   North. Farewell, good brother: we shall thrive, I trust.
   Hot. Uncle, adieu.—O, let the hours be short,
Till fields and blows and groans applaud our sport!
                               [Exeunt

ACT TWO

Scene I.—Rochester. An Inn Yard

Enter a Carrier with a lantern in his hand

   First Car. Heigh-ho! An't be not four by the day,
I'll be hanged: Charles' wain is over the new chimney, and
yet our horse not packed. What, ostler!
   Ostler. [*Within*] Anon, anon.
   First Car. I pr'ythee, Tom, beat Cut's saddle, put a
few flocks in the point; the poor jade is wrung in the
withers out of all cess.

Enter another Carrier

   Sec. Car. Peas and beans are as dank here as a dog,

and that is the next way to give poor jades the bots: this house is turned upside down since Robin ostler died.

First Car. Poor fellow! never joyed since the price of oats rose; it was the death of him.

Sec. Car. I think, this be the most villainous house in all London road for fleas: I am stung like a tench.

First Car. Like a tench? by the mass, there is ne'er a king in Christendom could be better bit than I have been since the first cock.

Sec. Car. Why, they will allow us ne'er a jordan, and then we leak in your chimney; and your chamber-lie breeds fleas like a loach.

First Car. What, ostler! come away, and be hanged; come away.

Sec. Car. I have a gammon of bacon and two races of ginger, to be delivered as far as Charing Cross.

First Car. 'Odsbody! the turkeys in my pannier are quite starved.—What, ostler!—A plague on thee! hast thou never an eye in thy head? canst not hear? An't were not as good a deed as drink, to break the pate of thee, I am a very villain. Come, and be hanged:—hast no faith in thee?

Enter GADSHILL

Gads. Good morrow, carriers. What's o'clock?

First Car. I think it be two o'clock.

Gads. I pr'ythee, lend me thy lantern, to see my gelding in the stable.

First Car Nay, soft, I pray ye: I know a trick worth two of that, i' faith.

Gads. I pr'ythee, lend me thine.

Sec. Car. Ay, when? canst tell?—Lend me thy lantern, quoth 'a?—marry, I'll see thee hanged first.

Gads. Sirrah carrier, what time do you mean to come to London?

Sec. Car. Time enough to go to bed with a candle, I warrant thee.—Come, neighbour Mugs, we'll call up the gentlemen: they will along with company, for they have great charge.   [*Exeunt Carriers*

Gads. What, ho! chamberlain!

Cham. [*Within*] At hand, quoth pickpurse.

Gads. That's even as fair as—at hand, quoth the chamberlain; for thou variest no more from picking of purses than giving direction doth from labouring: thou layest the plot how.

Enter Chamberlain

Cham. Good morrow, Master Gadshill. It holds current that I told you yesternight: there's a franklin in the wild of Kent hath brought three hundred marks with him in gold: I heard him tell it to one of his company last night at supper; a kind of auditor; one that hath abundance of charge too, God knows what. They are up already, and call for eggs and butter: they will away presently.

Gads. Sirrah, if they meet not with Saint Nicholas' clerks, I'll give thee this neck.

Cham. No, I'll none of it: I pr'ythee, keep that for the hangman; for, I know, thou worshipp'st Saint Nicholas as truly as a man of falsehood may.

Gads. What talkest thou to me of the hangman? if I hang, I'll make a fat pair of gallows; for, if I hang, old Sir John hangs with me, and thou knowest he's no starveling. Tut! there are other Trojans that thou dreamest not of, the which, for sport sake, are content to do the profession some grace, that would, if matters should be looked into, for their own credit sake, make all whole. I am joined with no foot land-rakers, no long-staff, sixpenny strikers, none of these mad, mustachio purple-hued malt-worms: but with nobility and tranquillity; burgomasters, and great oneyers: such as can hold in, such as will strike sooner than speak, and speak sooner than drink, and drink sooner than pray: and yet I lie; for they pray continually to their saint, the commonwealth; or, rather, not pray to her, but prey on her, for they ride up and down on her, and make her their boots.

Cham. What, the commonwealth their boots? will she hold out water in foul way?

Gads. She will, she will; justice hath liquored her. We steal as in a castle, cock-sure; we have the receipt of fern-seed,—we walk invisible.

Cham. Nay, by my faith; I think you are more beholding to the night, than to fern-seed, for your walking invisible.

Gads. Give me thy hand: thou shalt have a share in our purchase, as I am a true man.

Cham. Nay, rather let me have it, as you are a false thief.

Gads. Go to; *homo* is a common name to all men. Bid the ostler bring my gelding out of the stable.   Farewell, ye muddy knave.   [*Exeunt*

SCENE II.—The Road by Gadshill

Enter PRINCE HENRY *and* POINS; BARDOLPH *and* PETO, *at some distance*

Poins. Come, shelter, shelter: I have removed Falstaff's horse, and he frets like a gummed velvet

P. Hen. Stand close.

Enter FALSTAFF

Fal. Poins! Poins, and be hanged! Poins!

P. Hen. [*Coming forward*] Peace, ye fat-kidneyed rascal! What a brawling dost thou keep?

Fal. Where's Poins, Hal?

P. Hen. He is walked up to the top of the hill: I'll go seek him.   [*Pretends to seek Poins*

Fal. I am accursed to rob in that thief's company; the rascal hath removed my horse, and tied him I know not where. If I travel but four foot by the squire further afoot, I shall break my wind. Well, I doubt not but to die a fair death for all this, if I 'scape hanging for killing that rogue. I have forsworn his company hourly any time this two-and-twenty years, and yet I am betwitched with the rogue's company. If the rascal have not given me medicines to make me love him, I'll be hanged; it could not be else; I have drunk medicines.—Poins!—Hal!—a plague upon you both!—Bardolph!—Peto!—I'll starve, ere I'll rob a foot further. An't were not as good a deed as drink, to turn true man, and to leave these rogues, I am the veriest varlet that ever chewed with a tooth. Eight yards of uneven ground is threescore and ten miles afoot with me; and the stony-hearted villains know it well enough: a plague upon 't, when thieves cannot be true to one another! [*They whistle*] Whew!—A plague upon you all! Give me my horse, you rogues; give me my horse, and be hanged.

P. Hen: [*Coming forward*] Peace, ye fat-guts! lie down; lay thine ear close to the ground, and list if thou canst hear the tread of travellers.

Fal. Have you any levers to lift me up again, being down? 'Sblood, I'll not bear mine own flesh so far afoot again, for all the coin in thy father's exchequer. What a plague mean ye to colt me thus?

P. Hen. Thou liest; thou art not colted, thou art uncolted.

Fal. I pr'ythee, good Prince Hal, help me to my horse, good king's son.

P. Hen. Out, ye rogue! shall I be your ostler?

Fal. Go, hang thyself in thine own heir-apparent garters! If I be ta'en, I'll peach for this. An I have not ballads made on you all, and sung to filthy tunes, let a cup of sack be my poison: when a jest is so forward, and afoot too, I hate it.

Enter GADSHILL

Gad's. Stand.

Fal. So I do, against my will.

Poins. O, 't is our setter: I know his voice.
                    [*Coming forward with Bardolph and Peto*

Bard. What news?

31

Gads. Case ye, case ye: on with your visards: there's money of the king's coming down the hill; 't is going to the king's exchequer.

Fal. You lie, ye rogue: 't is going to the king's tavern.

Gads. There's enough to make us all.

Fal. To be hanged.

P. Hen. Sirs, you four shall front them in the narrow lane; Ned Poins and I will walk lower: if they 'scape from your encounter, then they light on us.

Peto. How many be there of them?

Gads. Some eight, or ten.

Fal. 'Zounds, will they not rob us?

P. Hen. What, a coward, Sir John Paunch?

Fal. Indeed, I am not John of Gaunt, your grandfather; but yet no coward, Hal.

P. Hen. Well, we leave that to the proof.

Poins. Sirrah Jack, thy horse stands behind the hedge: when thou needest him, there thou shalt find him. Farewell, and stand fast.

Fal. Now cannot I strike him, if I should be hanged.

P. Hen. [*Aside to Poins*] Ned, where are our disguises?

Poins. Here, hard by: stand close.

[*Exeunt Prince Henry and Poins*

Fal. Now, my masters, happy man be his dole, say I: every man to his business.

Enter the Travellers

First Trav. Come, neighbour;
The boy shall lead our horses down the hill;
We'll walk afoot awhile, and ease our legs.

Thieves. Stand!

Travellers. Jesu bless us!

Fal. Strike; down with them; cut the villains' throats. Ah, whoreson caterpillars! bacon-fed knaves! they hate us youth: down with them; fleece them.

Travellers. O, we are undone, both we and ours, for ever.

Fal. Hang ye, gorbellied knaves, are ye undone? No, ye fat chuffs; I would, your store were here! On, bacons, on! What, ye knaves, young men must live. You are grand-jurors, are ye? we'll jure ye, i' faith.

[*Exeunt Falstaff, etc., driving the Travellers out*

Re-enter PRINCE HENRY *and* POINS, *in buckram suits*

P. Hen. The thieves have bound the true men. Now could thou and I rob the thieves, and go merrily to London, it would be argument for a week, laughter for a month, and a good jest for ever.

Poins.   Stand close; I hear them coming.   [*They retire*

Enter the Thieves again

Fal.   Come, my masters; let us share, and then to horse before day.   An the Prince and Poins be not two arrant cowards, there's no equity stirring: there's no more valour in that Poins than in a wild duck.
P. Hen.   Your money!
Poins.   Villains!
　　[*As they are sharing, the Prince and Poins set upon them.   They all run away, and Falstaff, after a blow or two, runs away too, leaving the booty behind them*
P. Hen.   Got with much ease.   Now merrily to horse:
The thieves are scattered, and possessed with fear
So strongly, that they dare not meet each other;
Each takes his fellow for an officer.
Away, good Ned.   Falstaff sweats to death,
And lards the lean earth as he walks along:
Were't not for laughing, I should pity him.
　　Poins.   How the rogue roared!   [*Exeunt*

SCENE III.—Warkworth.   A Room in the Castle

Enter HOTSPUR, *reading a letter*

　—'But, for mine own part, my lord, I could be well contented to be there, in respect of the love I bear your house.'—He could be contented,—why is he not then?   In respect of the love he bears our house:—he shows in this, he loves his own barn better than he loves our house.   Let me see some more.   'The purpose you undertake, is dangerous;'—why, that's certain: 't is dangerous to take a cold, to sleep, to drink; but I tell you, my lord fool, out of this nettle, danger, we pluck this flower, safety. 'The purpose you undertake, is dangerous; the friends you have named, uncertain; the time itself unsorted; and your whole plot too light for the counterpoise of so great an opposition.'—Say you so, say you so?   I say unto you again, you are a shallow, cowardly hind, and you lie. What a lack-brain is this!   By the Lord, our plot is as good a plot as ever was laid; our friends true and constant: a good plot, good friends, and full of expectation; an excellent plot, very good friends.   What a frosty-spirited rogue is this!   Why, my Lord of York commends the plot and the general course of the action.   'Zounds! an I were now by this rascal, I could brain him with his lady's fan. Is there not my father, my uncle, and myself?   Lord Edmund Mortimer, my Lord of York, and Owen Glendower?   Is there not, besides, the Douglas?   Have I not

all their letters, to meet me in arms by the ninth of the
next month? and are they not, some of them, set forward
already? What a pagan rascal is this! an infidel! Ha!
you shall see now, in very sincerity of fear and cold heart,
will he to the king, and lay open all our proceedings. O,
I could divide myself and go to buffets, for moving such
a dish of skimmed milk with so honourable an action!
Hang him! let him tell the king: we are prepared. I will
set forward to-night.

Enter LADY PERCY

How now, Kate, I must leave you within these two hours.
   Lady. O, my good lord, why are you thus alone?
For what offence have I this fortnight been
A banished woman from my Harry's bed?
Tell me, sweet lord, what is't that takes from thee
Thy stomach, pleasure, and thy golden sleep?
Why dost thou bend thine eyes upon the earth,
And start so often when thou sitt'st alone?
Why hast thou lost the fresh blood in thy cheeks,
And given my treasures and my rights of thee
To thick-eyed musing, and cursed melancholy?
In thy faint slumbers I by thee have watched,
And heard thee murmur tales of iron wars,
Speak terms of manage to thy bounding steed,
Cry, 'Courage!—to the field!' And thou hast talked
Of sallies, and retires, of trenches, tents,
Of palisadoes, frontiers, parapets,
Of basilisks, of cannon, culverin,
Of prisoners ransomed, and of soldiers slain,
And all the occurrents of a heady fight.
Thy spirit within thee hath been so at war,
And thus hath so bestirred thee in thy sleep,
That beads of sweat have stood upon thy brow
Like bubbles in a late-disturbéd stream;
And in thy face strange motions have appeared
Such as we see when men restrain their breath
On some great sudden hest. O, what portents are these?
Some heavy business hath my lord in hand,
And I must know it, else he loves me not.
   Hot. What, ho!

Enter Servant

           Is Gilliams with the packet gone?
   Serv. He is, my lord, an hour ago.
   Hot. Hath Butler brought those horses from the sheriff?
   Serv. One horse, my lord, he brought even now.
   Hot. What horse? a roan, a crop-ear, is it not?
   Serv. It is, my lord.
   Hot.   That roan shall be my throne.

Well, I will back him straight: O, *esperance!*
Bid Butler lead him forth into the park.   *[Exit Servant*
    Lady. But hear you, my lord.
    Hot. What say'st thou, my lady?
    Lady. What is it carries you away?
    Hot. Why, my horse, my love, my horse.
    Lady. Out, you mad-headed ape!
A weasel hath not such a deal of spleen
As you are tossed with. But in faith, I'll know—
I'll know your business, Harry, that I will.
I fear, my brother Mortimer doth stir
About his title, and hath sent for you
To line his enterprise. But if you go—
    Hot. So far afoot, I shall be weary, love.
    Lady. Come, come, you paraquito, answer me
Directly unto this question that I ask.
In faith, I'll break thy little finger, Harry,
An if thou wilt not tell me true.
    Hot. Away.
Away, you trifler!—Love?—I love thee not,
I care not for thee, Kate: this is no world
To play with mammets and to tilt with lips:
We must have bloody noses and cracked crowns,
And pass them current too.—God's me, my horse!—
What say'st thou, Kate? what wouldst thou have. with
        me?
    Lady. Do you not love me? do you not, indeed?
Well, do not then; for since you love me not,
I will not love myself. Do you not love me?
Nay, tell me, if you speak in jest or no?
    Hot. Come, wilt thou see me ride?
And when I am o' horseback, I will swear
I love thee infinitely. But hark you, Kate;
I must not have you henceforth question me
Whither I go, nor reason whereabout:
Whither I must, I must; and, to conclude,
This evening must I leave you, gentle Kate.
I know you wise; but yet no further wise
Than Harry Percy's wife: constant you are,
But yet a woman: and for secrecy,
No lady closer; for I well believe
Thou wilt not utter what thou dost not know,—
And so far will I trust thee, gentle Kate.
    Lady. How! so far?
    Hot. Not an inch further. But hark you, Kate:
Whither I go, thither shall you go too;
To-day will I set forth, to-morrow you.
Will this content you, Kate?
    Lady.   It must of force.   *[Exeunt*

SCENE IV.—Eastcheap. A Room in the Boar's
Head Tavern

Enter PRINCE HENRY

P. Hen. Ned, pr'ythee, come out of that fat room, and
lend me thy hand to laugh a little.

Enter POINS

Poins. Where hast been, Hal?

P. Hen. With three or four loggerheads amongst three
or four score hogsheads. I have sounded the very base
string of humility. Sirrah, I am sworn brother to a leash
of drawers, and can call them all by their Christian names,
as—Tom, Dick, and Francis. They take it already upon
their salvation, that though I be but Prince of Wales, yet
I am the king of courtesy; and tell me flatly I am no proud
Jack, like Falstaff, but a Corinthian, a lad of mettle, a
good boy,—by the Lord, so they call me,—and when I am
King of England, I shall command all the good lads in
Eastcheap. They call drinking deep dying scarlet; and
when you breathe in your watering, they cry, 'Hem!'
and bid you play it off. To conclude, I am so good a
proficient in one quarter of an hour, that I can drink with
any tinker in his own language during my life. I tell thee,
Ned, thou hast lost much honour, that thou wert not with
me in this action. But, sweet Ned,—to sweeten which
name of Ned, I give thee this pennyworth of sugar, clapped
even now into my hand by an under-skinker, one that
never spake other English in his life, than—'Eight shillings
and sixpence,' and—'You are welcome;' with this shrill
addition,—'Anon, anon, sir! Score a pint of bastard in
the Half Moon,' or so. But, Ned, to drive away the time
till Falstaff come, I pr'ythee, do thou stand in some by-
room, while I question my puny drawer to what end he
gave me the sugar; and do thou never leave calling—
'Francis!' that his tale to me may be nothing but 'anon.'
Step aside, and I'll show thee a precedent.

Poins. Francis!

P. Hen. Thou art perfect.

Poins. Francis!   [*Exit*

Enter FRANCIS

Fran. Anon, anon, sir.—Look down into the Pome-
granate, Ralph.

P. Hen. Come hither, Francis.

Fran. My Lord?

P. Hen. How long hast thou to serve, Francis?

Fran. Forsooth, five years, and as much as to—

Poins. [*Within*] Francis!

Fran. Anon, anon, sir.

P. Hen. Five years! by'r lady, a long lease for the clinking of pewter. But, Francis, darest thou be so valiant as to play the coward with thy indenture and to show it a fair pair of heels and run from it?

Fran. O Lord, sir, I'll be sworn upon all the books in England, I could find in my heart—

Poins. [*Within*] Francis!

Fran. Anon, anon, sir.

P. Hen. How old art thou, Francis?

Fran. Let me see,—about Michaelmas next I shall be—

Poins. [*Within*] Francis!

Fran. Anon, sir.—Pray you, stay a little, my lord.

P. Hen. Nay, but hark you, Francis: for the sugar thou gavest me,—'t was a penny-worth, was't not?

Fran. O Lord, sir, I would it had been two!

P. Hen. I will give thee for it a thousand pound: ask me when thou wilt, and thou shalt have it.

Poins. [*Within*] Francis!

Fran. Anon, anon.

P. Hen. Anon, Francis? No, Francis; but to-morrow, Francis; or, Francis, on Thursday; or, indeed, Francis, when thou wilt. But, Francis,—

Fran. My Lord?

P. Hen. Wilt thou rob this leathern-jerkin, crystal-button, nott-pated, agate-ring, puke-stocking, caddis-garter, smooth-tongue, Spanish-pouch,—

Fran. O Lord, sir, what do you mean?

P. Hen. Why then, your brown bastard is your only drink; for, look you, Francis, your white canvas doublet will sully. In Barbary, sir, it cannot come to so much.

Fran. What, sir?

Poins. [*Within*] Francis!

P. Hen. Away, you rogue! Dost thou not hear them call?

[*Here they both call him: the Drawer stands amazed, not knowing which way to go*

Enter Vintner

Vint. What, standest thou still, and hearest such a calling? Look to the guests within. [*Exit Francis*] My lord, old Sir John, with half a dozen more, are at the door: shall I let them in?

P. Hen. Let them alone awhile, and then open the door. [*Exit Vintner*] Poins!

Re-enter POINS

Poins. Anon, anon, sir.

P. Hen. Sirrah, Falstaff and the rest of the thieves are
at the door: shall we be merry?

Poins. As merry as crickets, my lad. But hark ye:
what cunning match have you made with this jest of the
drawer? come, what's the issue?

P. Hen. I am now of all humours that have showed
themselves humours since the old days of goodman Adam
to the pupil age of this present twelve o'clock at midnight.
—What's o'clock, Francis?

Francis. [*Within*] Anon, anon, sir.

P. Hen. That ever this fellow should have fewer words
than a parrot, and yet the son of a woman! His industry
is up-stairs, and down-stairs; his eloquence the parcel of a
reckoning. I am not yet of Percy's mind, the Hotspur of
the North; he that kills me some six or seven dozen of
Scots at a breakfast, washes his hands, and says to his
wife,—'Fie upon this quiet life! I want work.' 'O my
sweet Harry,' says she, 'how many hast thou killed to-
day?' 'Give my roan horse a drench,' says he; and
answers, 'some fourteen,' an hour after, 'a trifle, a trifle.'
—I pr'ythee call in Falstaff: I'll play Percy, and that
damned brawn shall play Dame Mortimer his wife. 'Rivo!'
says the drunkard. Call in ribs, call in tallow.

Enter FALSTAFF, GADSHILL, BARDOLPH, *and* PETO, *followed
by* FRANCIS *with wine*

Poins. Welcome, Jack. Where hast thou been?

Fal. A plague of all cowards, I say, and a vengeance
too! marry, and amen!—Give me a cup of sack, boy.—
Ere I lead this life long, I'll sew nether-stocks, and mend
them and foot them too. A plague of all cowards!—give
me a cup of sack, rogue. Is there no virtue extant?

[*Drinks*

P. Hen. Didst thou never see Titan kiss a dish of
butter—pitiful-hearted Titan—that melted at the sweet
tale of the sun? if thou didst, then behold that compound.

Fal. You rogue, here's lime in this sack too: there is
nothing but roguery to be found in villainous man: yet a
coward is worse than a cup of sack with lime in it,—a
villainous coward.—Go thy ways, old Jack; die when thou
wilt, if manhood, good manhood, be not forgot upon the
face of the earth, then am I a shotten herring. There live
not three good men unhanged in England, and one of them
is fat, and grows old: God help the while! a bad world I
say. I would I were a weaver; I could sing psalms or
anything. A plague of all cowards I say still.

P. Hen. How now, wool-sack? what mutter you?

Fal. A king's son! If I do not beat thee out of thy
kingdom with a dagger of lath, and drive all thy subjects

afore thee like a flock of wild geese, I'll never wear hair on my face more. You Prince of Wales!

P. Hen. Why, you whoreson round man, what's the matter?

Fal. Are you not a coward? answer me to that; and Poins there.

Poins. 'Zounds, ye fat-paunch, an ye call me coward, I'll stab thee.

Fal. I call thee coward! I'll see thee damned ere I call thee coward; but I would give a thousand pound, I could run as fast as thou canst. You are straight enough in the shoulders; you care not who sees your back: call you that backing of your friends? A plague upon such backing! give me them that will face me.—Give me a cup of sack:—I am a rogue, if I drunk to-day.

P. Hen. O villain! thy lips are scarce wiped since thou drunk'st last.

Fal. All's one for that. [*Drinks*] A plague of all cowards, still say I.

P. Hen. What's the matter?

Fal. What's the matter! there be four of us here have ta'en a thousand pound this day morning.

P. Hen. Where is it, Jack? where is it?

Fal. Where is it! taken from us it is: a hundred upon poor four of us.

P. Hen. What, a hundred, man?

Fal. I am a rogue, if I were not at half-sword with a dozen of them two hours together. I have scaped by miracle. I am eight times thrust through the doublet, four through the hose; my buckler cut through and through; my sword hacked like a hand-saw,—*ecce signum!* I never dealt better since I was a man: all would not do. A plague of all cowards!—Let them speak: if they speak more or less than truth, they are villains, and the sons of darkness.

P. Hen. Speak, sirs: how was it?

Gads. We four set upon some dozen,—

Fal. Sixteen, at least, my lord.

Gads. And bound them.

Peto. No, no, they were not bound.

Fal. You rogue, they were bound, every man of them; or I am a Jew else, an Ebrew Jew.

Gads. As we were sharing, some six or seven fresh men set upon us,—

Fal. And unbound the rest, and then come in the other.

P. Hen. What, fought ye with them all?

Fal. All? I know not what ye call all; but if I fought not with fifty of them, I am a bunch of radish: if there were not two or three and fifty upon poor old Jack, then am I no two-legged creature.

P. Hen. Pray God you have not murdered some of them.

Fal. Nay, that's past praying for: I have peppered two of them; two I am sure I have paid, two rogues in buckram suits. I tell thee what, Hal,—if I tell thee a lie, spit in my face, call me horse. Thou knowest my old ward;—here I lay, and thus I bore my point. Four rogues in buckram let drive at me,—

P. Hen. What, four? thou saidst but two, even now.

Fal. Four, Hal; I told thee four.

Poins. Ay, ay, he said four.

Fal. These four came all a-front, and mainly thrust at me. I made me no more ado but took all their seven points in my target, thus.

P. Hen. Seven? why, there were but four, even now.

Fal. In buckram?

Poins. Ay, four, in buckram suits.

Fal. Seven, by these hilts, or I am a villain else.

P. Hen. Pr'ythee, let him alone: we shall have more anon.

Fal. Dost thou hear me, Hal?

P. Hen. Ay, and mark thee too, Jack.

Fal. Do so, for it is worth the listening to. These nine in buckram, that I told thee of,—

P. Hen. So, two more already.

Fal. Their points being broken,—

Poins. Down fell their hose.

Fal. Began to give me ground; but I followed me close, came in, foot and hand; and with a thought seven of the eleven I paid.

P. Hen. O monstrous! eleven buckram men grown out of two.

Fal. But, as the devil would have it, three misbegotten knaves in Kendal Green came at my back and let drive at me;—for it was so dark, Hal, that thou couldst not see thy hand.

P. Hen. These lies are like the father that begets them, —gross as a mountain, open, palpable. Why, thou clay-brained guts, thou knotty-pated fool, thou whoreson, obscene, greasy tallow-keech,—

Fal. What! art thou mad? art thou mad? is not the truth the truth?

P. Hen. Why, how couldst thou know these men in Kendal Green, when it was so dark thou couldst not see thy hand? come, tell us your reason: what sayest thou to this?

Poins. Come, your reason, Jack, your reason.

Fal. What, upon compulsion? No.; were I at the strappado, or all the racks in the world, I would not tell you on compulsion. Give you a reason on compulsion!

if reasons were as plenty as blackberries, I would give no man a reason upon compulsion, I.

P. Hen. I'll be no longer guilty of this sin: this sanguine coward, this bed-presser, this horseback-breaker, this huge hill of flesh;—

Fal. Away, you starveling, you elf-skin, you dried meat's-tongue, bull's-pizzle, you stock-fish,—O, for breath to utter what is like thee!—you tailor's-yard, you sheath, you bow-case, you vile standing tuck,—

P. Hen. Well, breathe awhile, and then to it again; and when thou hast tired thyself in base comparisons, hear me speak but this.

Poins. Mark, Jack.

P. Hen. We two saw—you four set on four, and bound them, and were masters of their wealth.—Mark now, how a plain tale shall put you down.—Then did we two set on you four, and, with a word, outfaced you from your prize, and have it, yea, and can show it you here in the house.— And, Falstaff, you carried your guts away as nimbly, with as quick dexterity, and roared for mercy, and still ran and roared, as ever I heard bull-calf. What a slave art thou, to hack thy sword as thou hast done, and then say, it was in fight! What trick, what device, what starting-hole canst thou now find out, to hide thee from this open and apparent shame?

Poins. Come, let's hear, Jack: what trick hast thou now?

Fal. By the Lord, I knew ye, as well as he that made ye. Why, hear ye, my masters. Was it for me to kill the heir-apparent? Should I turn upon the true prince? Why, thou knowest, I am as valiant as Hercules; but beware instinct; the lion will not touch the true prince. Instinct is a great matter; I was a coward on instinct. I shall think the better of myself and thee during my life; I for a valiant lion, and thou for a true prince. But, by the Lord, lads, I am glad you have the money.—Hostess, clap to the doors: [*to Hostess within*] watch to-night, pray to-morrow.—Gallants, lads, boys, hearts of gold, all the titles of good fellowship come to you! What! shall we be merry? shall we have a play extempore?

P. Hen. Content;—and the argument shall be, thy running away.

Fal. Ah! no more of that, Hal, an thou lovest me.

Enter Hostess

Host. O Jesu, my lord the prince,—

P. Hen. How now, my lady the hostess? what say'st thou to me?

Host. Marry, my lord, there is a nobleman of the court

at door would speak with you: he says, he comes from your father.

P. Hen. Give him as much as will make him a royal man, and send him back again to my mother.

Fal. What manner of man is he?

Host. An old man.

Fal. What doth gravity out of his bed at mid-night? —Shall I give him his answer?

P. Hen. Pr'ythee, do, Jack.

Fal. 'Faith, and I'll send him packing.   [*Exit*

P. Hen. Now, sirs:—by'r lady, you fought fair;—so did you, Peto;—so did you, Bardolph: you are lions too, you ran away upon instinct, you will not touch the true prince, no;—fie!

Bard. 'Faith, I ran when I saw others run.

P. Hen. 'Faith, tell me now in earnest, how came Falstaff's sword so hacked?

Peto. Why, he hacked it with his dagger, and said, he would swear truth out of England, but he would make you believe it was done in fight; and persuaded us to do the like.

Bard. Yea, and to tickle our noses with spear-grass, to make them bleed; and then to beslubber our garments with it, and to swear it was the blood of true men. I did that I did not this seven years before, I blushed, to hear his monstrous devices.

P. Hen. O villain, thou stolest a cup of sack eighteen years ago and wert taken with the manner, and ever since thou hast blushed extempore. Thou hadst fire and sword on thy side, and yet thou runn'st away: what instinct hadst thou for it?

Bard. My lord, do you see these meteors? do you behold these exhalations?

P. Hen. I do.

Bard. What think you they portend?

P. Hen. Hot livers and cold purses.

Bard. Choler, my lord, if rightly taken.

P. Hen. No, if rightly taken, halter.

Re-enter FALSTAFF

Here comes lean Jack, here comes bare-bone. How now, my sweet creature of bombast? How long is't ago, Jack, since thou sawest thine own knee?

Fal. My own knee? When I was about thy years, Hal, I was not an eagle's talon in the waist; I could have crept into any alderman's thumb-ring. A plague of sighing and grief! it blows a man up like a bladder. There's villainous news abroad: here was Sir John Bracy from your father; you must to the court in the morning. That same mad fellow of the north, Percy; and he of Wales, that gave Amaimon the bastinado, and made Lucifer cuckold, and swore the devil his true liegeman upon the cross of a Welsh hook,—what, a plague, call you him?—

Poins. O, Glendower.

Fal. Owen, Owen,—the same;—and his son-in-law, Mortimer; and old Northumberland; and that sprightly Scot of Scots, Douglas, that runs o' horseback up a hill perpendicular,—

P. Hen. He that rides at high speed, and with his pistol kills a sparrow flying.

Fal. You have hit it.

P. Hen. So did he never the sparrow.

Fal. Well, that rascal hath good mettle in him; he will not run.

P. Hen. Why, what a rascal art thou, then, to praise him for so running?

Fal. O' horseback, ye cuckoo! but afoot he will not budge a foot.

P. Hen. Yes, Jack, upon instinct.

Fal. I grant ye, upon instinct. Well, he is there too, and one Mordake, and a thousand blue-caps more: Worcester is stolen away to-night; thy father's beard is turned white with the news: you may buy land now as cheap as stinking mackerel.

P. Hen. Why, then, it is like, if there come a hot June, and this civil buffeting hold, we shall buy maidenheads as they buy hob-nails, by the hundreds.

Fal. By the mass, lad, thou sayest true; it is like we shall have good trading that way.—But, tell me, Hal, art thou not horribly afeard? thou being heir-apparent, could the world pick thee out three such enemies again as that fiend Douglas, that spirit Percy, and that devil Glendower? Art thou not horribly afraid? doth not thy blood thrill at it?

P. Hen. Not a whit, i' faith; I lack some of thy instinct.

Fal. Well, thou wilt be horribly chid to-morrow, when thou comest to thy father: if thou love me, practise an answer.

P. Hen. Do thou stand for my father, and examine me upon the particulars of my life.

Fal. Shall I? content:—This chair shall be my state, this dagger my sceptre, and this cushion my crown.

P. Hen. Thy state is taken from a joint-stool, thy golden sceptre for a leaden dagger, and thy precious rich crown for a pitiful bald crown!

Fal. Well, an the fire of grace be not quite out of thee, now thou shalt be moved.—Give me a cup of sack, to make mine eyes look red, that it may be thought I have wept;

for I must speak in passion, and I will do it in King
Cambyses' vein.   [*Drinks*

P. Hen. Well, here is my leg.

Fal. And here is my speech.—Stand aside, nobility.

Host. O Jesu, this is excellent sport, i' faith.

Fal. Weep not, sweet queen, for trickling tears are vain.

Host. O, the father, how he holds his countenance!

Fal. For God's sake, lords, convey my tristful queen;
For tears do stop the flood-gates of her eyes.

Host. O Jesu, he doth it as like one of these harlotry
players as ever I see.

Fal. Peace, good pint-pot; peace, good tickle-brain.—
Harry, I do not only marvel where thou spendest thy time,
but also how thou art accompanied: for though the
camomile, the more it is trodden on, the faster it grows,
yet youth, the more it is wasted, the sooner it wears.   That
thou art my son, I have partly thy mother's word, partly
my own opinion; but chiefly a villainous trick of thine eye,
and a foolish hanging of thy nether lip, that doth warrant
me.   If then thou be son to me, here lies the point:—why,
being son to me, art thou so pointed at? Shall the blessed
sun of heaven prove a micher, and eat blackberries? a
question not to be asked. Shall the son of England prove
a thief, and take purses? a question to be asked.   There
is a thing, Harry, which thou hast often heard of, and it is
known to many in our land by the name of pitch: this
pitch, as ancient writers do report, doth defile; so doth
the company thou keepest; for, Harry, now I do not speak
to thee in drink, but in tears; not in pleasure, but in
passion; not in words only, but in woes also:—and yet
there is a virtuous man, whom I have often noted in thy
company, but I know not his name.

P. Hen. What manner of man, an it like your majesty?

Fal. A goodly portly man, i' faith, and a corpulent;
of a cheerful look, a pleasing eye, and a most noble carriage;
and, as I think, his age some fifty, or, by'r lady, inclining
to threescore; and now I remember me, his name is
Falstaff: if that man should be lewdly given, he deceiveth
me; for, Harry, I see virtue in his looks. If then the tree
may be known by the fruit, as the fruit by the tree, then,
peremptorily I speak it, there is virtue in that Falstaff:
him keep with, the rest banish.—And tell me now, thou
naughty varlet, tell me, where hast thou been this month?

P. Hen. Dost thou speak like a king? Do thou stand
for me, and I'll play my father.

Fal. Depose me? If thou dost it half so gravely, so
majestically, both in word and matter, hang me up by the
heels for a rabbit-sucker or a poulter's hare.

P. Hen. Well, here I am set.

Fal. And here I stand.—Judge, my masters.

P. Hen. Now, Harry, whence come you?

Fal. My noble lord, from Eastcheap.

P. Hen. The complaints I hear of thee are grievous.

Fal. 'Sblood, my lord, they are false:—nay, I'll tickle ye for a young prince, i' faith.

P. Hen. Swearest thou, ungracious boy? henceforth ne'er look on me. Thou art violently carried away from grace: there is a devil haunts thee, in the likeness of a fat old man,—a tun of man is thy companion. Why dost thou converse with that trunk of humours, that bolting-hutch of beastliness, that swoln parcel of dropsies, that huge bombard of sack, that stuffed cloak-bag of guts, that roasted Manningtree ox with the pudding in his belly, that reverend vice, that grey iniquity, that father ruffian, that vanity in years? Wherein is he good, but to taste sack and drink it, wherein neat and cleanly, but to carve a capon and eat it? wherein cunning, but in craft? wherein crafty, but in villainy? wherein villainous, but in all things? wherein worthy, but in nothing?

Fal. I would your grace would take me with you. Whom means your grace?

P. Hen. That villainous abominable misleader of youth, Falstaff, that old white-bearded Satan.

Fal. My lord, the man I know.

P. Hen. I know thou dost.

Fal. But to say I know more harm in him than in myself, were to say more than I know. That he is old,— the more the pity,—his white hairs do witness it: but that he is,—saving your reverence,—a whoremaster, that I utterly deny. If sack and sugar be a fault, God help the wicked! If to be old and merry be a sin, then many an old host that I know is damned: if to be fat be to be hated, then Pharaoh's lean kine are to be loved. No, my good lord; banish Peto, banish Bardolph, banish Poins; but for sweet Jack Falstaff, kind Jack Falstaff, true Jack Falstaff, valiant Jack Falstaff, and therefore more valiant, being, as he is, old Jack Falstaff, banish not him thy Harry's company, banish not him thy Harry's company. Banish plump Jack, and banish all the world.

P. Hen. I do, I will.   [*A knocking heard*
                              [*Exeunt Hostess, Francis, and Bardolph*

Re-enter BARDOLPH, *running*

Bard. O, my lord, my lord! the sheriff with a most monstrous watch is at the door.

Fal. Out, ye rogue!—Play out the play: I have much to say in the behalf of that Falstaff.

Re-enter Hostess

Host. O Jesu, my lord, my lord,—

P. Hen. Heigh, heigh! the devil rides upon a fiddle-stick: what's the matter?

Host. The sheriff and all the watch are at the door: they are come to search the house. Shall I let them in?

Fal. Dost thou hear, Hal? never call a true piece of gold a counterfeit: thou art essentially mad, without seeming so.

P. Hen. And thou a natural coward, without instinct.

Fal. I deny your major: if you will deny the sheriff, so; if not, let him enter: if I become not a cart as well as another man, a plague on my bringing up! I hope I shall as soon be strangled with a halter as another.

P. Hen. Go, hide thee behind the arras:—the rest walk up above. Now, my masters, for a true face, and good conscience.

Fal. Both which I have had; but their date is out, and therefore I'll hide me.

> [*Exeunt all but the Prince and Poins*

P. Hen. Call in the sheriff.

Enter Sheriff and Carrier

Now, master sheriff, what's your will with me?

Sher. First, pardon me, my lord. A hue and cry
Hath followed certain men unto this house.

P. Hen. What men?

Sher. One of them is well known, my gracious lord,—
A gross fat man.

Car.   As fat as butter.

P. Hen. The man, I do assure you, is not here;
For I myself at this time have employed him,
And, sheriff, I will engage my word to thee,
That I will, by to-morrow dinner-time,
Send him to answer thee, or any man,
For anything he shall be charged withal:
And so, let me entreat you leave the house.

Sher. I will, my lord. There are two gentlemen
Have in this robbery lost three hundred marks.

P. Hen. It may be so: if he have robbed these men
He shall be answerable; and so, farewell.

Sher. Good night, my noble lord.

P. Hen. I think it is good morrow, is it not?

Sher. Indeed, my lord, I think it be two o'clock.

> [*Exeunt Sheriff and Carrier*

P. Hen. This oily rascal is known as well as Paul's. Go, call him forth.

Poins. Falstaff!—Fast asleep behind the arras, and snorting like a horse.

   P. Hen. Hark, how hard he fetches breath. Search his pockets. [*Poins searches*] What hast thou found?
   Poins. Nothing but papers, my lord.
   P. Hen. Let's see what they be: read them.
   Poins. [*Reads*] 'Item, A capon . . . **2s. 2d.**
Item, Sauce . . . . **4d.**
Item, Sack, two gallons . . . . **5s. 8d.**
Item, Anchovies, and sack after supper . . **2s. 6d.**
Item, Bread . . . . *ob.*'
   P. Hen. O monstrous, but one half-pennyworth of bread to this intolerable deal of sack!—What there is else, keep close; we'll read it at more advantage: there let him sleep till day. I'll to the court in the morning. We must all to the wars, and thy place shall be honourable. I'll procure this fat rogue a charge of foot; and I know his death will be a march of twelve-score. The money shall be paid back again with advantage. Be with me betimes in the morning; and so, good morrow, Poins.
   Poins. Good morrow, good my lord.   [*Exeunt*

ACT THREE

SCENE I.—Bangor. A Room in the Archdeacon's House

Enter HOTSPUR, WORCESTER, MORTIMER, *and* GLENDOWER

   Mort. These promises are fair, the parties sure,
And our induction full of prosperous hope.
   Hot. Lord Mortimer, and cousin Glendower,
Will you sit down?—
And, uncle Worcester:—a plague upon it!
I have forgot the map.
   Glend.   No, here it is.
Sit, cousin Percy; sir, good cousin Hotspur,
For by that name as oft as Lancaster
Doth speak of you, his cheek looks pale, and with
A rising sigh he wisheth you in heaven.
   Hot. And you in hell, as often as he hears
Owen Glendower spoke of.
   Glend. I cannot blame him.
At my nativity the front of heaven
Was full of fiery shapes, of burning cressets;
And at my birth the frame and huge foundations
Of the earth shaked like a coward.
   Hot. Why, so it would have done
At the same season, if your mother's cat
Had kittened, though yourself had ne'er been born.

Glend. I say, the earth did shake when I was born.
Hot. And I say, the earth was not of my mind,
If you suppose as fearing you it shook.
Glend. The heavens were all on fire, the earth did
          tremble.
Hot. O, then the earth shook to see the heavens on fire,
And not in fear of your nativity.
Diseaséd nature oftentimes breaks forth
In strange eruptions: oft the teeming earth
Is with a kind of colic pinched and vexed
By the imprisoning of unruly wind
Within her womb; which, for enlargement striving,
Shakes the old beldam earth, and topples down
Steeples, and moss-grown towers. At your birth,
Our grandam earth, having this distemperature,
In passion shook.
Glend.   Cousin, of many men
I do not bear these crossings. Give me leave
To tell you once again, that at my birth
The front of heaven was full of fiery shapes;
The goats ran from the mountains, and the herds
Were strangely clamorous to the frighted fields.
These signs have marked me extraordinary,
And all the courses of my life do show
I am not in the roll of common men.
Where is he living,—clipped in with sea
That chides the banks of England, Scotland, Wales,—
Which calls me pupil, or hath read to me?
And bring him out, that is but woman's son,
Can trace me in the tedious ways of art,
And hold me pace in deep experiments.
Hot. I think, there is no man speaks better Welsh.—
I'll to dinner.
Mort. Peace, cousin Percy; you will make him mad.
Glend. I can call spirits from the vasty deep.
Hot. Why, so can I, or so can any man;
But will they come, when you do call for them?
Glend. Why, I can teach you, cousin, to command the
          devil.
Hot. And I can teach thee, coz, to shame the devil
By telling truth: tell truth, and shame the devil.—
If thou have power to raise him, bring him hither,
And I'll be sworn, I've power to shame him hence.
O, while you live, tell truth, and shame the devil.
Mort. Come, come,
No more of this unprofitable chat.
Glend. Three times hath Henry Bolingbroke made head
Against my power: thrice from the banks of Wye,
And sandy bottomed Severn, have I sent
Him bootless home, and weather-beaten back.

   Hot.   Home without boots, and in foul weather too!
How 'scapes he agues, in the devil's name?
   Glend.   Come, here's the map. Shall we divide our
      right,
According to our three-fold order ta'en?
   Mort.   Aye, the archdeacon hath divided it
Into three limits very equally.
England, from Trent and Severn hitherto,
By south and east, is to my part assigned.
All westward, Wales, beyond the Severn shore,
And all the fertile land within that bound,
To Owen Glendower:—and, dear coz, to you
The remnant northward, lying off from Trent.
And our indentures tripartite are drawn,
Which being sealéd interchangeably—
A business that this night may execute—
To-morrow, cousin Percy, you and I,
And my good lord of Worcester, will set forth,
To meet your father and the Scottish power,
As is appointed us, at Shrewsbury.
My father Glendower is not ready yet,
Nor shall we need his help these fourteen days:—
Within that space you may have drawn together
Your tenants, friends, and neighbouring gentlemen.
   Glend.   A shorter time shall send me to you, lords:
And in my conduct shall your ladies come;
From whom you now must steal, and take no leave,
For there will be a world of water shed
Upon the parting of your wives and you.
   Hot.   Methinks my moiety, north from Burton here,
In quantity equals not one of yours.
See, how this river comes me cranking in,
And cuts me from the best of all my land
A huge half-moon, a monstrous cantle out.
I'll have the current in this place damned up,
And here the smug and silver Trent shall run
In a new channel, fair and evenly:
It shall not wind with such a deep indent,
To rob me of so rich a bottom here.
   Glend.   Not wind? it shall, it must; you see, it doth.
   Mort.   Yet, but
Mark, how he bears his course, and runs me up
With like advantage on the other side;
Gelding the opposéd continent as much
As on the other side it takes from you.
   Wor.   Yea, but a little charge will trench him here,
And on this north side win this cape of land;
And then he runs straightly and evenly.
   Hot.   I'll have it so; a little charge will do it.
   Glend.   I will not have it altered.

Hot.   Will not you?
Glend.   No, nor you shall not.
Hot.   Who shall say me nay?
Glend.   Why, that will I.
Hot.   Let me not understand you then:
Speak it in Welsh.
  Glend.   I can speak English, lord, as well as you,
For I was trained up in the English court;
Where, being but young, I faméd to the harp
Many an English ditty, lovely well,
And gave the tongue a helpful ornament,—
A virtue that was never seen in you.
  Hot.   Marry, and I'm glad of it with all my heart.
I had rather be a kitten, and cry mew,
Than one of these same metre ballad-mongers;
I had rather hear a brazen canstick turned,
Or a dry wheel grate on the axle-tree;
And that would set my teeth nothing on edge,
Nothing, so much as mincing poetry:—
'T is like the forced gait of a shuffling nag.
  Glend.   Come, you shall have Trent turned.
  Hot.   I do not care: I'll give thrice so much land
Away to any well-deserving friend;
But in the way of bargain, mark ye me,
I'll cavil on the ninth part of a hair.
Are the indentures drawn? shall we be gone?
  Glend.   The moon shines fair, you may away by night:
I'll haste the writer, and withal
Break with your wives of your departure hence.
I am afraid my daughter will run mad,
So much she doteth on her Mortimer.   [*Exit*
  Mort. Fie, cousin Percy, how you cross my father!
  Hot.   I cannot choose: sometime he angers me
With telling me of the moldwarp and the ant,
Of the dreamer Merlin and his prophecies,
And of a dragon, and a finless fish,
A clip-winged griffin, and a moulten raven,
A couching lion, and a ramping cat,
And such a deal of skimble-skamble stuff
As puts me from my faith.   I tell you what,—
He held me, last night, at the least nine hours,
In reckoning up the several devils' names
That were his lackeys: I cried, 'Humph,' and 'Well, go
      to,'
But marked him not a word.   O, he's as tedious
As is a tired horse, a railing wife;
Worse than a smoky house.   I had rather live
With cheese and garlic in a windmill, far
Then feed on cates and have him talk to me
In any summer-house in Christendom.

Mort.   In faith, he is a worthy gentleman,
Exceedingly well read, and profited
In strange concealments, valiant as a lion,
And wondrous affable, and as bountiful
As mines of India.   Shall I tell you, cousin?
He holds your temper in a high respect,
And curbs himself even of his natural scope,
When you do cross his humour; 'faith, he does:
I warrant you, that man is not alive
Might so have tempted him as you have done,
Without the taste of danger and reproof:
But do not use it oft, let me entreat you.
        Wor.   In faith, my lord, you are too wilful-blame;
And since your coming hither have done enough
To put him quite beside his patience.
You must needs learn, lord, to amend this fault:
Though sometimes it show greatness, courage, blood,—
And that's the dearest grace it renders you,—
Yet oftentimes it doth present harsh rage,
Defect of manners, want of government,
Pride, haughtiness, opinion, and disdain;
The least of which haunting a nobleman
Loseth men's hearts, and leaves behind a stain
Upon the beauty of all parts besides,
Beguiling them of commendation.
        Hot.   Well, I am schooled: good manners be your speed!
Here come our wives, and let us take our leave.

Re-enter GLENDOWER, *with* LADY MORTIMER *and* LADY
                    PERCY

        Mort.   This is the deadly spite that angers me,
My wife can speak no English, I no Welsh.
        Glend.   My daughter weeps: she will not part with you:
She'll be a soldier too; she'll to the wars.
        Mort.   Good father, tell her, she and my aunt Percy,
Shall follow in your conduct speedily.
                    [*Glendower speaks to her in Welsh, and
                        she answers him in the same*
        Glend.   She's   desperate   here;   a peevish self-willed
            harlotry,
One no persuasion can do good upon.
                    [*She speaks to Mortimer in Welsh*
        Mort.   I understand thy looks: that pretty Welsh
Which thou pourest down from these swelling heavens,
I am too perfect in: and, but for shame,
In such a parley should I answer thee.   [*She speaks again*
I understand thy kisses, and thou mine,
And that's a feeling disputation:
But I will never be a truant, love,

51

Till I have learned thy language; for thy tongue
Makes Welsh as sweet as ditties highly penned
Sung by a fair queen in a summer's bower
With ravishing division to her lute.
    Glend. Nay, if you melt, then will she run mad.
                                  [She speaks again
    Mort. O, I am ignorance itself in this.
    Glend. She bids you
Upon the wanton rushes lay you down,
And rest your gentle head upon her lap,
And she will sing the song that pleaseth you,
And on your eyelids crown the god of sleep,
Charming your blood with pleasing heaviness:
Making such difference 'twixt wake and sleep
As is the difference betwixt day and night
The hour before the heavenly-harnessed team
Begins his golden progress in the east.
    Mort. With all my heart I'll sit and hear her sing:
By that time will our book, I think, be drawn.
    Glend. Do so;
And those musicians that shall play to you,
Hang in the air a thousand leagues from hence;
And straight they shall be here. Sit, and attend.
    Hot. Come, Kate, thou art perfect in lying down:
come, quick, quick; that I may lay my head in thy lap.
    Lady P. Go, ye giddy goose.   *[The music plays*
    Hot. Now I perceive the devil understands Welsh;
And 't is no marvel, he's so humorous.
By'r lady, he's a good musician.
    Lady. P. Then should you be nothing but musical,
for you are altogether governed by humours. Lie still, ye
thief, and hear the lady sing in Welsh.
    Hot. I had rather hear, Lady, my brach howl in Irish.
    Lady P. Wouldst have thy head broken?
    Hot. No.
    Lady P. Then be still.
    Hot. Neither: 't is a woman's fault.
    Lady P. Now, God help thee!
    Hot. To the Welsh lady's bed.
    Lady P. What's that?
    Hot. Peace! she sings.
              [A Welsh song sung by Lady Mortimer
    Hot. Come, Kate, I'll have your song too.
    Lady P. Not mine, in good sooth.
    Hot. Not yours, in good sooth! 'Heart! you swear
like a comfit-maker's wife. 'Not you, in good sooth';
and, 'As true as I live;' and, 'As God shall mend me;'
and, 'As sure as day:'
And giv'st such sarcenet surety for thy oaths,
As if thou never walk'dst further than Finsbury.

Swear me, Kate, like a lady as thou art,
A good mouth-filling oath; and leave 'in sooth,'
And such protest of pepper-gingerbread,
To velvet-guards and Sunday-citizens.
Come, sing.
    Lady P. I will not sing.
    Hot. 'T is the next way to turn tailor, or be redbreast
teacher. An the indentures be drawn, I'll away within
these two hours; and so, come in when ye will.   [*Exit*
    Glend. Come, come, Lord Mortimer; you are as slow
As hot Lord Percy is on fire to go.
By this our book's drawn; we'll but seal, and then
To horse immediately.
    Mort. With all my heart.   [*Exeunt*

SCENE II.—London. A Room in the Palace

Enter KING HENRY, PRINCE OF WALES, *and* LORDS

    K. Hen. Lords, give us leave; the Prince of Wales
        and I
Must have some conference: but be near at hand,
For we shall presently have need of you.— [*Exeunt Lords*
I know not whether God will have it so,
For some displeasing service I have done,
That, in his secret doom, out of my blood
He'll breed revengement and a scourge for me;
But thou dost, in thy passages of life,
Make me believe, that thou art only marked
For the hot vengeance and the rod of Heaven
To punish my mistreadings. Tell me else,
Could such inordinate and low desires,
Such poor, such bare, such lewd, such mean attempts,
Such barren pleasures, rude society,
As thou art matched withal and grafted to,
Accompany the greatness of thy blood,
And hold their level with thy princely heart?
    P. Hen. So please your majesty, I would I could
Quit all offences with as clear excuse
As well as, I am doubtless, I can purge
Myself of many I am charged withal:
Yet such extenuation let me beg
As in reproof of many tales devised—
Which oft the ear of greatness needs must hear—
By smiling pick-thanks and base newsmongers,
I may for some things true wherein my youth
Hath faulty wandered and irregular
Find pardon on my true submission.
    K. Hen. God pardon thee!—yet let me wonder, Harry

At thy affections, which do hold a wing
Quite from the flight of all thy ancestors.
Thy place in council thou hast rudely lost,
Which by thy younger brother is supplied;
And art almost an alien to the hearts
Of all the court and princes of my blood.
The hope and expectation of thy time
Is ruined; and the soul of every man
Prophetically does forethink thy fall.
Had I so lavish of my presence been,
So common-hackneyed in the eyes of men,
So stale and cheap to vulgar company,
Opinion, that did help me to the crown,
Had still kept loyal to possession,
And left me in reputeless banishment,
A fellow of no mark nor likelihood.
By being seldom seen, I could not stir,
But like a comet I was wondered at;
That men would tell their children, 'This is he;'
Others would say,—'Where? which is Bolingbroke?'
And then I stole all courtesy from Heaven,
And dressed myself in such humility
That I did pluck allegiance from men's hearts,
Loud shouts and salutations from their mouths,
Even in the presence of the crownéd king.
Thus did I keep my person fresh and new;
My presence, like a robe pontifical,
Ne'er seen but wondered at: and so my state
Seldom but sumptuous, showed like a feast,
And won by rareness such solemnity.
The skipping king, he ambled up and down
With shallow jesters and rash bavin wits,
Soon kindled and soon burned; carded his state;
Mingled his royalty with capering fools,
Had his great name profanéd with their scorns,
And gave his countenance, against his name,
To laugh at gibing boys, and stand the push
Of every beardless vain comparative;
Grew a companion to the common streets,
Enfeoffed himself to popularity,
That, being daily swallowed by men's eyes,
They surfeited with honey, and began
To loathe the taste of sweetness, whereof a little
More than a little is by much too much.
So, when he had occasion to be seen,
He was but as the cuckoo is in June,
Heard, not regarded; seen, but with such eyes
As, sick and blunted with community,
Afford no extraordinary gaze
Such as is bent on sun-like majesty

When it shines seldom in admiring eyes;
But rather drowsed, and hung their eyelids down,
Slept in his face, and rendered such aspect
As cloudy men use to their adversaries,
Being with his presence glutted, gorged, and full.
And in that very line, Harry, stand'st thou;
For thou hast lost thy princely privilege
With vile participation: not an eye
But is aweary of thy common sight,
Save mine, which hath desired to see thee more;
Which now doth that I would not have it do,—
Make blind itself with foolish tenderness.
    P. Hen.   I shall hereafter, my thrice gracious lord,
Be more myself.
    K. Hen.   For all the world,
As thou art to this hour, was Richard then
When I from France set foot at Ravenspurg;
And even as I was then, is Percy now.
Now, by my sceptre, and my soul to boot,
He hath more worthy interest to the state
Than thou the shadow of succession:
For, of no right, nor colour like to right,
He doth fill fields with harness in the realm,
Turns head against the lion's arméd jaws,
And, being no more in debt to years than thou,
Leads ancient lords and reverend bishops on
To bloody battles and to bruising arms.
What never-dying honour hath he got
Against renownéd Douglas, whose high deeds,
Whose hot incursions, and great name in arms,
Holds from all soldiers chief majority
And military title capital
Through all the kingdoms that acknowledge Christ.
Thrice hath this Hotspur, Mars in swathing-clothes,
This infant warrior, in his enterprises
Discomfited great Douglas: ta'en him once,
Enlargéd him, and made a friend of him,
To fill the mouth of deep defiance up,
And shake the peace and safety of our throne.
And what say you to this?   Percy, Northumberland,
The Archbishop's Grace of York, Douglas, and Mortimer,
Capitulate against us, and are up.
But wherefore do I tell these news to thee?
Why, Harry, do I tell thee of my foes,
Which art my near'st and dearest enemy?
Thou that art like enough, through vassal fear,
Base inclination, and the start of spleen,
To fight against me under Percy's pay,
To dog his heels, and court'sy at his frowns,
To show how much thou art degenerate.

P. Hen.   Do not think so; you shall not find it so:
And God forgive them that so much have swayed
Your majesty's good thoughts away from me!
I will redeem all this on Percy's head,
And, in the closing of some glorious day,
Be bold to tell you that I am your son;
When I will wear a garment all of blood,
And stain my favours in a bloody mask,
Which, washed away, shall scour my shame with it:
And that shall be the day, whene'er it lights,
That this same child of honour and renown,
This gallant Hotspur, this all praiséd knight,
And your unthought-of Harry, chance to meet.
For every honour sitting on his helm,
'Would they were multitudes, and on my head
My shames redoubled! for the time will come
That I shall make this northern youth exchange
His glorious deeds for my indignities.
Percy is but my factor, good my lord,
To engross up glorious deeds on my behalf;
And I will call him to so strict account,
That he shall render every glory up,
Yea, even the slightest worship of his time,
Or I will tear the reckoning from his heart.
This, in the name of God, I promise here:
The which, if he be pleased I shall perform,
I do beseech your majesty, may salve
The long-grown wounds of my intemperance:
If not, the end of life cancels all bands,
And I will die a hundred thousand deaths
Ere break the smallest parcel of this vow.
K. Hen.   A hundred thousand rebels die in this:—
Thou shalt have charge and sovereign trust herein.

Enter BLUNT

How, now, good Blunt? thy looks are full of speed.
Blunt.   So is the business that I come to speak of.
Lord Mortimer of Scotland hath sent word
That Douglas and the English rebels met
The eleventh of this month at Shrewsbury.
A mighty and a fearful head they are,
If promises be kept on every hand,
As ever offered foul play in a state.
K. Hen.   The Earl of Westmoreland set forth to-day
With him my son, Lord John of Lancaster;
For this advertisement is five days old.—
On Wednesday next, Harry, you shall set forward;
On Thursday we ourselves will march:
Our meeting is Bridgnorth: and, Harry, you

56

Shall march through Glostershire; by which account
Our business valuéd, some twelve days hence
Our general forces at Bridgnorth shall meet.
Our hands are full of business: let's away;
Advantage feeds him fat while men delay.   *[Exeunt*

SCENE III.—Eastcheap. A Room in the Boar's
Head Tavern

Enter FALSTAFF *and* BARDOLPH

Fal. Bardolph, am I not fallen away vilely since this last
action? do I not bate? do I not dwindle? Why, my skin
hangs about me like an old lady's loose gown: I am
withered like an old apple-John. Well, I'll repent, and
that suddenly, while I am in some liking; I shall be out of
heart shortly, and then I shall have no strength to repent.
An I have not forgotten what the inside of a church is made
of, I am a peppercorn, a brewer's horse: the inside of a
church! Company, villainous company, hath been the spoil
of me.

Bard. Sir John, you are so fretful, you cannot live long.

Fal. Why, there is it:—come, sing me a bawdy song;
make me merry. I was as virtuously given as a gentleman
need to be; virtuous enough: swore little; diced not above
seven times a week; went to a bawdy-house not above once
in a quarter—of an hour; paid money that I borrowed—
three or four times, lived well, and in good compass: and
now I live out of all order, out of all compass.

Bard. Why, you are so fat, Sir John, that you must
needs be out of all compass,—out of all reasonable compass,
Sir John.

Fal. Do thou amend thy face, and I'll amend my life.
Thou art our admiral, thou bearest the lantern in the poop,—
but 't is in the nose of thee; thou art the Knight of the
Burning Lamp.

Bard. Why, Sir John, my face does you no harm.

Fal. No, I'll be sworn, I make as good use of it as many
a man doth of a death's-head or a *memento mori*. I never see
thy face but I think upon hell-fire, and Dives that lived in
purple; for there he is in his robes, burning, burning. If
thou wert any way given to virtue, I would swear by thy face;
my oath should be, 'By this fire, that's God's angel.' But
thou art altogether given over, and wert indeed, but for the
light in thy face, the sun of utter darkness. When thou
rann'st up Gadshill in the night to catch my horse, if I did
not think thou hadst been an *ignis fatuus* or a ball of wild-
fire, there's no purchase in money. O, thou art a perpetual
triumph, an everlasting bonfire-light. Thou hast saved me

a thousand marks in links and torches, walking with thee in the night betwixt tavern and tavern: but the sack that thou hast drunk me would have bought me lights as good cheap at the dearest chandler's in Europe. I have maintained that salamander of yours with fire any time this two-and-thirty years; God reward me for it!

Bard. 'Sblood, I would my face were in your belly!

Fal. God-a-mercy! so should I be sure to be heart-burned.

Enter Hostess

How now, Dame Partlet the hen? have you inquired yet who picked my pocket?

Host. Why, Sir John, what do you think, Sir John? Do you think I keep thieves in my house? I have searched, I have inquired, so has my husband, man by man, boy by boy, servant by servant: the tithe of a hair was never lost in my house before.

Fal. Ye lie, hostess; Bardolph was shaved, and lost many a hair; and I'll be sworn my pocket was picked. Go to, you are a woman, go.

Host. Who, I? No, I defy thee: God's light, I was never called so in mine own house before.

Fal. Go to, I know you well enough.

Host. No, Sir John; you do not know me, Sir John. I know you, Sir John: you owe me money, Sir John, and now you pick a quarrel to beguile me of it. I bought you a dozen of shirts to your back.

Fal. Dowlas, filthy dowlas: I have given them away to bakers' wives, and they have made boulters of them.

Host. Now, as I am a true woman, holland of eight shillings an ell. You owe money here besides, Sir John, for your diet, and by-drinkings, and money lent you, four-and-twenty pound.

Fal. He had his part of it; let him pay.

Host. He? alas, he is poor: he had nothing.

Fal. How! poor? look upon his face; what call you rich? let them coin his nose, let them coin his cheeks, I'll not pay a denier. What, will you make a younker of me? shall I not take mine ease in mine inn, but I shall have my pocket picked? I have lost a seal-ring of my grandfather's, worth forty mark.

Host. O Jesu, I have heard the prince tell him, I know not how oft, that that ring was copper.

Fal. How! the prince is a Jack, a sneakcup: 'sblood, an he were here, I would cudgel him like a dog, if he would say so.

Enter PRINCE HENRY *and* POINS, *marching.* FALSTAFF
meets the PRINCE, *playing on his truncheon, like a fife*

Fal.   How now, lad? is the wind in that door, i' faith?
must we all march?

Bard.   Yea, two and two, Newgate-fashion.

Host.   My lord, I pray you, hear me.

P. Hen.   What sayest thou, Mistress Quickly? How
does thy husband? I love him well, he is an honest
man.

Host.   Good my lord, hear me.

Fal.   Pr'ythee, let her alone, and list to me.

P. Hen.   What sayest thou, Jack?

Fal.   The other night I fell asleep, here, behind the arras,
and had my pocket picked: this house is turned bawdy-
house; they pick pockets.

P. Hen.   What didst thou lose, Jack?

Fal.   Wilt thou believe me, Hal? three or four bonds of
forty pounds a-piece, and a seal-ring of my grandfather's.

P. Hen.   A trifle; some eight-penny matter.

Host.   So I told him, my lord; and I said I heard your
grace say so: and, my lord, he speaks most vilely of you,
like a foul-mouthed man as he is, and said he would cudgel
you.

P. Hen.   What! he did not?

Host.   There's neither faith, truth, nor womanhood in
me else.

Fal.   There's no more faith in thee than in a stewed
prune; nor no more truth in thee than in a drawn fox;
and for womanhood, Maid Marian may be the deputy's
wife of the ward to thee. Go, you thing, go.

Host.   Say, what thing? what thing?

Fal.   What thing? why, a thing to thank God on.

Host.   I am no thing to thank God on, I would thou
shouldst know it; I am an honest man's wife; and, setting
thy knighthood aside, thou art a knave to call me so.

Fal.   Setting thy womanhood aside, thou art a beast to
say otherwise.

Host.   Say, what beast, thou knave, thou?

Fal.   What beast? why, an otter.

P. Hen.   An otter, Sir John! why an otter?

Fal.   Why, she's neither fish nor flesh; a man knows not
where to have her.

Host.   Thou art an unjust man in saying so: thou or
any man knows where to have me, thou knave thou!

P. Hen.   Thou sayest true, hostess; and he slanders thee
most grossly.

Host.   So he doth you, my lord; and said this other
day, you ought him a thousand pound.

P. Hen.   Sirrah, do I owe you a thousand pound?

Fal. A thousand pound, Hal! a million: thy love is worth a million; thou owest me thy love.

Host. Nay, my lord, he called you Jack, and said he would cudgel you.

Fal. Did I, Bardolph?

Bard. Indeed, Sir John, you said so.

Fal. Yea,—if he said my ring was copper.

P. Hen. I say, 't is copper: darest thou be as good as thy word now?

Fal. Why, Hal, thou knowest, as thou art but a man, I dare; but as thou art a prince, I fear thee as I fear the roaring of the lion's whelp.

P. Hen. And why not as the lion?

Fal. The king himself is to be feared as the lion. Dost thou think, I'll fear thee as I fear thy father? nay, an I do, I pray God my girdle break!

P. Hen. O, if it should, how would thy guts fall about thy knees! But, sirrah, there's no room for faith, truth, nor honesty in this bosom of thine,—it is filled up with guts and midriff. Charge an honest woman with picking thy pocket! why, thou whoreson, impudent, embossed rascal, if there were anything in thy pocket but tavern-reckonings, memorandums of bawdy-houses, and one poor pennyworth of sugar-candy to make thee long-winded,—if thy pocket were enriched with any other injuries but these, I am a villain. And yet you will stand to it; you will not pocket up wrong. Art thou not ashamed?

Fal. Dost thou hear, Hal? thou knowest, in the state of innocency Adam fell; and what should poor Jack Falstaff do in the days of villainy? Thou seest I have more flesh than another man; and therefore more frailty. You confess, then, you picked my pocket?

P. Hen. It appears so by the story.

Fal. Hostess, I forgive thee: go, make ready breakfast; love thy husband, look to thy servants, cherish thy guests: thou shalt find me tractable to any honest reason; thou seest I am pacified.—Still?—Nay, pr'ythee, be gone. [*Exit Hostess*] Now, Hal, to the news at court. For the robbery, lad,—how is that answered?

P. Hen. O! my sweet beef, I must still be good angel to thee:—the money is paid back again.

Fal. O, I do not like that paying back; 't is a double labour.

P. Hen. I am good friends with my father, and may do anything.

Fal. Rob me the exchequer the first thing thou doest, and do it with unwashed hands too.

Bard. Do, my lord.

P. Hen. I have procured thee, Jack, a charge of foot.

Fal. I would it had been of horse. Where shall I find

one that can steal well? O, for a fine thief, of the age of
two-and-twenty, or thereabouts! I am heinously un-
provided. Well, God be thanked for these rebels,—they
offend none but the virtuous: I laud them, I praise them.

 P. Hen. Bardolph!
 Bard. My lord.
 P. Hen. Go bear this letter to Lord John of Lancaster,
To my brother John; this to my Lord of Westmoreland.
            [Exit Bardolph
Go, Poins, to horse, to horse! for thou and I
Have thirty miles to ride ere dinner-time. *[Exit Poins*
Meet me to-morrow in the Temple Hall
At two o'clock, Jack, in the afternoon:
There shalt thou know thy charge, and there receive
Money, and order for their furniture.
The land is burning, Percy stands on high;
And either they or we must lower lie.   *[Exit*
 Fal. Rare words! brave world!—Hostess, my break-
   fast; come:—
O! I could wish this tavern were my drum. *[Exit*

ACT FOUR

SCENE I.—The Rebel Camp near Shrewsbury

Enter HOTSPUR, WORCESTER, *and* DOUGLAS

 Hot. Well said, my noble Scot: if speaking truth
In this fine age were not thought flattery,
Such attribution should the Douglas have,
As not a soldier of this season's stamp
Should go so general current through the world.
By God, I cannot flatter; I defy
The tongues of soothers; but a braver place
In my heart's love hath no man than yourself.
Nay, task me to my word; approve me, lord.
 Doug. Thou art the king of honour:
No man so potent breathes upon the ground
But I will beard him.
 Hot.   Do so, and 't is well.—

Enter a Messenger with letters

What letters hast thou there?—I can but thank you.
 Mess. These letters come from your father,—
 Hot. Letters from him! why comes he not himself?
 Mess. He cannot come, my lord: he's grievous sick.
 Hot. Zounds! how has he the leisure to be sick

In such a justling time?   Who leads his power?
Under whose government come they along?
    Mess.   His letters bear his mind, not I, my lord.
    Wor.   I pr'ythee, tell me, doth he keep his bed?
    Mess.   He did, my lord, four days ere I set forth;
And at the time of my departure thence
He was much feared by his physicians.
    Wor.   I would the state of time had first been whole
Ere he by sickness had been visited:
His health was never better worth than now.
    Hot.   Sick now! droop now! this sickness doth infect
The very life-blood of our enterprise;
'T is catching hither, even to our camp.
He writes me here, that inward sickness—
And that his friends by deputation could not
So soon be drawn; nor did he think it meet,
To lay so dangerous and dear a trust
On any soul removed, but on his own.
Yet doth he give us bold advertisement,
That with our small conjunction we should on,
To see how fortune is disposed to us;
For, as he writes, there is no quailing now,
Because the king is certainly possessed
Of all our purposes.   What say you to it?
    Wor.   Your father's sickness is a maim to us.
    Hot.   A perilous gash, a very limb lopped off:—
And yet, in faith, it's not; his present want
Seems more than we shall find it:—were it good
To set the exact wealth of all our states
All at one cast? to set so rich a main
On the nice hazard of one doubtful hour?
It were not good; for therein should we read
The very bottom and the soul of hope,
The very list, the very utmost bound
Of all our fortunes.
    Doug.   'Faith, and so we should
Where now remains a sweet reversion;
And we may boldly spend upon the hope
Of what is to come in:
A comfort of retirement lives in this.
    Hot.   A rendezvous, a home to fly unto,
If that the devil and mischance look big
Upon the maidenhead of our affairs.
    Wor.   But yet, I would your father had been here.
The quality and hair of our attempt
Brooks no division: it will be thought
By some, that know not why he is away,
That wisdom, loyalty, and mere dislike
Of our proceedings, kept the earl from hence:
And think how such an apprehension

May turn the tide of fearful faction,
And breed a kind of question in our cause:
For well you know we of the offering side
Must keep aloof from strict arbitrement,
And stop all sight-holes, every loop from whence
The eye of reason may pry in upon us.
This absence of your father's draws a curtain,
That shows the ignorant a kind of fear
Before not dreamt of.
   Hot.   You strain too far.
I rather of his absence make this use:—
It lends a lustre, and more great opinion,
A larger dare to our great enterprise,
Than if the earl were here; for men must think,
If we, without his help, can make a head
To push against the kingdom, with his help
We shall o'erturn it topsy-turvy down.—
Yet all goes well, yet all our joints are whole.
   Doug.   As heart can think: there is not such a word
Spoke of in Scotland as this term of fear.

            Enter SIR RICHARD VERNON

   Hot.   My cousin Vernon! welcome, by my soul.
   Ver.   Pray God, my news be worth a welcome, lord.
The Earl of Westmoreland, seven thousand strong,
Is marching hitherwards; with him, Prince John.
   Hot.   No harm: what more?
   Ver.   And further, I have learned,
The king himself in person is set forth,
Or hitherwards intended speedily,
With strong and mighty preparation.
   Hot.   He shall be welcome too.   Where is his son,
The nimble-footed madcap Prince of Wales,
And his comrádes, that daffed the world aside,
And bid it pass?
   Ver.   All furnished, all in arms,
All plumed like estridges that wing the wind:
Bated like eagles having lately bathed,
Glittering in golden coats, like images;
As full of spirit as the month of May,
And gorgeous as the sun at midsummer;
Wanton as youthful goats, wild as young bulls.
I saw young Harry, with his beaver on,
His cuisses on his thighs, gallantly armed,
Rise from the ground like feathered Mercury,
And vaulted with such ease into his seat,
As if an angel dropped down from the clouds
To turn and wind a fiery Pegasus
And witch the world with noble horsemanship.

Hot. No more, no more: worse than the sun in March
This praise doth nourish agues. Let them come;
They come like sacrifices in their trim,—
And to the fire-eyed maid of smoky war,
All hot and bleeding, will we offer them:
The mailéd Mars shall on his altar sit
Up to the ears in blood. I am on fire
To hear this rich reprisal is so nigh,
And yet not ours.—Come, let me taste my horse,
Who is to bear me like a thunderbolt
Against the bosom of the Prince of Wales:
Harry to Harry shall, hot horse to horse,
Meet, and ne'er part till one drop down a corse.—
O, that Glendower were come!
Ver.   There is more news:
I learned in Worcester, as I rode along,
He cannot draw his power this fourteen days.
    Doug. That's the worst tidings that I hear of yet.
    Wor. Ay, by my faith, that bears a frosty sound.
    Hot. What may the king's whole battle reach unto?
    Ver. To thirty thousand.
    Hot.   Forty let it be:
My father and Glendower being both away,
The powers of us may serve so great a day.
Come, let us take a muster speedily:
Doomsday is near; die all, die merrily.
    Doug. Talk not of dying: I am out of fear
Of death or death's hand for this one half year.   [*Exeunt*

SCENE II.—A Public Road near Coventry

Enter FALSTAFF *and* BARDOLPH

    Fal. Bardolph, get thee before to Coventry; fill me a
bottle of sack: our soldiers shall march through; we'll
to Sutton Co'fil' to-night.
    Bard. Will you give me money, captain?
    Fal. Lay out, lay out.
    Bard. This bottle makes an angel.
    Fal. An if it do, take it for thy labour; and if it make
twenty, take them all; I'll answer the coinage. Bid
my lieutenant Peto meet me at the town's end.
    Bard. I will, captain: farewell.   [*Exit*
    Fal. If I be not ashamed of my soldiers, I am a soused
gurnet. I have misused the king's press damnably. I
have got, in exchange of a hundred and fifty soldiers, three
hundred and odd pounds. I press me none but good
householders, yeomen's sons: inquire me out contracted
bachelors, such as had been asked twice on the banns;

such a commodity of warm slaves as had as lief hear the
devil as a drum; such as fear the report of a caliver worse
than a struck fowl or a hurt wild duck. I pressed me none
but such toasts-and-butter, with hearts in their bellies no
bigger than pins' heads, and they have bought out their
services; and now my whole charge consists of ancients,
corporals, lieutenants, gentlemen of companies, slaves as
ragged as Lazarus in the painted cloth, where the glutton's
dogs lick at his sores; and such as, indeed, were never soldiers,
but discarded unjust serving-men, younger sons to younger
brothers, revolted tapsters, and ostlers trade-fallen; the
cankers of a calm world, and a long peace; ten times more
dishonourable ragged than an old faced ancient: and such
have I, to fill up the rooms of them that have bought out
their services, that you would think that I had a hundred
and fifty tattered prodigals lately come from swine-keeping,
from eating draff and husks. A mad fellow met me on
the way, and told me I had unloaded all the gibbets and
pressed the dead bodies. No eye hath seen such scare-
crows. I'll not march through Coventry with them,
that's flat:—nay, and the villains march wide betwixt
the legs, as if they had gyves on; for indeed, I had the
most of them out of prison. There's not a shirt and a
half in all my company: and the half-shirt is two napkins
tacked together, and thrown over the shoulders like a
herald's coat without sleeves; and the shirt, to say the
truth, stolen from my host at St. Albans, or the red-nose
inn-keeper of Daventry. But that's all one; they'll find
linen enough on every hedge.

Enter PRINCE HENRY *and* WESTMORELAND

P. Hen. How now, blown Jack? how now, quilt?
   Fal. What, Hal! How now, mad wag? what a devil
dost thou in Warwickshire?—My good Lord of Westmoreland, I cry you mercy; I thought your honour had already
been at Shrewsbury.
   West. 'Faith, Sir John, 't is more than time that I were
there, and you too; but my powers are there already.
The king, I can tell you, looks for us all: we must away
all to-night.
   Fal. Tut, never fear me; I am as vigilant as a cat to
steal cream.
   P. Hen. I think, to steal cream indeed; for thy theft
hath already made thee butter. But tell me, Jack; whose
fellows are these that come after?
   Fal. Mine, Hal, mine.
   P. Hen. I did never see such pitiful rascals.
   Fal. Tut, tut! good enough to toss; food for powder,
food for powder; they'll fill a pit, as well as better; tush,
man, mortal men, mortal men.

West. Ay, but Sir John, methinks they are exceeding poor and bare,—too beggarly.

Fal. 'Faith, for their poverty, I know not where they had that; and for their bareness, I am sure, they never learned that of me.

P. Hen. No, I'll be sworn; unless you call three fingers on the ribs, bare. But, sirrah, make haste; Percy is already in the field.   [*Exit*

Fal. What, is the king encamped?

West. He is, Sir John: I fear we shall stay too long.
                                                          [*Exit*

Fal. Well,
To the latter end of a fray, and the beginning of a feast,
Fits a dull fighter, and a keen guest.   [*Exit*

Scene III.—The Rebel Camp near Shrewsbury

Enter Hotspur, Worcester, Douglas, *and* Vernon

Hot. We'll fight with him to-night.

Wor.   It may not be.

Doug. You give him, then, advantage.

Ver.   Not a whit.

Hot. Why say you so? looks he not for supply?

Ver. So do we.

Hot.   His is certain, ours is doubtful.

Wor. Good cousin, be advised, stir not to-night.

Ver. Do not, my lord.

Doug.   You do not counsel well.
You speak it out of fear and a cold heart.

Ver. Do me no slander, Douglas; by my life,—
And I dare well maintain it with my life,—
If well-respected honour bid me on,
I hold as little counsel with weak fear
As you, or any Scot that this day lives:
Let it be seen to-morrow in the battle,
Which of us fears.

Doug.   Yea, or to-night.

Ver.   Content.

Hot. To-night, say I.

Ver. Come, come, it may not be. I wonder much,
Being men of such great leading as you are,
That you foresee not what impediments
Drag back our expedition: certain horse
Of my cousin Vernon's are not yet come up;
Your uncle Worcester's horse came but to-day,
And now their pride and mettle is asleep,
Their courage with hard labour tame and dull.
That not a horse is half the half of himself.

Hot.   So are the horses of the enemy
In general, journey bated, and brought low:
The better part of ours are full of rest.
   Wor.   The number of the king exceedeth ours;
For God's sake, cousin, stay till all come in.
                    [*The trumpet sounds a parley*

Enter SIR WALTER BLUNT

   Blunt.   I come with gracious offers from the king,
If you vouchsafe me hearing and respect.
   Hot.   Welcome, Sir Walter Blunt; and would to God
You were of our determination!
Some of us love you well; and even those some
Envy your great deservings and good name,
Because you are not of our quality
But stand against us like an enemy.
   Blunt.   And God defend but still I should stand so,
So long as out of limit and true rule
You stand against anointed majesty.
But, to my charge.—The king hath sent to know
The nature of your griefs, and whereupon
You conjure from the breast of civil peace
Such bold hostility, teaching his duteous land
Audacious cruelty?   If that the king
Have any way your good deserts forgot,
Which he confesseth to be manifold,
He bids you name your griefs, and, with all speed
You shall have your desires with interest,
And pardon absolute for yourself and these
Herein misled by your suggestion.
   Hot.   The king is kind; and well we know the king
Knows at what time to promise, when to pay.
My father and my uncle and myself
Did give him that same royalty he wears;
And, when he was not six-and-twenty strong,
Sick in the world's regard, wretched and low,
A poor unminded outlaw sneaking home,
My father gave him welcome to the shore;
And when he heard him swear and vow to God,
He came but to be Duke of Lancaster,
To sue his livery and beg his peace,
With tears of innocence and terms of zeal,
My father, in kind heart and pity moved,
Swore him assistance, and performed it too.
Now, when the lords and barons of the realm
Perceived Northumberland did lean to him,
The more and less came in with cap and knee;
Met him in boroughs, cities, villages,
Attended him on bridges, stood in lanes,

Laid gifts before him, proffered him their oaths,
Gave him their heirs as pages, followed him
Even at the heels in golden multitudes.
He presently,—as greatness knows itself,—
Steps me a little higher than his vow
Made to my father while his blood was poor,
Upon the naked shore at Ravenspurg;
And now, forsooth, takes on him to reform
Some certain edicts and some strait decrees
That lie too heavy on the commonwealth;
Cries out upon abuses, seems to weep
Over his country's wrongs; and, by this face,
This seeming brow of justice, did he win
The hearts of all that he did angle for;
Proceeded further; cut me off the heads
Of all the favourites that the absent king
In deputation left behind him here
When he was personal in the Irish war.
   Blunt.   Tut, I came not to hear this.
   Hot.   Then, to the point.
In short time after he deposed the king;
Soon after that, deprived him of his life;
And, in the neck of that, tasked the whole state:
To make that worse, suffered his kinsman March—
Who is, if every owner were well placed,
Indeed his king—to be engaged in Wales,
There without ransom to lie forfeited;
Disgraced me in my happy victories;
Sought to entrap me by intelligence;
Rated my uncle from the council-board;
In rage dismissed my father from the court;
Broke oath on oath, committed wrong on wrong,
And, in conclusion, drove us to seek out
This head of safety; and, withal, to pry
Into his title, which we find to be
Too indirect for long continuance.
   Blunt.   Shall I return this answer to the king?
   Hot.   Not so, Sir Walter; we'll withdraw a while.
Go to the king, and let there be impawned
Some surety for a safe return again,
And in the morning early shall mine uncle
Bring him our purposes; and so farewell.
   Blunt.   I would you would accept of grace and love.
   Hot.   And, may be, so we shall.
   Blunt.   'Pray God, you do!
                               [Exeunt

SCENE IV.—York. A Room in the Archbishop's
House

Enter the ARCHBISHOP OF YORK *and* SIR MICHAEL

Arch. Hie, good Sir Michael; bear this sealéd brief
With wingéd haste to the lord marshal;
This to my cousin Scroop; and all the rest
To whom they are directed. If you knew
How much they do import, you would make haste.
    Sir M. My good lord,
I guess their tenor.
    Arch.   Like enough, you do.
To-morrow, good Sir Michael, is a day
Wherein the fortune of ten thousand men
Must bide the touch. For, sir, at Shrewsbury,
As I am truly given to understand,
The king, with mighty and quick-raiséd power,
Meets with Lord Harry: and, I fear, Sir Michael,
What with the sickness of Northumberland,
Whose power was in the first proportion,
And what with Owen Glendower's absence thence,
Who with them was a rated sinew too,
And comes not in, o'er-ruled by prophecies,
I fear the power of Percy is too weak
To wage an instant trial with the king.
    Sir M. Why, my good lord, you need not fear; there's
        Douglas
And Mortimer.
    Arch. No, Mortimer's not there.
    Sir M. But there is Mordake, Vernon, Lord Harry
        Percy,
And there's my Lord of Worcester, and a head
Of gallant warriors, noble gentlemen.
    Arch. And so there is; but yet the king hath drawn
The special head of all the land together;—
The Prince of Wales, Lord John of Lancaster,
The noble Westmoreland, and warlike Blunt,
And many more corrivals and dear men
Of estimation and command in arms.
    Sir M. Doubt not, my lord, they shall be well opposed.
    Arch. I hope no less, yet needful 't is to fear;
And, to prevent the worst, Sir Michael, speed:
For, if Lord Percy thrive not, ere the king
Dismiss his power, he means to visit us,
For he hath heard of our confederacy,—
And 't is but wisdom to make strong against him:
Therefore, make haste. I must go write again
To other friends; and so farewell, Sir Michael.   [*Exeunt*

ACT FIVE

SCENE I.—The King's Camp near Shrewsbury

Enter KING HENRY, PRINCE HENRY, PRINCE JOHN OF LAN-
CASTER, SIR WALTER BLUNT, *and* SIR JOHN FALSTAFF

  K. Hen.   How bloodily the sun begins to peer
Above yon bosky hill! the day looks pale
At his distemperature.
  P. Hen.   The southern wind
Doth play the trumpet to his purposes;
And by his hollow whistling in the leaves
Foretells a tempest and a blustering day.
  K. Hen.   Then with the losers let it sympathise,
For nothing can seem foul to those that win.—
                            [*Trumpet sounds*

Enter WORCESTER *and* VERNON

How now, my Lord of Worcester! 't is not well
That you and I should meet upon such terms
As now we meet.   You have deceived our trust,
And made us doff our easy robes of peace,
To crush our old limbs in ungentle steel:
This is not well, my lord; this is not well.
What say you to it? will you again unknit
This churlish knot of all-abhorréd war,
And move in that obedient orb again
Where you did give a fair and natural light,
And be no more an exhaled meteor,
A prodigy of fear, and a portent
Of broachéd mischief to the unborn times?
  Wor.   Hear me, my liege.
For mine own part, I could be well content
To entertain the lag end of my life
With quiet hours; for, I do protest,
I have not sought the day of this dislike.
  K. Hen.   You have not sought it!—How comes it then?
  Fal.   Rebellion lay in his way, and he found it.
  P. Hen.   Peace, chewet, peace!
  Wor.   It pleased your majesty to turn your looks
Of favour from myself and all our house;
And yet I must remember you, my lord,
We were the first and dearest of your friends.
For you my staff of office did I break
In Richard's time; and posted day and night
To meet you on the way and kiss your hand
When yet you were in place and in account

Nothing so strong and fortunate as I.
It was myself, my brother, and his son,
That brought you home, and boldly did outdare
The dangers of the time. You swore to us,
And you did swear that oath at Doncaster,
That you did nothing purpose 'gainst the state,
Nor claim no further than your new-fallen right,
The seat of Gaunt, dukedom of Lancaster:
To this we swore our aid. But in short space
It rained down fortune showering on your head;
And such a flood of greatness fell on you,
What with our help, what with the absent king,
What with the injuries of a wanton time,
The seeming sufferances that you had borne,
And the contrarious winds that held the king
So long in his unlucky Irish wars
That all in England did repute him dead:
And, from this swarm of fair advantages,
You took occasion to be quickly wooed
To gripe the general sway into your hand;
Forgot your oath to us at Doncaster;
And, being fed by us, you used us so
As that ungentle gull, the cuckoo's bird,
Useth the sparrow,—did oppress our nest,
Grew by our feeding to so great a bulk,
That even our love durst not come near your sight
For fear of swallowing; but with nimble wing
We were enforced, for safety sake, to fly
Out of your sight and raise this present head;
Whereby we stand oppos√©d by such means
As you yourself have forced against yourself,
By unkind usage, dangerous countenance,
And violation of all faith and troth
Sworn to us in your younger enterprise.

    K. Hen. These things, indeed, you have articulated,
Proclaimed at market-crosses, read in churches,
To face the garment of rebellion
With some fine colour that may please the eye
Of fickle changelings and poor discontents,
Which gape and rub the elbow at the news
Of hurly-burly innovation:
And never yet did insurrection want
Such water-colours to impaint his cause;
Nor moody beggars, starving for a time
Of pell-mell havoc and confusion.

    P. Hen. In both our armies there is many a soul
Shall pay full dearly for this encounter,
If once they join in trial. Tell your nephew,
The Prince of Wales doth join with all the world
In praise of Henry Percy: by my hopes.

This present enterprise set off his head,
I do not think a braver gentleman,
More active-valiant, or more valiant-young,
More daring or more bold, is now alive
To grace this latter age with noble deeds.
For my part, I may speak it to my shame,
I have a truant been to chivalry;
And so, I hear, he doth account me too;
Yet this before my father's majesty,—
I am content that he shall take the odds
Of his great name and estimation,
And will, to save the blood on either side,
Try fortune with him in a single fight.
    K. Hen.   And, Prince of Wales, so dare we venture thee,
Albeit considerations infinite
Do make against it.—No, good Worcester, no,
We love our people well; even those we love
That are misled upon your cousin's part;
And, will they take the offer of our grace,
Both he, and they, and you, yea, every man,
Shall be my friend again, and I'll be his.
So tell your cousin, go, and bring me word
What he will do: but if he will not yield,
Rebuke and dread correction wait on us,
And they shall do their office.   So, be gone.
We will not now be troubled with reply:
We offer fair; take it advisedly.
                  [Exeunt Worcester and Vernon
    P. Hen.   It will not be accepted, on my life,
The Douglas and the Hotspur both together
Are confident against the world in arms.
    K. Hen.   Hence, therefore, every leader to his charge;
For on their answer, will we set on them:
And God befriend us, as our cause is just!
            [Exeunt King, Blunt, and Prince John
    Fal.   Hal, if thou see me down in the battle, and bestride
me, so; 't is a point of friendship.
    P. Hen.   Nothing but a colossus can do thee that
friendship.   Say thy prayers, and farewell.
    Fal.   I would it were bed-time, Hal, and all well.
    P. Hen.   Why, thou owest God a death.   *[Exit*
    Fal.   'T is not due yet; I would be loath to pay him
before his day.   What need I be so forward with him that
calls not on me.   Well, 't is no matter; honour pricks me
on.   Yea, but how if honour prick me off when I come on?
how then?   Can honour set to a leg?   No: or an arm?
No: or take away the grief of a wound?   No.   Honour
hath no skill in surgery then?   No.   What is honour?
A word.   What is that word honour?   Air.   A trim
reckoning!—Who hath it?   He that died o' Wednesday.

Doth he feel it? No. Doth he hear it? No. Is it
insensible then? Yea, to the dead. But will it not live
with the living? No. Why? Detraction will not suffer
it.—Therefore, I'll none of it: honour is a mere scutcheon,
and so ends my catechism.   [*Exit*

Scene II.—The Rebel Camp

Enter Worcester *and* Vernon

Wor.   O, no! my nephew must not know, Sir Richard,
The liberal kind offer of the king.
Ver.   'T were best he did.
Wor.   Then are we all undone.
It is not possible, it cannot be,
The king should keep his word in loving us;
He will suspect us still, and find a time
To punish this offence in other faults:
Suspicion all our lives stuck full of eyes—
For treason is but trusted like the fox,
Who, ne'er so tame, so cherished, and locked up,
Will have a wild trick of his ancestors—
Look how we can, or sad, or merrily,
Interpretation will misquote our looks,
And we shall feed like oxen at a stall,
The better cherished, still the nearer death.
My nephew's trespass may be well forgot,
It hath the excuse of youth and heat of blood,
And an adopted name of privilege,
A hare-brained Hotspur governed by a spleen.
All his offences live upon my head
And on his father's: we did train him on;
And his corruption being ta'en from us,
We, as the spring of all, shall pay for all.
Therefore, good cousin, let not Harry know
In any case the offer of the king.
Ver.   Deliver what you will, I'll say 't is so.
Here comes your cousin.

Enter Hotspur *and* Douglas; *Officers and
Soldiers behind*

Hot.   My uncle is returned: deliver up
My Lord of Westmoreland.—Uncle, what news?
Wor.   The king will bid you battle presently.
Doug.   Defy him by the Lord of Westmoreland.
Hot.   Lord Douglas, go you and tell him so.
Doug.   Marry, and shall, and very willingly.   [*Exit*
Wor.   There is no seeming mercy in the king.

Hot. Did you beg any? God forbid!
  Wor. I told him gently of our grievances,
Of his oath-breaking; which he mended thus,
By now forswearing that he is forsworn:
He calls us rebels, traitors; and will scourge
With haughty arms this hateful name in us.

Re-enter DOUGLAS

  Doug. Arm, gentlemen! to arms! for I have thrown
A brave defiance in King Henry's teeth,
And Westmoreland, that was engaged, did bear it;
Which cannot choose but bring him quickly on.
  Wor. The Prince of Wales stepped forth before the king,
And, nephew, challenged you to single fight.
  Hot. O, 'would the quarrel lay upon our heads,
And that no man might draw short breath to-day,
But I and Harry Monmouth! Tell me, tell me,
How showed his tasking? seemed it in contempt?
  Ver. No, by my soul; I never in my life
Did hear a challenge urged more modestly,
Unless a brother should a brother dare
To gentle exercise and proof of arms.
He gave you all the duties of a man,
Trimmed up your praises with a princely tongue,
Spoke your deservings like a chronicle,
Making you ever better than his praise,
By still dispraising praise, valued with you;
And, which became him like a prince indeed,
He made a blushing cital of himself,
And chid his truant youth with such a grace
As if he mastered there a double spirit
Of teaching, and of learning, instantly.
There did he pause. But let me tell the world,—
If he outlive the envy of this day,
England did never owe so sweet a hope,
So much misconstrued in his wantonness.
  Hot. Cousin, I think thou art enamouréd
Upon his follies: never did I hear
Of any prince so wild a libertine;
But be he as he will, yet once ere night
I will embrace him with a soldier's arm,
That he shall shrink under my courtesy.—
Arm, arm, with speed!—And, fellows, soldiers, friends,
Better consider what you have to do
Than I, that have not well the gift of tongue,
Can lift your blood up with persuasion.

Enter a Messenger

  Mess. My lord,
Here are letters for you.

Hot. I cannot read them now,—
O gentlemen! the time of life is short;
To spend that shortness basely were too long,
If life did ride upon a dial's point,
Still ending at the arrival of an hour.
An if we live, we live to tread on kings;
If die, brave death, when princes die with us.
Now, for our consciences,—the arms are fair,
When the intent of bearing them is just.

Enter another Messenger

Mess. My lord, prepare; the king comes on apace.
Hot. I thank him, that he cuts me from my tale,
For I profess not talking.   Only this,—
Let each man do his best: and here draw I
A sword, whose temper I intend to stain
With the best blood that I can meet withal
In the adventure of this perilous day.
Now,—*Esperance !*—Percy!—and set on!—
Sound all the lofty instruments of war,
And by that music let us all embrace;
For, heaven to earth, some of us never shall
A second time do such a courtesy.
          [*The trumpets sound.   They embrace, and exeunt*

SCENE III.—Plain near Shrewsbury

*Excursions and parties fighting.   Alarum to the battle.
Then enter* DOUGLAS *and* BLUNT, *meeting*

Blunt. What is thy name, that in the battle thus
Thou crosses me? what honour dost thou seek
Upon my head?
Doug. Know then, my name is Douglas;
And I do haunt thee in the battle thus
Because some tell me that thou art a king.
Blunt. They tell thee true.
Doug. The Lord of Stafford dear to-day hath bought
Thy likeness; for, instead of thee, King Harry,
This sword hath ended him: so shall it thee,
Unless thou yield thee as my prisoner.
Blunt. I was not born a yielder, thou proud Scot;
And thou shalt find a king that will revenge
Lord Stafford's death.   [*They fight, and Blunt is slain*

Enter HOTSPUR

Hot. O Douglas! hadst thou fought at Holmedon thus,
I never had triumphed upon a Scot.

75

Doug. All's done, all's won: here breathless lies the
    king.
Hot. Where?
Doug. Here.
Hot. This, Douglas? no; I know this face full well:
A gallant knight he was, his name was Blunt,
Semblably furnished like the king himself.
Doug. A fool go with thy soul, whither it goes!
A borrowed title hast thou bought too dear:
Why did'st thou tell me that thou wert a king?
Hot. The king hath many marching in his coats.
Doug. Now, by my sword, I will kill all his coats;
I'll murder all his wardrobe, piece by piece,
Until I meet the king
    Hot.   Up, and away!
Our soldiers stand full fairly for the day.   *[Exeunt*

Alarums. Enter FALSTAFF

Fal. Though I could 'scape shot-free at London, I fear
the shot here; here's no scoring, but upon the pate.—
Soft! who are you? Sir Walter Blunt:—there's honour
for you; here's no vanity.—I am as hot as molten lead,
and as heavy too: God keep lead out of me! I need
no more weight than mine own bowels.—I have led my
ragamuffins where they are peppered: there's not three
of my hundred and fifty left alive, and they are for the
town's end, to beg during life. But who comes here?

Enter PRINCE HENRY

P. Hen. What! stand'st thou idle here? lend me thy
    sword:
Many a noble man lies stark and stiff
Under the hoofs of vaunting enemies,
Whose deaths are unrevenged: pr'ythee, lend me thy
    sword.
Fal. O Hal! I pr'ythee, give me leave to breathe
awhile.—Turk Gregory never did such deeds in arms as I
have done this day. I have paid Percy, I have made him
sure.
P. Hen. He is, indeed; and living to kill thee. I
pr'ythee, lend me thy sword.
Fal. Nay, before God, Hal, if Percy be alive, thou
gett'st not my sword; but take my pistol, if thou wilt.
P. Hen. Give it me. What, is it in the case?
Fal. Ay, Hal. 'T is hot, 't is hot: there's that will
sack a city.   *[The Prince draws out a bottle of sack*
P. Hen. What, is't a time to jest and dally now?
                  [Throws it at him, and exit
Fal. Well, if Percy be alive, I'll pierce him. If he do

come in my way, so: if he do not, if I come in his willingly,
let him make a carbonado of me.   I like not such grinning
honour as Sir Walter hath: give me life; which if I can
save, so; if not, honour comes unlooked for, and there's
an end.   *[Exit*

SCENE IV.—Another Part of the Field

Alarums.   Excursions.   Enter the KING, PRINCE HENRY,
PRINCE JOHN, *and* WESTMORELAND

    K. Hen.   I pr'ythee,
Harry, withdraw thyself; thou bleed'st too much.—
Lord John of Lancaster, go you with him.
    P. John.   Not I, my lord, unless I did bleed too.
    P. Hen.   I do beseech your majesty, make up,
Lest your retirement do amaze your friends.
    K. Hen.   I will do so.—
My Lord of Westmoreland, lead him to his tent.
    West.   Come, my lord, I'll lead you to your tent.
    P. Hen.   Lead me, my lord?   I do not need your help:
And Heaven forbid, a shallow scratch should drive
The Prince of Wales from such a field as this,
Where stained nobility lies trodden on,
And rebels' arms triúmph in massacres!
    P. John.   We breathe too long.—Come, cousin West-
           moreland,
Our duty this way lies: for God's sake, come.
           [Exeunt Prince John and Westmoreland
    P. Hen.   By God, thou hast deceived me, Lancaster,
I did not think thee lord of such a spirit:
Before, I loved thee as a brother, John;
But now, I do respect thee as my soul.
    K. Hen.   I saw him hold Lord Percy at the point
With lustier maintenance than I did look for
Of such an ungrown warrior.
    P. Hen.   O, this boy
Lends mettle to us all.   *[Exit*

Alarums.   Enter DOUGLAS

    Doug.   Another king! they grow like Hydra's heads.
I am the Douglas, fatal to all those
That wear those colours on them.—What art thou,
That counterfeit'st the person of a king?
    K. Hen.   The king himself; who, Douglas, grieves at
           heart,
So many of his shadows thou hast met,
And not the very king.   I have two boys

Seek Percy and thyself about the field:
But seeing thou fall'st on me so luckily,
I will assay thee; so defend thyself.
  Doug. I fear thou art another counterfeit,
And yet, in faith, thou bear'st thee like a king:
But mine I am sure thou art whoe'er thou be,
And thus I win thee.
                    [*They fight: the King being in danger, re-enter
                                              Prince Henry*
  P. Hen. Hold up thy head, vile Scot, or thou art like
Never to hold it up again! the spirits
Of Shirley, Stafford, Blunt, are in my arm;
It is the Prince of Wales, that threatens thee,
Who never promiseth but he means to pay.—
                              [*They fight: Douglas flies*
Cheerly, my lord: how fares your grace?—
Sir Nicholas Gawsey hath for succour sent,
And so hath Clifton; I'll to Clifton straight.
  K. Hen. Stay, and breathe awhile.—
Thou hast redeemed thy lost opinion;
And showed thou mak'st some tender of my life,
In this fair rescue thou hast brought to me.
  P. Hen. O God, they did me too much injury
That ever said I hearkened for your death.
If it were so, I might have let alone
The insulting hand of Douglas over you,
Which would have been as speedy in your end
As all the poisonous potions in the world,
And saved the treacherous labour of your son.
  K. Hen. Make up to Clifton: I'll to Sir Nicholas
     Gawsey.   [*Exit*

Enter HOTSPUR

  Hot. If I mistake not, thou art Harry Monmouth.
  P. Hen. Thou speak'st as if I would deny my name.
  Hot. My name is Harry Percy.
  P. Hen.   Why, then I see
A very valiant rebel of that name.
I am the Prince of Wales; and think not, Percy,
To share with me in glory any more:
Two stars keep not their motion in one sphere;
Nor can one England brook a double reign,
Of Harry Percy and the Prince of Wales.
  Hot. Nor shall it, Harry, for the hour is come
To end the one of us; and 'would to God,
Thy name in arms were now as great as mine!
  P. Hen. I'll make it greater ere I part from thee;
And all the budding honours on thy crest
I'll crop, to make a garland for my head.
  Hot. I can no longer brook thy vanities.   [*They fight*
                       78

Enter FALSTAFF

Fal. Well said, Hal! to it, Hal!—Nay, you shall find no boy's play here, I can tell you.

Re-enter DOUGLAS; *he fights with* FALSTAFF, *who falls down as if he were dead, and exit* DOUGLAS. HOTSPUR *is wounded, and falls*

Hot. O Harry, thou hast robbed me of my youth!
I better brook the loss of brittle life
Than those proud titles thou hast won of me;
They wound my thoughts worse than thy sword my flesh:—
But thought's the slave of life, and life time's fool,
And time that takes survey of all the world,
Must have a stop. O, I could prophesy,
But that the earthy and cold hand of death
Lies on my tongue:—no, Percy, thou art dust,
And food for—   [*Dies*
P. Hen. For worms, brave Percy: fare thee well, great heart!—
Ill-weaved ambition, how much art thou shrunk!
When that this body did contain a spirit,
A kingdom for it was too small a bound;
But now, two paces of the vilest earth
Is room enough:—this earth, that bears thee dead,
Bears not alive so stout a gentleman.
If thou wert sensible of courtesy,
I should not make so dear a show of zeal:—
But let my favours hide thy mangled face;
And, even in thy behalf, I'll thank myself
For doing these fair rites of tenderness.
Adieu, and take thy praise with thee to heaven!
Thy ignomy sleep with thee in the grave,
But not remembered in thy epitaph!—
     [*He spieth Falstaff on the ground*
What, old acquaintance! could not all this flesh
Keep in a little life? Poor Jack, farewell!
I could have better spared a better man.
O, I should have a heavy miss of thee,
If I were much in love with vanity.
Death hath not struck so fat a deer to-day,
Though many dearer, in this bloody fray.
Embowelled will I see thee by-and-by;
Till then, in blood by noble Percy lie.   [*Exit*
Fal. [*Rising*] Embowelled! if thou embowel me to-day, I'll give you leave to powder me, and eat me too, to-morrow. 'Sblood, 't was time to counterfeit, or that hot termagant Scot had paid me scot and lot too. Counterfeit? I lie; I am no counterfeit: to die, is to be a counter-

feit; for he is but the counterfeit of a man, who hath not the life of a man; but to counterfeit dying, when a man thereby liveth, is to be no counterfeit, but the true and perfect image of life indeed. The better part of valour is discretion; in the which better part I have saved my life. Zounds, I am afraid of this gunpowder Percy, though he be dead. How, if he should counterfeit too, and rise? by my faith, I am afraid he would prove the better counterfeit. Therefore I'll make him sure; yea, and I'll swear I killed him. Why may not he rise, as well as I? Nothing confutes me but eyes, and nobody sees me: therefore, sirrah [*stabbing him*], with a new wound in your thigh come you along with me.   [*He takes Hotspur on his back*

Re-enter PRINCE HENRY *and* PRINCE JOHN

   P. Hen. Come, brother John; full bravely hast thou fleshed
Thy maiden sword.
   P. John.   But, soft! whom have we here?
Did you not tell me this fat man was dead?
   P. Hen. I did; I saw him dead, breathless and bleeding
On the ground.—
Art thou alive? or is it fantasy
That plays upon our eyesight? pr'ythee, speak;
We will not trust our eyes without our ears.
Thou art not what thou seem'st.
   Fal. No, that's certain; I am not a double man; but if I be not Jack Falstaff, then am I Jack. There is Percy; [*throwing the body down*] if your father will do me any honour; if not, let him kill the next Percy himself. I look to be either earl or duke, I can assure you.
   P. Hen. Why, Percy, I killed myself, and saw thee dead.
   Fal. Didst thou?—Lord, Lord, how this world is given to lying!—I grant you I was down, and out of breath, and so was he; but we rose both at an instant, and fought a long hour by Shrewsbury clock. If I may be believed, so; if not, let them that should reward valour bear the sin upon their own heads. I'll take it upon my death, I gave him this wound in the thigh: if the man were alive, and would deny it, zounds, I would make him eat a piece of my sword.
   P. John. This is the strangest tale that e'er I heard.
   P. Hen. This is the strangest fellow, brother John.—
Come, bring your luggage nobly on your back:
For my part, if a lie may do thee grace,
I'll gild it with the happiest terms I have.
                       [*A retreat is sounded*
The trumpet sounds retreat; the day is ours.

Come, brother, let's to th' highest of the field,
To see what friends are living, who are dead.
                    [*Exeunt Prince Henry and Prince John*
    Fal. I'll follow, as they say, for reward. He that
rewards me, God reward him! If I do grow great, I'll
grow less; for I'll purge, and leave sack, and live cleanly
as a nobleman should do.   [*Exit, bearing off the body*

SCENE V.—Another Part of the Field

The trumpets sound. Enter KING HENRY, PRINCE HENRY,
    PRINCE JOHN, WESTMORELAND, *and others, with* WOR-
    CESTER, *and* VERNON, *prisoners*

    K. Hen. Thus ever did rebellion find rebuke,—
Ill-spirited Worcester, did we not send grace,
Pardon, and terms of love to all of you?
And wouldst thou turn our offers contrary?
Misuse the tenor of thy kinsman's trust?
Three knights upon our party slain to-day,
A noble earl, and many a creature else,
Had been alive this hour,
If, like a Christian, thou hadst truly borne
Betwixt our armies true intelligence.
    Wor. What I have done, my safety urged me to,
And I embrace this fortune patiently,
Since not to be avoided it falls on me.
    K. Hen. Bear Worcester to the death, and Vernon too;
Other offenders we will pause upon.—
                    [*Exeunt Worcester and Vernon guarded*
How goes the field?
    P. Hen. The noble Scot, Lord Douglas, when he saw
The fortune of the day quite turned from him,
The noble Percy slain, and all his men
Upon the foot of fear, fled with the rest;
And falling from a hill he was so bruised,
That the pursuers took him. At my tent
The Douglas is, and I beseech your grace
I may dispose of him.
    K. Hen.   With all my heart.
    P. Hen. Then, brother John of Lancaster, to you
This honourable bounty shall belong.
Go to the Douglas, and deliver him
Up to his pleasure, ransomless, and free:
His valour shown upon our crests to-day
Hath taught us how to cherish such high deeds
Even in the bosom of our adversaries.
    P. John. I thank your grace for this high courtesy,
Which I shall give away immediately.

K. Hen. Then this remains,—that we divide our
   power.—
You, son John, and my cousin Westmoreland,
Towards York shall bend you with your dearest speed,
To meet Northumberland and the prelate Scroop,
Who, as we hear, are busily in arms:
Myself,—and you, son Harry,—will towards Wales,
To fight with Glendower and the Earl of March.
Rebellion in this land shall lose his sway,
Meeting the check of such another day:
And since this business so fair is done,
Let us not leave till all our own be won.   [*Exeunt*

KING HENRY THE FOURTH

SECOND PART

DRAMATIS PERSONÆ

KING HENRY THE FOURTH
HENRY, *Prince of Wales, after-
    wards King Henry V* ⎞
THOMAS, *Duke of Clarence* ⎬ *His sons*
PRINCE JOHN OF LANCASTER ⎟
PRINCE HUMPHREY OF GLOSTER ⎠
EARL OF WARWICK ⎞
EARL OF WESTMORELAND ⎟
EARL OF SURREY ⎬ *Of the King's Party*
GOWER ⎟
HARCOURT ⎠
BLUNT
Lord Chief-Justice of the King's Bench
A Gentleman attending on the Chief-Justice
EARL OF NORTHUMBERLAND ⎞
SCROOP, *Archbishop of York* ⎟
LORD MOWBRAY ⎬ *opposites to the King*
LORD HASTINGS ⎟
LORD BARDOLPH ⎠
SIR JOHN COLEVILLE
TRAVERS *and* MORTON, *retainers of Northumberland*
SIR JOHN FALSTAFF
His Page
BARDOLPH
PISTOL
POINS
PETO
SHALLOW *and* SILENCE, *Country Justices*
DAVY, *servant to Shallow*
MOULDY, SHADOW, WART, FEEBLE, *and* BULL-CALF, *Recruits*
FANG *and* SNARE, *sheriff's officers*
RUMOUR, *the Presenter*

LADY NORTHUMBERLAND
LADY PERCY
Hostess QUICKLY
DOLL TEAR-SHEET

Lords, and Attendants; Porter, Officers, Soldiers, Mes-
    senger, Drawers, Beadles, Grooms, etc.

A Dancer, speaker of the Epilogue

SCENE—*England*

THE SECOND PART OF

KING HENRY IV

INDUCTION

Warkworth. Before NORTHUMBERLAND'S Castle

Enter RUMOUR, *painted full of tongues*

  Rum. Open your ears; for which of you will stop
The vent of hearing when loud Rumour speaks?
I, from the orient to the drooping west,
Making the wind my post-horse, still unfold
The acts commencéd on this ball of earth:
Upon my tongues continual slanders ride,
The which in every language I pronounce,
Stuffing the ears of men with false reports.
I speak of peace, while covert enmity,
Under the smile of safety, wounds the world:
And who but Rumour, who but only I,
Make fearful musters and prepared defence,
Whilst the big year, swoln with some other grief,
Is thought with child by the stern tyrant war,
And no such matter? Rumour is a pipe
Blown by surmises, jealousies, conjectures;
And of so easy and so plain a stop
That the blunt monster with uncounted heads,
The still-discordant wavering multitude,
Can play upon it. But what need I thus
My well-known body to anatomise
Among my household? Why is Rumour here?
I run before King Harry's victory;
Who in a bloody field by Shrewsbury
Hath beaten down young Hotspur and his troops,
Quenching the flame of bold rebellion
Even with the rebel's blood. But what mean I
To speak so true at first? my office is
To noise abroad, that Harry Monmouth fell
Under the wrath of noble Hotspur's sword,
And that the king before the Douglas' rage
Stooped his anointed head as low as death.

This have I rumoured through the pleasant towns
Between that royal field of Shrewsbury
And this worm-eaten hold of ragged stone,
Where Hotspur's father, old Northumberland,
Lies crafty sick.   The posts come tiring on,
And not a man of them brings other news
Than they have learned of me: from Rumour's tongues
They bring smooth comforts false, worse than true wrongs.

[*Exit*

ACT ONE

SCENE I.—The Same

Enter LORD BARDOLPH

L. Bard.   Who keeps the gate here? ho!

The Porter opens the gate

Where is the earl?
Port.   What shall I say you are?
L. Bard.   Tell thou the earl
That the Lord Bardolph doth attend him here.
Port.   His lordship is walked forth into the orchard:
Please it your honour, knock but at the gate,
And he himself will answer.

Enter NORTHUMBERLAND

L. Bard.   Here comes the earl.
North.   What news, Lord Bardolph? every minute now
Should be the father of some stratagem.
The times are wild; contention, like a horse
Full of high feeding, madly hath broke loose,
And bears down all before him.
L. Bard.   Noble earl,
I bring you certain news from Shrewsbury.
North.   Good, an God will!
L. Bard.   As good as heart can wish:—
The king is almost wounded to the death;
And, in the fortune of my lord your son,
Prince Harry slain outright; and both the Blunts
Killed by the hand of Douglas; young Prince John,
And Westmoreland, and Stafford, fled the field;
And Harry Monmouth's brawn, the hulk Sir John,
Is prisoner to your son.   O, such a day,
So fought, so followed, and so fairly won,
Came not till now to dignify the times
Since Cæsar's fortunes.
North.   How is this derived?

86

Saw you the field? came you from Shrewsbury?
    L. Bard. I spake with one, my lord, that came from
        thence;
A gentleman well bred, and of good name,
That freely rendered me these news for true.
    North. Here comes my servant Travers, whom I sent
On Tuesday last to listen after news.
    L. Bard. My lord, I over-rode him on the way;
And he is furnished with no certainties,
More than he haply may retail from me.

Enter TRAVERS

    North. Now, Travers, what good tidings come with you?
    Tra. My lord, Sir John Umfrevile turned me back
With joyful tidings; and, being better horsed,
Out-rode me. After him came spurring hard
A gentleman, almost forspent with speed,
That stopped by me to breathe his bloodied horse.
He asked the way to Chester; and of him
I did demand, what news from Shrewsbury.
He told me that rebellion had ill luck,
And that young Harry Percy's spur was cold.
With that, he gave his able horse the head,
And, bending forward, struck his arméd heels
Against the panting sides of his poor jade
Up to the rowel-head; and starting so,
He seemed in running to devour the way,
Staying no longer question.
    North.   Ha!—Again.
Said he, young Harry Percy's spur was cold?
Of Hotspur, Coldspur? that rebellion
Had met ill luck?
    L. Bard.   My lord, I'll tell you what:
If my young lord your son have not the day,
Upon mine honour, for a silken point
I'll give my barony: never talk of it.
    North. Why should the gentleman that rode by Travers
Give then such instances of loss?
    L. Bard.   Who, he?
He was some hilding fellow, that had stolen
The horse he rode on, and, upon my life,
Spoke at a venture. Look, here comes more news.

Enter MORTON

    North. Yea, this man's brow, like to a title-leaf,
Foretells the nature of a tragic volume:
So looks the strond whereon the imperious flood
Hath left a witnessed usurpation.
Say, Morton, didst thou come from Shrewsbury?

Mor. I ran from Shrewsbury, my noble lord,
Where hateful death put on his ugliest mask
To fright our party.
     North.   How doth my son, and brother?
Thou tremblest; and the whiteness in thy cheek
Is apter than thy tongue to tell thy errand.
Even such a man, so faint, so spiritless,
So dull, so dead in look, so woe-begone,
Drew Priam's curtain in the dead of night,
And would have told him half his Troy was burned:
But Priam found the fire ere he his tongue,
And I my Percy's death ere thou report'st it.
This thou wouldst say,—'Your son did thus, and thus;
Your brother, thus; so fought the noble Douglas;'
Stopping my greedy ear with their bold deeds:
But in the end, to stop mine ear indeed,
Thou hast a sigh to blow away this praise
Ending with—'Brother, son, and all are dead.'
    Mor. Douglas is living, and your brother, yet;
But for my lord your son,—
    North.   Why, he is dead.
See, what a ready tongue suspicion hath!
He that but fears the thing he would not know
Hath, by instinct, knowledge from others' eyes
That what he feared is chancéd. Yet speak Morton;
Tell thou thy earl his divination lies,
And I will take it as a sweet disgrace,
And make thee rich for doing me such wrong.
    Mor. You are too great to be by me gainsaid:
Your spirit is too true, your fears too certain.
    North. Yet, for all this, say not that Percy's dead.
I see a strange confession in thine eye:
Thou shak'st thy head, and hold'st it fear or sin
To speak a truth. If he be slain, say so:
The tongue offends not that reports his death;
And he doth sin that doth belie the dead,
Not he which says the dead is not alive.
Yet the first bringer of unwelcome news
Hath but a losing office; and his tongue
Sounds ever after as a sullen bell,
Remembered knolling a departed friend.
    L. Bard. I cannot think, my lord, your son is dead.
    Mor. I'm sorry I should force you to believe
That which I would to Heaven I had not seen;
But these mine eyes saw him in bloody state,
Rendering faint quittance, wearied and out-breathed,
To Harry Monmouth; whose swift wrath beat down
The never-daunted Percy to the earth,
From whence with life he never more sprung up.
In few, his death—whose spirit lent a fire

Even to the dullest peasant in his camp—
Being bruited once, took fire and heat away
From the best-tempered courage in his troops;
For from his metal was his party steeled;
Which once in him abated, all the rest
Turned on themselves, like dull and heavy lead:
And as the thing that's heavy in itself,
Upon enforcement flies with greatest speed,
So did our men, heavy in Hotspur's loss,
Lend to this weight such lightness with their fear,
That arrows fled not swifter toward their aim,
Than did our soldiers, aiming at their safety,
Fly from the field.   Then was that noble Worcester
Too soon ta'en prisoner; and that furious Scot,
The bloody Douglas, whose well-labouring sword
Had three times slain the appearance of the king,
Gan vail his stomach, and did grace the shame
Of those that turned their backs; and in his flight,
Stumbling in fear, was took.   The sum of all
Is, that the king hath won, and hath sent out
A speedy power, to encounter you, my lord,
Under the conduct of young Lancaster
And Westmoreland.   This is the news at full.
    North.   For this I shall have time enough to mourn.
In poison there is physic; and these news,
Having been well, that would have made me sick,
Being sick, have in some measure made me well:
And as the wretch whose fever-weakened joints,
Like strengthless hinges, buckle under life,
Impatient of his fit, breaks like a fire
Out of his keeper's arms, even so my limbs,
Weakened with grief, being now enraged with grief,
Are thrice themselves.   Hence, therefore, thou nice
        crutch!
A scaly gauntlet now, with joints of steel,
Must glove this hand: and hence, thou sickly quoif!
Thou art a guard too wanton for the head
Which princes, fleshed with conquest, aim to hit.
Now bind my brows with iron; and approach
The ragged'st hour that time and spite dare bring,
To frown upon the enraged Northumberland!
Let heaven kiss earth! now, let not Nature's hand
Keep the wild flood confined! let order die!
And let this world no longer be a stage,
To feed contention in a lingering act;
But let one spirit of the first-born Cain
Reign in all bosoms, that, each heart being set
On bloody courses, the rude scene may end,
And darkness be the burier of the dead!
    Tra.   This strainéd passion doth you wrong, my lord.

L. Bard. Sweet earl, divorce not wisdom from your
    honour.
  Mor. The lives of all your loving complices
Lean on your health; the which, if you give o'er
To stormy passion, must perforce decay.
You cast the event of war, my noble lord,
And summed the account of chance before you said,
'Let us make head.' It was your presurmise
That in the dole of blows your son might drop;
You knew he walked o'er perils, on an edge,
More likely to fall in than to get o'er:
You were advised his flesh was capable
Of wounds and scars, and that his forward spirit
Would lift him where most trade of danger ranged;
Yet did you say,—'Go forth;' and none of this,
Though strongly apprehended, could restrain
The stiff-borne action: what hath then befallen,
Or what hath this bold enterprise brought forth,
More than that being which was like to be?
  L. Bard. We all that are engagéd to this loss,
Knew that we ventured on such dangerous seas,
That, if we wrought out life, 't was ten to one;
And yet we ventured, for the gain proposed
Choked the respect of likely peril feared,—
And, since we are o'erset, venture again.
Come, we will all put forth, body and goods.
  Mor. 'T is more than time: and, my most noble lord,
I hear for certain, and do speak the truth,
The gentle Archbishop of York is up,
With well-appointed powers; he is a man
Who with a double surety binds his followers.
My lord your son had only but the corpse,
But shadows and the shows of men, to fight;
For that same word, rebellion, did divide
The action of their bodies from their souls,
And they did fight with queasiness, constrained,
As men drink potions; that their weapons only
Seemed on our side, but, for their spirits and souls,
This word, rebellion, it had froze them up,
As a fish are in a pond. But now the bishop
Turns insurrection to religion:
Supposed sincere and holy in his thoughts,
He's followed both with body and with mind,
And doth enlarge his rising with the blood
Of fair King Richard, scraped from Pomfret stones;
Derives from Heaven his quarrel and his cause;
Tells them he doth bestride a bleeding land,
Gasping for life under great Bolingbroke;
And more and less do flock to follow him.
  North. I knew of this before; but, to speak truth,

This present grief had wiped it from my mind.
Go in with me; and counsel every man
The aptest way for safety and revenge:
Get posts and letters, and make friends with speed:
Never so few, nor never yet more need.   [*Exeunt*

SCENE II.—London. A Street

Enter FALSTAFF, *with his Page bearing his sword
and buckler*

Fal.   Sirrah, you giant, what says the doctor to my
water?
Page.   He said, sir, the water itself was a good healthy
water; but for the party that owed it, he might have more
diseases than he knew for.
Fal.   Men of all sorts take a pride to gird at me:
the brain of this foolish-compounded clay, man, is not
able to invent anything that tends to laughter, more than
I invent or is invented on me: I am not only witty in
myself, but the cause that wit is in other men.   I do here
walk before thee, like a sow that hath overwhelmed all
her litter but one.   If the prince put thee into my service
for any other reason than to set me off, why then I have
no judgment.   Thou whoreson mandrake, thou art fitter
to be worn in my cap than to wait at my heels.   I was never
manned with an agate till now: but I will set you neither in
gold nor silver, but in vile apparel, and send you back again
to your master, for a jewel,—the juvenal, the prince your
master, whose chin is not yet fledged.   I will sooner have
a beard grow in the palm of my hand than he shall get
one on his cheek; and yet he will not stick to say his face
is a face-royal.   God may finish it when he will, it is not
a hair amiss yet: he may keep it still as a face-royal, for
a barber shall never earn sixpence out of it; and yet he
will be crowing, as if he had writ man ever since his father
was a bachelor.   He may keep his own grace, but he is
almost out of mine, I can assure him—What said Master
Dombledon about the satin for my short cloak and my
slops?
Page.   He said, sir, you should procure him better
assurance than Bardolph: he would not take his bond and
yours; he liked not the security.
Fal.   Let him be damned, like the glutton! pray God
his tongue be hotter!—A whoreson Achitophel!   A rascally
'yea-forsooth' knave, to bear a gentleman in hand, and
then stand upon security!—The whoreson smooth-pates
do now wear nothing but high shoes, and bunches of keys
at their girdles; and if a man is thoroughly with them in

honest taking up, then they must stand upon security. I
had as lief they would put ratsbane in my mouth, as offer
to stop it with security. I looked he should have sent me
two-and-twenty yards of satin, as I am a true knight, and
he sends me security. Well, he may sleep in security; for
he hath the horn of abundance, and the lightness of his
wife shines through it: and yet cannot he see, though he
have his own lantern to light him.—Where's Bardolph?

Page. He's gone into Smithfield to buy your worship a
horse.

Fal. I bought him in Paul's, and he'll buy me a horse
in Smithfield: an I could get me but a wife in the stews,
I were manned, horsed, and wived.

Page. Sir, here comes the nobleman that committed
the prince for striking him about Bardolph.

Fal. Wait close; I will not see him.

Enter the LORD CHIEF-JUSTICE *and an Attendant*

Ch. Just. What's he that goes there?

Atten. Falstaff, an 't please your lordship.

Ch. Just. He that was in question for the robbery?

Atten. He, my lord; but he hath since done good
service at Shrewsbury; and, as I hear, is now going with
some charge to the Lord John of Lancaster.

Ch. Just. What, to York? Call him back again.

Atten. Sir John Falstaff!

Fal. Boy, tell him I am deaf.

Page. You must speak louder; my master is deaf.

Ch. Just. I am sure he is, to the hearing of anything
good.—Go, pluck him by the elbow; I must speak with
him.

Atten. Sir John,—

Fal. What! a young knave, and beg? Is there not
wars? is there no employment? doth not the king lack
subjects? do not the rebels want soldiers. Though it be
a shame to be on any side but one, it is worse shame to beg
than to be on the worst side, were it worse than the name
of rebellion can tell how to make it.

Atten. You mistake me, sir.

Fal. Why, sir, did I say you were an honest man?
setting my knighthood and soldiership aside, I had lied
in my throat if I had said so.

Atten. I pray you, sir, then set your knighthood and
your soldiership aside, and give me leave to tell you, you
lie in your throat, if you say I am any other than an honest
man.

Fal. I give thee leave to tell me so? I lay aside that
which grows to me? If thou gett'st any leave of me,
hang me: if thou tak'st leave, thou wert better be hanged.
You hunt-counter, hence! avaunt!

Atten.   Sir, my lord would speak with you.

Ch. Just.   Sir John Falstaff, a word with you.

Fal.   My good lord!—God give your lordship good time of day. I am glad to see your lordship abroad; I heard say, your lordship was sick; I hope, your lordship goes abroad by advice. Your lordship, though not clean past your youth, hath yet some smack of age in you, some relish of the saltness of time; and I most humbly beseech your lordship to have a reverent care of your health.

Ch. Just.   Sir John, I sent for you before your expedition to Shrewsbury.

Fal.   An 't please your lordship, I hear his majesty is returned with some discomfort from Wales.

Ch. Just.   I talk not of his majesty:—You would not come when I sent for you.

Fal.   And I hear, moreover, his highness is fallen into this same whoreson apoplexy.

Ch. Just.   Well, God mend him!—I pray you, let me speak with you.

Fal.   This apoplexy is, as I take it, a kind of lethargy. an 't please your lordship; a kind of sleeping in the blood, a whoreson tingling.

Ch. Just.   What tell you me of it? be it as it is.

Fal.   It hath its original from much grief; from study, and perturbation of the brain. I have read the cause of his effects in Galen: it is a kind of deafness.

Ch. Just.   I think you are fallen into the disease, for you hear not what I say to you.

Fal.   Very well, my lord, very well: rather, an 't please you, it is the disease of not listening, the malady of not marking, that I am troubled withal.

Ch. Just.   To punish you by the heels would amend the attention of your ears: and I care not if I do become your physician.

Fal.   I am as poor as Job, my lord, but not so patient: your lordship may minister the potion of imprisonment to me, in respect of poverty; but how I should be your patient to follow your prescriptions, the wise may make some dram of a scruple, or, indeed, a scruple itself.

Ch. Just.   I sent for you, when there were matters against you for your life, to come speak with me.

Fal.   As I was then advised by my learned counsel in the laws of this land-service, I did not come.

Ch. Just.   Well, the truth is, Sir John, you live in great infamy.

Fal.   He that buckles him in my belt cannot live in less.

Ch. Just.   Your means are very slender, and your waste is great.

Fal.   I would it were otherwise: I would my means were greater, and my waist slenderer.

Ch. Just. You have misled the youthful prince.

Fal. The young prince hath misled me: I am the fellow with the great belly, and he my dog.

Ch. Just. Well, I am loath to gall a new-healed wound. Your day's service at Shrewsbury hath a little gilded over your night's exploit on Gadshill: you may thank the unquiet time for your quiet o'er-posting that action.

Fal. My lord,—

Ch. Just. But since all is well, keep it so: wake not a sleeping wolf.

Fal. To wake a wolf is as bad as to smell a fox.

Ch. Just. What, you are as a candle, the better part burnt out.

Fal. A wassail candle, my lord; all tallow: if I did say of wax, my growth would approve the truth.

Ch. Just. There is not a white hair on your face but should have his effect of gravity.

Fal. His effect of gravy, gravy, gravy.

Ch. Just. You follow the young prince up and down, like his ill angel.

Fal. Not so, my lord; your ill angel is light, but, I hope, he that looks upon me will take me without weighing: and yet, in some respects, I grant, I cannot go:—I cannot tell. Virtue is of so little regard in these costermonger times, that true valour is turned bearherd. Pregnancy is made a tapster, and hath his quick wit wasted in giving reckonings: all the other gifts appertinent to man, as the malice of this age shapes them, are not worth a gooseberry. You, that are old, consider not the capacities of us that are young; you measure the heat of our livers with the bitterness of your galls: and we that are in the vaward of our youth, I must confess, are wags too.

Ch. Just. Do you set down your name in the scroll of youth, that are written down old with all the characters of age? Have you not a moist eye? a dry hand? a yellow cheek? a white beard? a decreasing leg? an increasing belly? Is not your voice broken? your wind short? your chin double? your wit single? and every part about you blasted with antiquity? and will you yet call yourself young? Fie, fie, fie, Sir John!

Fal. My lord, I was born about three of the clock in the afternoon, with a white head, and something a round belly. For my voice, I have lost it with hallooing, and singing of anthems. To approve my youth further, I will not: the truth is, I am only old in judgment and understanding; and he that will caper with me for a thousand marks, let him lend me the money, and have at him. For the box o' the ear that the prince gave you, he gave it like a rude prince, and you took it like a sensible lord. I have checked him for it; and the young lion repents,—

marry, not in ashes and sackcloth, but in new silk and old sack.

Ch. Just. Well, God send the prince a better companion!

Fal. God send the companion a better prince! I cannot rid my hands of him.

Ch. Just. Well, the king hath severed you and Prince Harry. I hear, you are going with Lord John of Lancaster against the archbishop, and the Earl of Northumberland.

Fal. Yea: I thank your pretty sweet wit for it. But look you, pray, all you that kiss my lady. Peace at home, that our armies join not in a hot day: for, by the Lord, I take but two shirts out with me, and I mean not to sweat extraordinarily: if it be a hot day, and I brandish anything but my bottle, I would I might never spit white again. There is not a dangerous action can peep out his head, but I am thrust upon it. Well, I cannot last ever. But it was always yet the trick of our English nation, if they have a good thing, to make it too common. If you will needs say I am an old man, you should give me rest. I would to God, my name were not so terrible to the enemy as it is: I were better to be eaten to death with a rust, than to be scoured to nothing with perpetual motion.

Ch. Just. Well be honest, be honest; and God bless your expedition.

Fal. Will your lordship lend me a thousand pound to furnish me forth?

Ch. Just. Not a penny, not a penny; you are too impatient to bear crosses. Fare you well: commend me to my cousin Westmoreland. [*Exeunt Chief-Justice and Attendant*

Fal. If I do, fillip me with a three-man beetle.—A man can no more separate age and covetousness than he can part young limbs and lechery; but the gout galls the one, and the pox pinches the other; and so both the degrees prevent by curses.—Boy!

Page. Sir?

Fal. What money is in my purse?

Page. Seven groats and twopence.

Fal. I can get no remedy against this consumption of the purse: borrowing only lingers and lingers it out, but the disease is incurable.—Go bear this letter to my Lord of Lancaster; this to the Prince; this to the Earl of Westmoreland; and this to old Mistress Ursula, whom I have weekly sworn to marry since I perceived the first white hair on my chin. About it: you know where to find me. [*Exit Page*] A pox of this gout! or, a gout of this pox! for the one or the other plays the rogue with my great toe. 'T is no matter if I do halt; I have the wars for my colour, and my pension shall seem the more reasonable. A good wit will make use of anything: I will turn diseases to commodity. [*Exit*

SCENE III.—York. A Room in the Archbishop's Palace.

Enter the ARCHBISHOP OF YORK, *the* LORDS HASTINGS,
MOWBRAY, *and* BARDOLPH

    Arch. Thus have you heard our cause and known our
        means;
And, my most noble friends, I pray you all
Speak plainly your opinions of our hopes:—
And first, lord marshal, what say you to it?
    Mowb. I well allow the occasion of our arms;
But gladly would be better satisfied
How, in our means, we should advance ourselves
To look with forehead bold and big enough
Upon the power and puissance of the king.
    Hast. Our present musters grow upon the file
To five-and-twenty thousand men of choice;
And our supplies live largely in the hope
Of great Northumberland, whose bosom burns
With an incensèd fire of injuries.
    L. Bard. The question, then, Lord Hastings, standeth
        thus:—
Whether our present five-and-twenty thousand
May hold up head without Northumberland.
    Hast. With him, we may.
    L. Bard.   Ay, marry, there's the point:
But if without him we be thought too feeble,
My judgment is, we should not step too far
Till we had his assistance by the hand;
For in a theme so bloody-faced as this,
Conjecture, expectation, and surmise
Of aids incertain, should not be admitted.
    Arch. 'T is very true, Lord Bardolph; for, indeed,
It was young Hotspur's case at Shrewsbury.
    L. Bard. It was, my lord; who lined himself with hope,
Eating the air on promise of supply,
Flattering himself with project of a power
Much smaller than the smallest of his thoughts:
And so, with great imagination,
Proper to madmen, led his powers to death,
And winking leaped into destruction.
    Hast. But, by your leave, it never yet did hurt
To lay down likelihoods and forms of hope.
    L. Bard. Yes, if this present quality of war—
Indeed the instant action, a cause on foot—
Lives so in hope as in an early spring
We see the appearing buds, which to prove fruit,
Hope gives not so much warrant as despair
That frosts will bite them.   When we mean to build,

We first survey the plot, then draw the model;
And when we see the figure of the house,
Then must we rate the cost of the erection,
Which if we find outweighs ability,
What do we then, but draw anew the model
In fewer offices, or, at least, desist
To build at all?   Much more, in this great work—
Which is, almost, to pluck a kingdom down,
And set another up—should we survey
The plot of situation, and the model,
Consent upon a sure foundation,
Question surveyors, know our own estate,
How able such a work to undergo,
To weigh against his opposite; or else
We fortify in paper and in figures,
Using the names of men instead of men:
Like one that draws the model of a house
Beyond his power to build it; who, half through,
Gives o'er, and leaves his part-created cost
A naked subject to the weeping clouds
And waste for churlish winter's tyranny.
      Hast.   Grant that our hopes, yet likely of fair birth,
Should be still-born, and that we now possessed
The utmost man of expectation;
I think we are a body strong enough,
Even as we are, to equal with the king.
      L. Bard.   What, is the king but five-and-twenty thou-
            sand?
      Hast.   To us no more; nay, not so much, Lord Bardolph.
For his divisions, as the times do brawl,
Are in three heads: one power against the French,
And one against Glendower; perforce, a third
Must take up us: so is the unfirm king
In three divided; and his coffers sound
With hollow poverty and emptiness.
      Arch.   That he should draw his several strengths to-
            gether
And come against us in full puissance,
Need not be dreaded.
      Hast.   If he should do so,
He leaves his back unarmed, the French and Welsh
Baying him at the heels: never fear that.
      L. Bard.   Who is it like should lead his forces hither?
      Hast.   The Duke of Lancaster and Westmoreland:
Against the Welsh, himself and Harry Monmouth;
But who is substituted 'gainst the French,
I have no certain notice.
      Arch.   Let us on,
And publish the occasion of our arms.
The commonwealth is sick of their own choice;

Their over-greedy love hath surfeited.—
An habitation giddy and unsure
Hath he that buildeth on the vulgar heart.
O thou fond many! with what loud applause
Didst thou beat heaven with blessing Bolingbroke,
Before he was what thou wouldst have him be,
And being now trimmed in thine own desires,
Thou, beastly feeder, art so full of him,
That thou provok'st thyself to cast him up.
So, so, thou common dog, didst thou disgorge
Thy glutton bosom of the royal Richard;
And now thou wouldst eat thy dead vomit up,
And howl'st to find it.   What trust is in these times?
They that, when Richard lived, would have him die,
Are now become enamoured on his grave:
Thou, that threw'st dust upon his goodly head,
When through proud London he came sighing on
After the admiréd heels of Bolingbroke,
Cry'st now, 'O earth, yield us that king again,
And take thou this!'   O thoughts of men accurst!
Past, and to come, seems best; things present, worst.
    Mowb.   Shall we go draw our numbers and set on?
    Hast.   We are time's subjects, and time bids be gone.
                            [*Exeunt*

ACT TWO

Scene I.—London.   A Street

Enter Hostess, Fang *and his Boy with her, and* Snare *following*

    Host.   Master Fang, have you entered the action?
    Fang.   It is entered.
    Host.   Where's your yeoman?   Is 't a lusty yeoman? will 'a stand to 't?
    Fang.   Sirrah, where's Snare?
    Host.   O Lord, ay: good Master Snare.
    Snare.   Here, here.
    Fang.   Snare, we must arrest Sir John Falstaff.
    Host.   Yes, good Master Snare; I have entered him and all.
    Snare.   It may chance cost some of us our lives, for he will stab.
    Host.   Alas the day! take heed of him; he stabbed me in mine own house, and that most beastly.   In good faith, a' cares not what mischief he doth, if his weapon be out: he will foin like any devil; he will spare neither man, woman, nor child.

Fang.   If I can close with him, I care not for his thrust.
Host.   No, nor I neither: I'll be at your elbow.
Fang.   An I but fist him once; an he come but within my vice,—
Host.   I am undone by his going; I warrant you, he's an infinitive thing upon my score.—Good Master Fang' hold him sure:—good Master Snare, let him not 'scape. 'A comes continuantly to Pie Corner (saving your manhoods) to buy a saddle; and he's indited to dinner to the Lubbar's Head in Lumbert Street, to Master Smooth's the silkman: I pray you, since my exion is entered, and my case so openly known to the world, let him be brought in to his answer. A hundred mark is a long one for a poor lone woman to bear; and I have borne, and borne, and borne, and have been fubbed off, and fubbed off, and fubbed off, from this day to that day, that it is a shame to be thought on. There is no honesty in such dealing, unless a woman should be made an ass, and a beast to bear every knave's wrong.—Yonder he comes; and that arrant malmsey-nose, Bardolph, with him.

Enter SIR JOHN FALSTAFF, *Page and* BARDOLPH

Do your offices, do your offices, Master Fang, and Master Snare: do me, do me, do me your offices.
Fal.   How now? whose mare's dead? what's the matter?
Fang.   Sir John, I arrest you at the suit of Mistress Quickly.
Fal.   Away, varlets!—Draw, Bardolph: cut me off the villain's head; throw the quean in the channel.
Host.   Throw me in the channel? I'll throw thee there. Wilt thou? wilt thou? thou bastardly rogue!— Murder, murder! O, thou honey-suckle villain! wilt thou kill God's officers, and the king's? O, thou honey-seed rogue! thou art a honey-seed; a man queller, and a woman queller.
Fal.   Keep them off, Bardolph.
Fang.   A rescue! a rescue!
Host.   Good people, bring a rescue or two.—Thou wo 't, wo 't ta? do, do, thou rogue! do, thou hemp-seed!
Fal.   Away, you scullion! you rampallian! you fusti-larian! I'll tickle your catastrophe.

Enter the Lord Chief-Justice, *attended*

Ch. Just.   What is the matter? keep the peace here, ho!
Host.   Good my lord, be good to me! I beseech you, stand to me!
Ch. Just.   How now, Sir John! what are you brawling here?

Doth this become your place, your time, and business?
You should have been well on your way to York.—
Stand from him, fellow: wherefore hang'st upon him?

Host. O my most worshipful lord, an't please your grace, I am a poor widow of Eastcheap, and he is arrested at my suit.

Ch. Just. For what sum?

Host. It is more than for some, my lord; it is for all,—all I have. He hath eaten me out of house and home; he hath put all my substance into that fat belly of his;—but I will have some of it out again, or I will ride thee o' nights, like the mare.

Fal. I think, I am as like to ride the mare, if I have any vantage of ground to get up.

Ch. Just. How comes this, Sir John? Fie! what man of good temper would endure this tempest of exclamation? Are you not ashamed to enforce a poor widow to so rough a course by her own?

Fal. What is the gross sum that I owe thee?

Host. Marry, if thou wert an honest man, thyself and the money too. Thou didst swear to me upon a parcel-gilt goblet, sitting in my Dolphin-chamber, at the round table, by a sea-coal fire, upon Wednesday in Wheeson week, when the prince broke thy head for liking his father to a singing-man of Windsor,—thou didst swear to me then, as I was washing thy wound, to marry me, and make me my lady thy wife. Canst thou deny it? Did not goodwife Keech, the butcher's wife, come in then, and call me gossip Quickly? coming in to borrow a mess of vinegar; telling us, she had a good dish of prawns, whereby thou didst desire to eat some, whereby I told thee, they were ill for a green wound? And didst thou not, when she was gone downstairs, desire me to be no more so familiarity with such poor people; saying that ere long they should call me madam? And didst thou not kiss me, and bid me fetch thee thirty shillings? I put thee now to thy book-oath: deny it, if thou canst.

Fal. My lord, this is a poor mad soul; and she says, up and down the town, that her eldest son is like you. She hath been in good case, and the truth is, poverty hath distracted her. But for these foolish officers, I beseech you I may have redress against them.

Ch. Just. Sir John, Sir John, I am well acquainted with your manner of wrenching the true cause the false way. It is not a confident brow, nor the throng of words that come with such more than impudent sauciness from you, can thrust me from a level consideration; you have, as it appears to me, practised upon the easy-yielding spirit of this woman, and made her serve your uses both in purse and person.

Host. Yes, in troth, my lord.

Ch. Just. Pr'ythee, peace.—Pay her the debt you owe her, and unpay the villainy you have done with her: the one you may do with sterling money, and the other with current repentance.

Fal. My lord, I will not undergo this sneap without reply. You call honourable boldness, impudent sauciness: if a man will make court'sy, and say nothing, he is virtuous. No, my lord, my humble duty remembered, I will not be your suitor: I say to you, I do desire deliverance from these officers, being upon hasty employment in the king's affairs.

Ch. Just. You speak as having power to do wrong: but answer in the effect of your reputation, and satisfy the poor woman.

Fal. Come hither, hostess.   *[Taking her aside*

Enter GOWER

Ch. Just. Now, Master Gower,—what news?

Gow. The king, my lord, and Harry Prince of Wales Are near at hand: the rest the paper tells.   *[Gives a letter*

Fal. As I am a gentleman,—

Host. Nay, you said so before.

Fal. As I am a gentleman;—come no more words of it.

Host. By this heavenly ground I tread on, I must be fain to pawn both my plate and the tapestry of my dining-chambers.

Fal. Glasses, glasses, is the only drinking: and for thy walls,—a pretty slight drollery, or the story of the Prodigal, or the German hunting in water-work is worth a thousand of these bed-hangings and these fly-bitten tapestries. Let it be ten pound, if thou canst. Come, an't were not for thy humours, there's not a better wench in England. Go, wash thy face, and draw thy action. Come, thou must not be in this humour with me; dost not know me? Come, come, I know thou wast set on to this.

Host. Pray thee, Sir John, let it be but twenty nobles: i' faith I am loath to pawn my plate, in good earnest, la.

Fal. Let it alone; I'll make other shift: you'll be a fool still.

Host. Well, you shall have it, though I pawn my gown. I hope you'll come to supper. You'll pay me all to-gether?

Fal. Will I live?—[*To Bardolph*] Go, with her, with her; hook on, hook on.

Host. Will you have Doll Tear-sheet meet you at supper?

Fal. No more words; let's have her.

      [Exeunt Hostess, Bardolph, Officers, and Page

Ch. Just. I have heard better news.

Fal. What's the news, my good lord?

Ch. Just. Where lay the king last night?

Gow. At Basingstoke, my lord.

Fal. I hope, my lord, all's well: what is the news, my lord?

Ch. Just. Come all his forces back?

Gow. No; fifteen hundred foot, five hundred horse,
Are marched up to my Lord of Lancaster,
Against Northumberland and the Archbishop.

Fal. Comes the king back from Wales, my noble lord?

Ch. Just. You shall have letters of me presently. Come, go along with me, good Master Gower.

Fal. My lord!

Ch. Just. What's the matter?

Fal. Master Gower, shall I entreat you with me to dinner?

Gow. I must wait upon my good lord here: I thank you, good Sir John.

Ch. Just. Sir John, you loiter here too long, being you are to take soldiers up in counties as you go.

Fal. Will you sup with me, Master Gower.

Ch. Just. What foolish master taught you these manners, Sir John?

Fal. Master Gower, if they become me not, he was a fool that taught them me.—This is the right fencing grace, my lord! tap for tap, and so, part fair.

Ch. Just. Now, the lord lighten thee! thou art a great fool.   [*Exeunt*

SCENE II.—The Same. Another Street

Enter PRINCE HENRY *and* POINS

P. Hen. Trust me, I am exceeding weary.

Poins. Is it come to that? I had thought, weariness durst not have attached one of so high blood.

P. Hen. 'Faith, it does me; though it discolours the complexion of my greatness to acknowledge it. Doth it not show vilely in me to desire small beer?

Poins. Why, a prince should not be so loosely studied as to remember so weak a composition.

P. Hen. Belike, then, my appetite was not princely got; for, by my troth, I do now remember the poor creature, small beer. But, indeed, these humble considerations make me out of love with my greatness. What a disgrace it is to me to remember thy name? or to know thy face to-morrow? or to take note of how many pair of silk stockings thou hast; namely, these, and those that were thy peach-coloured ones? or to bear the inventory of thy shirts; as, one for superfluity, and one other for use?—but that the tennis-court-keeper knows better than I, for it is a low ebb of linen with thee, when thou keepest not racket there; as thou hast not done a great while, because the rest of thy low-countries have made a shift to eat up thy holland: and God knows whether those that bawl out the ruins of thy linen shall inherit his kingdom; but the midwives say, the children are not in the fault; whereupon the world increases, and kindreds are mightily strengthened.

Poins. How ill it follows, after you have laboured so hard, you should talk so idly! Tell me, how many good young princes would do so, their fathers being so sick as yours at this time is?

P. Hen. Shall I tell thee one thing, Poins?

Poins. Yes, faith, and let it be an excellent good thing.

P. Hen. It shall serve among wits of no higher breeding than thine.

Poins. Go to; I stand the push of your one thing that you will tell.

P. Hen. Marry, I tell thee,—it is not meet that I should be sad, now my father is sick: albeit I could tell to thee—as to one it pleases me, for fault of a better, to call my friend—I could be sad, and sad indeed too.

Poins. Very hardly upon such a subject.

P. Hen. By this hand, thou think'st me as far in the devil's book as thou and Falstaff for obduracy and persistency: let the end try the man. But I tell thee, my heart bleeds inwardly that my father is so sick; and keeping such vile company as thou art hath in reason taken from me all ostentation of sorrow.

Poins. The reason?

P. Hen. What wouldst thou think of me, if I should weep?

Poins. I would think thee a most princely hypocrite.

P. Hen. It would be every man's thought; and thou art a blessed fellow to think as every man thinks: never a man's thought in the world keeps the roadway better than thine: every man would think me an hypocrite indeed. And what accites your most worshipful thought to think so?

Poins. Why, because you have been so lewd, and so much engraffed to Falstaff.

P. Hen. And to thee.

Poins. By this light, I am well spoke on; I can hear it with mine own ears: the worst that they can say of me is, that I am a second brother, and that I am a proper fellow of my hands; and those two things, I confess, I cannot help. By the mass, here comes Bardolph.

Enter BARDOLPH *and Page*

P. Hen.   And the boy that I gave Falstaff: he had
him from me Christian; and look, if the fat villain have
not transformed him ape.

Bard.   God save your grace.

P. Hen.   And yours, most noble Bardolph.

Bard.   [*To the Page*]   Come, you virtuous ass, you
bashful fool, must you be blushing? wherefore blush you
now? What a maidenly man-at-arms are you become!
Is it such a matter to get a pottle-pot's maidenhead?

Page.   'A called me even now, my lord, through a red
lattice, and I could discern no part of his face from the
window: at last, I spied his eyes; and, methought, he
had made two holes in the ale-wife's new petticoat, and
peeped through.

P. Hen.   Hath not the boy profited?

Bard.   Away, you whoreson upright rabbit, away!

Page.   Away, you rascally Althæa's dream, away!

P. Hen.   Instruct us, boy; what dream, boy?

Page.   Marry, my lord, Althæa dreamed she was delivered
of a fire-brand; and therefore I call him her dream.

P. Hen.   A crown's worth of good interpretation.—
There it is, boy.   [*Gives him money*

Poins.   O, that this good blossom could be kept from
cankers!—Well, there is sixpence to preserve thee.

Bard.   An you do not make him be hanged among you,
the gallows shall have wrong.

P. Hen.   And how doth thy master, Bardolph?

Bard.   Well, my good lord. He heard of your grace's
coming to town: there's a letter for you.

Poins.   Delivered with good respect.—And how doth
the martlemas, your master?

Bard.   In bodily health, sir.

Poins.   Marry, the immortal part needs a physician;
but that moves not him: though that be sick, it dies
not.

P. Hen.   I do allow this wen to be as familiar with me
as my dog; and he holds his place, for look you how
he writes.

Poins.   [*Reads*]   'John Falstaff, knight,'—every man
must know that, as oft as he has occasion to name himself;
even like those that are kin to the king, for they never
prick their finger, but they say, 'There is some of the
king's blood spilt:' 'How comes that?' says he, that
takes upon him not to conceive: the answer is as ready
as a borrower's cap; 'I am the king's poor cousin, sir.'

P. Hen.   Nay, they will be kin to us, or they will fetch it
from Japhet. But to the letter:—

Poins.   'Sir John Falstaff, knight, to the son of the king nearest his father, Harry Prince of Wales, greeting.'—Why, this is a certificate.

P. Hen. Peace!

Poins. 'I will imitate the honourable Romans in brevity:'—he sure means brevity in breath, short-winded. —'I commend me to thee, I commend thee, and I leave thee. Be not too familiar with Poins; for he misuses thy favours so much, that he swears thou art to marry his sister Nell. Repent at idle times as thou may'st, and so, farewell.

> Thine, by yea and no, (which is as much as to say, as thou usest him,) JACK FALSTAFF, with my familiars; JOHN, with my brothers and sisters; and SIR JOHN with all Europe.'

My lord, I will steep this letter in sack, and make him eat it.

P. Hen. That's to make him eat twenty of his words. But do you use me thus, Ned? must I marry your sister?

Poins. God send the wench no worse fortune! but I never said so.

P. Hen. Well, thus we play the fools with the time; and the spirits of the wise sit in the clouds, and mock us.—Is your master here in London?

Bard. Yes, my lord.

P. Hen. Where sups he? doth the old boar feed in the old frank?

Bard. At the old place, my lord,—in Eastcheap.

P. Hen. What company?

Page. Ephesians, my lord,—of the old church.

P. Hen. Sup any women with him?

Page. None, my lord, but old Mistress Quickly, and Mistress Doll Tear-sheet.

P. Hen. What pagan may that be?

Page. A proper gentlewoman, sir, and a kinswoman of my master's.

P. Hen. Even such kin as the parish-heifers are to the town-bull.—Shall we steal upon them, Ned, at supper?

Poins. I am your shadow, my lord; I'll follow you.

P. Hen. Sirrah, you boy,—and Bardolph,—no word to your master that I am yet come to town: there's for your silence.

Bard. I have no tongue, sir.

Page. And for mine, sir,—I will govern it.

P. Hen. Fare ye well; go. [*Exeunt Bardolph and Page*]—This Doll Tear-sheet should be some road.

Poins. I warrant you, as common as the way between St. Albans and London.

P. Hen. How might we see Falstaff bestow himself to-night in his true colours, and not ourselves be seen?

Poins. Put on two leathern jerkins and aprons, and wait upon him at his table as drawers.

P. Hen. From a god to a bull, a heavy declension: it was Jove's case. From a prince to a prentice, a low transformation: that shall be mine; for in everything the purpose must weigh with the folly. Follow me, Ned.

[*Exeunt*

SCENE III.—Warkworth. Before the Castle

Enter NORTHUMBERLAND, LADY NORTHUMBERLAND, *and* LADY PERCY

North. I pray thee, loving wife and gentle daughter,
Give even way unto my rough affairs:
Put not you on the visage of the times
And be, like them, to Percy troublesome.
Lady N. I have given over, I will speak no more:
Do what you will; your wisdom be your guide.
North. Alas, sweet wife, my honour is at pawn;
And, but my going, nothing can redeem it.
Lady P. O, yet, for God's sake, go not to these wars!
The time was, father, that you broke your word,
When you were more endeared to it than now;
When your own Percy, when my heart's dear Harry,
Threw many a northward look to see his father
Bring up his powers; but he did long in vain
Who then persuaded you to stay at home?
There were two honours lost,—yours and your son's:
For yours,—may heavenly glory brighten it!
For his,—it stuck upon him, as the sun
In the grey vault of heaven: and by his light
Did all the chivalry of England move
To do brave acts; he was, indeed, the glass
Wherein the noble youth did dress themselves.
He had no legs that practised not his gait;
And speaking thick, which nature made his blemish,
Became the accents of the valiant;
For those that could speak low and tardily
Would turn their own perfection to abuse,
To seem like him; so that, in speech, in gait,
In diet, in affections of delight,
In military rules, humours of blood,
He was the mark and glass, copy and book,
That fashioned others. And him,—O wondrous him!
O miracle of men!—him did you leave—
Second to none, unseconded by you—
To look upon the hideous god of war
In disadvantage; to abide a field
106

Where nothing but the sound of Hotspur's name
Did seem defensible:—so you left him.
Never, O, never, do his ghost the wrong
To hold your honour more precise and nice
With others than with him: let them alone.
The marshal, and the árchbishop, are strong:
Had my sweet Harry had but half their numbers,
To-day might I, hanging on Hotspur's neck,
Have talked of Monmouth's grave.
  North.   Beshrew your heart,
Fair daughter, you do draw my spirits from me,
With new lamenting ancient oversights.
But I must go, and meet with danger there;
Or it will seek me in another place,
And find me worse provided.
  Lady N.   O, fly to Scotland
Till that the nobles and the arméd commons
Have of their puissance made a little taste.
  Lady P. If they get ground and vantage of the king,
Then join you with them, like a rib of steel,
To make strength stronger; but, for all our loves,
First let them try themselves. So did your son;
He was so suffered; so came I a widow;
And never shall have length of life enough
To rain upon remembrance with mine eyes
That it may grow and sprout as high as heaven,
For recordation to my noble husband.
  North. Come, come, go in with me. 'T is with my mind
As with the tide swelled up unto its height,
That makes a still-stand, running neither way:
Fain would I go to meet the árchbishop,
But many thousand reasons hold me back.
I will resolve for Scotland: there am I,
Till time and vantage crave my company.   [*Exeunt*

SCENE IV.—London.   A Room in the Boar's
Head Tavern, in Eastcheap

Enter two Drawers

First Draw. What the devil hast thou brought there?
apple-Johns? thou know'st Sir John cannot endure an
apple-John.
Sec. Draw. Mass, thou sayest true. The prince once
set a dish of apple-Johns before him, and told him, there
were five more Sir Johns; and, putting off his hat, said,
'I will now take my leave of these six dry, round, old,
withered knights.' It angered him to the heart; but he
hath forgot that.

First Draw. Why then, cover, and set them down: and see if thou canst find out Sneak's noise; Mistress Tearsheet would fain have some music. Despatch:—the room where they supped is too hot; they'll come in straight.

Sec. Draw. Sirrah, here will be the Prince, and Master Poins anon; and they will put on two of our jerkins and aprons, and Sir John must not know of it: Bardolph hath brought word.

First Draw. By the mass, here will be old utis: it will be an excellent stratagem.

Sec. Draw. I'll see if I can find out Sneak.   [*Exit*

Enter Hostess and DOLL TEAR-SHEET

Host. I' faith, sweetheart, methinks now, you are in an excellent good temperality: your pulsidge beats as extraordinarily as heart would desire; and your colour, I warrant you, is as red as any rose, in good truth, la; but, i' faith, you have drunk too much canaries, and that's a marvellous searching wine, and it perfumes the blood ere one can say,—'What's this?'—How do you now?

Doll. Better than I was:—Hem.

Host. Why, that's well said; a good heart's worth of gold.—Lo, here comes Sir John.

Enter FALSTAFF, *singing*

Fal. 'When Arthur first in court'—Empty the jordan [*Exit Drawer*]—'And was a worthy king.' How now, Mistress Doll?

Host. Sick of a calm; yea, good sooth.

Fal. So is all her sect; an they be once in a calm, they are sick.

Doll. You muddy rascal, is that all the comfort you give me?

Fal. You make fat rascals, Mistress Doll.

Doll. I make them! gluttony and diseases make them; I make them not.

Fal. If the cook help to make the gluttony, you help to make the diseases, Doll; we catch of you, Doll, we catch of you; grant that, my poor virtue, grant that.

Doll. Ay, marry,—our chains, and our jewels.

Fal. 'Your brooches, pearls, and owches:'—for to serve bravely, is to come halting off, you know: to come off the breach with his pike bent bravely, and to surgery bravely; to venture upon the charged chambers bravely,—

Doll. Hang yourself, you muddy conger, hang yourself!

Host. By my troth, this is the old fashion; you two never meet, but you fall to some discord. You are both, in good troth, as rheumatic as two dry toasts; you cannot one bear with another's confirmities. What the good-year!

one must bear, and that must be you: you are the weaker vessel, as they say, the emptier vessel.

Doll. Can a weak empty vessel bear such a huge full hogshead? there's a whole merchant's venture of Bourdeaux stuff in him; you have not seen a hulk better stuffed in the hold.—Come, I'll be friends with thee, Jack: thou art going to the wars; and whether I shall ever see thee again or no, there is nobody cares.

Re-enter Drawer

Draw. Sir, Ancient Pistol's below, and would speak with you.

Doll. Hang him, swaggering rascal! let him not come hither: it is the foul-mouth'dst rogue in England.

Host. If he swagger, let him not come here: no, by my faith; I must live among my neighbours; I'll no swaggerers: I am in good name and fame with the very best:—shut the door;—there comes no swaggerers here: I have not lived all this while, to have swaggering now:—shut the door, I pray you.

Fal. Dost thou hear, hostess?—

Host. Pray you, pacify yourself, Sir John: there comes no swaggerers here.

Fal. Dost thou hear? it is mine ancient.

Host. Tilly-fally, Sir John, ne'er tell me: your ancient swaggerer comes not in my doors. I was before Master Tisick, the deputy, t' other day; and, as he said to me,—'t was no longer ago than Wednesday last,—'Neighbour Quickly,' says he;—Master Dumb, our minister, was by then;—'Neighbour Quickly,' says he, 'receive those that are civil; for,' saith he, 'you are in an ill name:'—now a' said so, I can tell whereupon; 'for,' says he, 'you are an honest woman, and well thought on; therefore take heed what guests you receive: receive,' says he, 'no swaggering companions.'—There comes none here:—you would bless you to hear what he said.—No, I'll no swaggerers.

Fal. He's no swaggerer, hostess; a tame cheater, i' faith; you may stroke him as gently as a puppy greyhound: he'll not swagger with a Barbary hen, if her feathers turn back in any show of resistance.—Call him up, drawer.   [*Exit Drawer*

Host. Cheater, call you him? I will bar no honest man my house, nor no cheater; but I do not love swaggering: by my troth, I am the worse, when one says—'swagger.' Feel, masters, how I shake; look you, I warrant you.

Doll. So you do, hostess.

Host. Do I? yea, in very truth do I, an't were an aspen-leaf: I cannot abide swaggerers.

Enter PISTOL, BARDOLPH, *and Page*

Pist. God save you, Sir John!

Fal. Welcome, Ancient Pistol. Here, Pistol, I charge you with a cup of sack: do you discharge upon mine hostess.

Pist. I will discharge upon her, Sir John, with two bullets.

Fal. She is pistol-proof, sir; you shall hardly offend her.

Host. Come, I'll drink no proofs, nor no bullets: I'll drink no more than will do me good, for no man's pleasure, I.

Pist. Then to you, Mistress Dorothy; I will charge you.

Doll. Charge me! I scorn you, scurvy companion. What! you poor, base, rascally, cheating, lack-linen mate! Away, you mouldy rogue, away! I am meat for your master.

Pist. I know you, Mistress Dorothy.

Doll. Away, you cut-purse rascal! you filthy bung, away! By this wine, I'll thrust my knife in your mouldy chaps, an you play the saucy cuttle with me. Away, you bottle-ale rascal! you basket-hilt stale juggler, you!—Since when, I pray you, sir?—God's light? with two points on your shoulder? much!

Pist. I will murder your ruff for this.

Fal. No more, Pistol; I would not have you go off here. Discharge yourself of our company, Pistol.

Host. No, good Captain Pistol; not here, sweet captain.

Doll. Captain! thou abominable damned cheater, art thou not ashamed to be called captain? An captains were of my mind, they would truncheon you out, for taking their names upon you before you have earned them. You a captain, you slave! for what? for tearing a poor whore's ruff in a bawdy-house?—He a captain! hang him, rogue! he lives upon mouldy stewed prunes, and dried cakes. A captain! these villains will make the word captain as odious as the word 'occupy,' which was an excellent good word before it was ill-sorted: therefore captains had need look to 't.

Bard. Pray thee, go down, good ancient.

Fal. Hark thee hither, Mistress Doll.

Pist. Not I: I tell thee what, Corporal Bardolph; I could tear her.—I'll be revenged on her.

Page. Pray thee, go down.

Pist. I'll see her damned first;—to Pluto's damned lake, by this hand, to the infernal deep, with Erebus and tortures vile also. Hold hook and line, say I. Down, down, dogs! down fates! Have we not Hiren here?

Host. Good Captain Peesel, be quiet; it is very late, i' faith. I beseek you now, aggravate your choler.

Pist.   These be good humours, indeed!   Shall pack-
          horses,
And hollow pamper'd jades of Asia,
Which cannot go but thirty miles a day,
Compare with Cæsars, and with Cannibals,
And Trojan Greeks?   nay, rather damn them with
King Cerberus, and let the welkin roar.
Shall we fall foul for toys?
   Host.   By my troth, captain, these are very bitter words.
   Bard.   Be gone, good ancient: this will grow to a brawl
anon.
   Pist.   Die men like dogs; give crowns like pins!   Have
we not Hiren here?
   Host.   On my word, captain, there's none such here.
What the good-year!   do you think I would deny her?
For God's sake, be quiet.
   Pist.   Then feed and be fat, my fair Calipolis.
Come, give's some sack.
Si fortune me tormente, sperato me contente.—
Fear we broadsides?   no, let the fiend give fire:
Give me some sack; and, sweetheart, lie thou there.
                              [*Laying down his sword*
Come we to full points here, and are *et ceteras* nothing?
   Fal.   Pistol, I would be quiet.
   Pist.   Sweet knight, I kiss thy neif; what!   we have
seen the seven stars.
   Doll.   For God's sake, thrust him down-stairs!   I
cannot endure such a fustian rascal.
   Pist.   Thrust him down-stairs!   know we not Galloway
nags?
   Fal.   Quoit him down, Bardolph, like a shove-groat
shilling: nay, an 'a nothing but speak nothing, 'a shall be
nothing here.
   Bard.   Come, get you down-stairs.
   Pist.   What!   shall we have incision?   shall we im-
          brue?—   [*Snatching up his sword*
Then, death, rock me asleep, abridge my doleful days!
Why then, let grievous, ghastly, gaping wounds
Untwine the Sisters Three!   Come, Atropos, I say!
   Host.   Here's goodly stuff toward!
   Fal.   Give me my rapier, boy.
   Doll.   I pray thee, Jack, I pray thee do not draw.
   Fal.   Get you down-stairs.   [*Drawing*
   Host.   Here's a goodly tumult!   I'll forswear keeping
house, afore I'll be in these tirrits and frights.   So;
murder, I warrant now.—Alas, alas! put up your naked
weapons, put up your naked weapons.
                    [*Exeunt Bardolph and Pistol*
   Doll.   I pray thee, Jack, be quiet; the rascal is gone.
Ah! you whoreson little valiant villain, you.

111

Host. Are you not hurt i' the groin? methought 'a made a shrewd thrust at your belly.

Re-enter BARDOLPH

Fal. Have you turned him out o' doors?
Bard. Yes, sir: the rascal's drunk. You have hurt him, sir, in the shoulder.
Fal. A rascal, to brave me!
Doll. Ah, you sweet little rogue, you! Alas, poor ape, how thou sweat'st! Come, let me wipe thy face;—come on, you whoreson chops:—ah, rogue! i' faith, I love thee: thou art as valorous as Hector of Troy, worth five of Agamemnon, and ten times better than the Nine Worthies: ah, villain?
Fal. A rascally slave! I will toss the rogue in a blanket.
Doll. Do, if thou darest for thy heart: an thou dost, I'll canvass thee between a pair of sheets.

Enter Music

Page. The music is come, sir.
Fal. Let them play:—play, sirs.—Sit on my knee, Doll.—A rascal bragging slave! the rogue fled from me like quicksilver.
Doll. I' faith, and thou followedst him like a church. Thou whoreson little tidy Bartholomew boar-pig, when wilt thou leave fighting o' days and foining o' nights, and begin to patch up thine old body for heaven?

Enter behind, PRINCE HENRY *and* POINS, *disguised like Drawers*

Fal. Peace, good Doll! do not speak like a death's head; do not bid me remember mine end.
Doll. Sirrah, what humour is the prince of?
Fal. A good shallow young fellow: 'a would have made a good pantler, 'a would ha' chipped bread well.
Doll. They say, Poins has a good wit.
Fal. He a good wit? hang him, baboon! his wit is as thick as Tewksbury mustard; there's no more conceit in him than is in a mallet.
Doll. Why does the prince love him so, then?
Fal. Because their legs are both of a bigness; and 'a plays at quoits well; and eats conger and fennel; and drinks off candles' ends for flap-dragons; and rides the wild mare with the boys; and jumps upon joint-stools; and swears with a good grace; and wears his boot very smooth, like unto the sign of the leg; and breeds no bate

112

with telling of discreet stories; and such other gambol faculties 'a has, that show a weak mind and an able body, for the which the prince admits him: for the prince himself is such another; the weight of a hair will turn the scales between their avoirdupois.

P. Hen. Would not this nave of a wheel have his ears cut off!

Poins. Let's beat him before his whore.

P. Hen. Look, whether the withered elder hath not his poll clawed like a parrot.

Poins. Is it not strange, that desire should so many years outlive performance?

Fal. Kiss me, Doll.

P. Hen. Saturn and Venus this year in conjunction! what says the almanac to that?

Poins. And, look, whether the fiery Trigon, his man, be not lisping to his master's old tables, his note-book, his counsel-keeper.

Fal. Thou dost give me flattering busses.

Doll. By my troth, I kiss thee with a most constant heart.

Fal. I am old, I am old.

Doll. I love thee better than I love e'er a scurvy young boy of them all.

Fal. What stuff wilt have a kirtle of? I shall receive money o' Thursday; shalt have a cap to-morrow. A merry song, come: it grows late; we'll to bed. Thou'lt forget me, when I am gone.

Doll. By my troth, thou'lt set me a-weeping, an thou say'st so: prove that ever I dress myself handsome till thy return.—Well, hearken the end.

Fal. Some sack, Francis!

P. Hen., Poins. Anon, anon, sir.   [*Advancing*

Fal. Ha! a bastard son of the king's.—And art not thou Poins his brother?

P. Hen. Why, thou globe of sinful continents, what a life dost thou lead!

Fal. A better than thou: I am a gentleman; thou art a drawer.

P. Hen. Very true, sir; and I come to draw you out by the ears.

Host. O, the Lord preserve thy good grace! by my troth, welcome to London.—Now, the Lord bless that sweet face of thine! O Jesu, are you come from Wales?

Fal. Thou whoreson mad compound of majesty,—by this light flesh and corrupt blood, thou art welcome.

[*Leaning his hand upon Doll*

Doll. How, you fat fool! I scorn you.

Poins. My lord, he will drive you out of your revenge, and turn all to a merriment, if you take not the heat.

P. Hen. You whoreson candle-mine, you, how vilely did you speak of me even now, before this honest, virtuous, civil gentlewoman!

Host. God's blessing of your good heart! and so she is, by my troth.

Fal. Didst thou hear me?

P. Hen. Yes; and you knew me, as you did when you ran away by Gadshill: you knew I was at your back, and spoke it on purpose to try my patience.

Fal. No, no, no; not so; I did not think thou wast within hearing.

P. Hen. I shall drive you, then, to confess the wilful abuse; and then I know how to handle you.

Fal. No abuse, Hal, o' mine honour; no abuse.

P. Hen. Not!—to dispraise me, and call me pantler, and bread-chipper, and I know not what?

Fal. No abuse, Hal.

Poins. No abuse!

Fal. No abuse, Ned, i' the world: honest Ned, none. I dispraised him before the wicked, that the wicked might not fall in love with him;—in which doing, I have done the part of a careful friend and a true subject, and thy father is to give me thanks for it. No abuse, Hal;—none, Ned, none; no, 'faith, boys, none.

P. Hen. See now, whether pure fear, and entire cowardice, doth not make thee wrong this virtuous gentlewoman to close with us? Is she of the wicked? Is thine hostess here of the wicked? Or is thy boy of the wicked? Or honest Bardolph, whose zeal burns in his nose, of the wicked?

Poins. Answer, thou dead elm, answer.

Fal. The fiend hath pricked down Bardolph irrecoverable; and his face is Lucifer's privy-kitchen, where he doth nothing but roast malt-worms. For the boy,—there is a good angel about him, but the devil outbids him too.

P. Hen. For the women?

Fal. For one of them,—she is in hell already, and burns poor souls. For the other,—I owe her money, and whether she be damned for that, I know not.

Host. No, I warrant you.

Fal. No, I think thou art not; I think, thou art quit for that. Marry, there is another indictment upon thee, for suffering flesh to be eaten in thy house, contrary to the law; for the which I think thou wilt howl.

Host. All victuallers do so: what's a joint of mutton or two in a whole Lent?

P. Hen. You, gentlewoman,—

Doll. What says your grace?

Fal. His grace says that which his flesh rebels against.

[Knocking heard

Host. Who knocks so loud at door ? look to the door there, Francis.

Enter PETO

P. Hen. Peto, how now! what news?
Peto. The king your father is at Westminster;
And there are twenty weak and wearied posts
Come from the north: and, as I came along,
I met and overtook a dozen captains,
Bare-headed, sweating, knocking at the taverns,
And asking every one for Sir John Falstaff.
P. Hen. By Heavens, Poins, I feel me much to blame,
So idly to profane the precious time
When tempest of commotion, like the south
Borne with black vapour, doth begin to melt
And drop upon our bare unarmèd heads.
Give me my sword and cloak.—Falstaff, good-night.
          [*Exeunt Prince Henry, Poins, Peto, and Bardolph*
Fal. Now comes in the sweetest morsel of the night,
and we must hence, and leave it unpicked. [*Knocking
heard*] More knocking at the door!

Re-enter BARDOLPH

How now? what's the matter?
Bard. You must away to court, sir, presently;
A dozen captains stay at door for you.
Fal. [*To the Page*] Pay the musicians, sirrah.—Farewell, hostess;—farewell, Doll. You see, my good wenches,
how men of merit are sought after: the undeserver may
sleep, when the man of action is called on. Farewell, good
wenches: if I be not sent away post, I will see you again
ere I go.
Doll. I cannot speak;—if my heart be not ready to
burst,—well, sweet Jack, have a care of thyself.
Fal. Farewell, farewell. [*Exeunt Falstaff and Bardolph*
Host. Well, fare thee well: I have known thee these
twenty-nine years, come peascod-time; but an honester,
and truer-hearted man,—well, fare thee well.
Bard. [*Within*] Mistress Tear-sheet,—
Host. What's the matter?
Bard. [*Within*] Bid Mistress Tear-sheet come to my
master.
Host. O! run, Doll, run; run, good Doll: come. [*Doll
comes blubbered*] Yea, will you come, Doll?   [*Exeunt*

ACT THREE

SCENE I.—A Room in the Palace

Enter KING HENRY *in his night-gown, with a Page*

K. Hen.   Go, call the Earls of Surrey and of Warwick;
But, ere they come, bid them o'er-read these letters
And well consider of them.   Make good speed.   [*Exit Page*
How many thousands of my poorest subjects
Are at this hour asleep!—O sleep, O gentle sleep,
Nature's soft nurse, how have I frighted thee
That thou no more wilt weigh my eyelids down
And steep my senses in forgetfulness?
Why, rather, sleep, liest thou in smoky cribs,
Upon uneasy pallets stretching thee
And hushed with buzzing night-flies to thy slumber,
Than in the perfumed chambers of the great,
Under the canopies of costly state
And lulled with sounds of sweetest melody?
O thou dull god, why liest thou with the vile
In loathsome beds, and leav'st the kingly couch
A watch-case or a common 'larum bell?
Wilt thou upon the high and giddy mast
Seal up the ship-boy's eyes, and rock his brains
In cradle of the rude imperious surge,
And in the visitation of the winds
Who take the ruffian billows by the top,
Curling their monstrous heads and hanging them
With deafening clamours in the slippery clouds
That with the hurly death itself awakes,—
Canst thou, O partial sleep! give thy repose
To the wet sea boy in an hour so rude;
And in the calmest and most stillest night,
With all appliances and means to boot,
Deny it to a king?   Then, happy low, lie down!
Uneasy lies the head that wears a crown.

Enter WARWICK *and* SURREY

War.   Many good-morrows to your majesty!
K. Hen.   Is it good-morrow, lords?
War.   'T is one o'clock, and past.
K. Hen.   Why then, good-morrow to you all, my lords.
Have you read o'er the letters that I sent you?
War.   We have, my liege.
K. Hen.   Then you perceive, the body of our kingdom
How foul it is; what rank diseases grow,
And with what danger, near the heart of it.

116

War. It is but as a body yet distempered,
Which to his former strength may be restored
With good advice and little medicine.
My Lord Northumberland will soon be cooled.
    K. Hen. O God, that one might read the book of
      fate,
And see the revolution of the times
Make mountains level, and the continent,
Weary of solid firmness, melt itself
Into the sea; and, other times, to see
The beachy girdle of the ocean
Too wide for Neptune's hips; how chances mock,
And changes fill the cup of alteration
With divers liquors! O, if this were seen,
The happiest youth—viewing his progress through,
What perils past, what crosses to ensue—
Would shut the book and sit him down and die.
It is not ten years gone,
Since Richard and Northumberland, great friends,
Did feast together, and in two years after
Were they at wars. It is but eight years since
This Percy was the man nearest my soul;
Who like a brother toiled in my affairs,
And laid his love and life under my foot;
Yea, for my sake, even to the eyes of Richard,
Gave him defiance. But which of you was by—
[*To Warwick*] (You, cousin Nevil, as I may remember)—
When Richard, with his eyes brimful of tears,
Then checked and rated by Northumberland,
Did speak these words, now proved a prophecy?
'Northumberland, thou ladder, by the which
My cousin Bolingbroke ascends my throne;'—
Though then, God knows, I had no such intent,
But that necessity so bowed the state
That I and greatness were compelled to kiss.
'The time shall come,' thus did he follow it,
'The time will come, that foul sin, gathering head,
Shall break into corruption;'—so went on,
Foretelling this same time's condition,
And the division of our amity.
    War. There is a history in all men's lives,
Figuring the nature of the times deceased;
The which observed, a man may prophesy
With a near aim of the main chance of things
As yet not come to life, which in their seeds
And weak beginnings lie intreasuréd.
Such things become the hatch and brood of time;
And, by the necessary form of this,
King Richard might create a perfect guess
That great Northumberland, then false to him,

Would, of that seed, grow to a greater falseness
Which should not find a ground to root upon
Unless on you.
 K. Hen. Are these things then necessities?
Then let us meet them like necessities;—
And that same word even now cries out on us.
They say, the bishop and Northumberland
Are fifty thousand strong.
 War.   It cannot be, my lord;
Rumour doth double, like the voice and echo,
The numbers of the feared.—Please it your grace
To go to bed; upon my life, my lord,
The powers that you already have sent forth
Shall bring this prize in very easily.
To comfort you the more, I have received
A certain instance that Glendower is dead.
Your majesty hath been this fortnight ill,
And these unseasoned hours, perforce, must add
Unto your sickness.
 K. Hen.   I will take your counsel:
And were these inward wars once out of hand,
We would, dear lords, unto the Holy Land.   [*Exeunt*

SCENE II.—Court before JUSTICE SHALLOW'S House
in Glostershire

Enter SHALLOW *and* SILENCE *meeting ;* MOULDY, SHADOW,
WART, FEEBLE, BULL-CALF, *and Servants, behind*

 Shal. Come on, come on, come on, sir; give me your
hand, sir, give me your hand, sir: an early stirrer, by the
rood. And how doth my good cousin Silence?
 Sil. Good morrow, good cousin Shallow.
 Shal. And how doth my cousin, your bed-fellow? and
your fairest daughter, and mine, my god-daughter Ellen?
 Sil. Alas, a black ousel, cousin Shallow.
 Shal. By yea and nay, sir, I dare say, my cousin William
is become a good scholar. He is at Oxford still, is he not?
 Sil. Indeed, sir; to my cost.
 Shal. He must then to the inns o' court shortly. I
was once of Clement's Inn, where I think they will talk of
mad Shallow yet.
 Sil. You were called lusty Shallow then, cousin.
 Shal. By the mass, I was called anything; and I would
have done anything indeed too, and roundly too. There
was I, and little John Doit of Staffordshire, and black
George Bare, and Francis Pickbone, and Will Squele, a
Cotsol' man; you had not four such swinge-bucklers in all

the inns o' court again: and, I may say to you, we knew where the bona-robas were, and had the best of them all at commandment. Then was Jack Falstaff, now Sir John, a boy, and page to Thomas Mowbray, Duke of Norfolk.

Sil. This Sir John, cousin, that comes hither anon about soldiers?

Shal. The same Sir John, the very same. I saw him break Skogan's head at the court gate, when 'a was a crack, not thus high: and the very same day did I fight with one Sampson Stockfish, a fruiterer, behind Gray's Inn. Jesu, Jesu, the mad days that I have spent! and to see how many of my old acquaintance are dead!

Sil. We shall all follow, cousin.

Shal. Certain, 't is certain; very sure, very sure: death, as the Psalmist saith, is certain to all; all shall die.—How a good yoke of bullocks at Stamford fair!

Sil. Truly, cousin, I was not there.

Shal. Death is certain.—Is old Double of your town living yet?

Sil. Dead, sir.

Shal. Jesu, Jesu, dead!—'a drew a good bow;—and dead!—'a shot a fine shoot:—John o' Gaunt loved him well, and betted much money on his head. Dead!—'a would have clapped i' the clout at twelve score; and carried you a forehand shaft a fourteen and fourteen and a half, that it would have done a man's heart good to see.—How a score of ewes now?

Sil. Thereafter as they be; a score of good ewes may be worth ten pounds.

Shal. And is old Double dead?

Sil. Here come two of Sir John Falstaff's men, as I think.

Enter BARDOLPH, *and one with him*

Bard. Good morrow, honest gentlemen: I beseech you, which is Justice Shallow?

Shal. I am Robert Shallow, sir; a poor esquire of this county, and one of the king's justices of the peace: What is your good pleasure with me?

Bard. My captain, sir, commends him to you; my captain, Sir John Falstaff: a tall gentleman, by Heaven, and a most gallant leader.

Shal. He greets me well, sir. I knew him a good back-sword man. How doth the good knight? may I ask, how my lady his wife doth?

Bard. Sir, pardon; a soldier is better accommodated than with a wife.

Shal. It is well said, in faith, sir; and it is well said indeed, too. Better accommodated!—it is good; yea, indeed, it is: a good phrases are surely, and ever were, very commendable. Accommodated! it comes of *accommodo*: very good; a good phrase.

Bard. Pardon me, sir; I have heard the word. Phrase, call you it? By this good day, I know not the phrase; but I will maintain the word with my sword to be a soldier-like word, and a word of exceeding good command, by Heaven. Accommodated; that is, when a man is, as they say, accommodated; or, when a man is, being, whereby, 'a may be thought to be accommodated; which is an excellent thing.

Shal. It is very just.—Look, here comes good Sir John.

Enter FALSTAFF

Give me your good hand, give me your worship's good hand: by my troth, you like well, and bear your years very well: welcome, good Sir John.

Fal. I am glad to see you well, good Master Robert Shallow.—Master Sure-card, as I think.

Shal. No, Sir John; it is my cousin Silence, in commission with me.

Fal. Good Master Silence, it well befits you should be of the peace.

Sil. Your good worship is welcome.

Fal. Fie! this is hot weather.—Gentlemen, have you provided me here half a dozen sufficient men?

Shal. Marry, have we, sir. Will you sit?

Fal. Let me see them, I beseech you.

Shal. Where's the roll? where's the roll? where's the roll?—Let me see, let me see, let me see: so, so, so, so: yea, marry, sir:—Ralph Mouldy!—let them appear as I call; let them do so, let them do so.—Let me see; where is Mouldy?

Moul. Here, an't please you.

Shal. What think you, Sir John? a good-limbed fellow; young, strong, and of good friends.

Fal. Is thy name Mouldy?

Moul. Yea, an't please you.

Fal. 'T is the more time thou wert used.

Shal. Ha, ha, ha! most excellent, i' faith! things that are mouldy lack use: very singular good!—In faith, well said, Sir John; very well said.

Fal. [*To Shallow*] Prick him.

Moul. I was pricked well enough before, an you could have let me alone: my old dame will be undone now, for one to do her husbandry and her drudgery. You need not to have pricked me; there are other men fitter to go out than I.

Fal. Go to; peace, Mouldy: you shall go. Mouldy, it is time you were spent.

Moul. Spent!
Shal. Peace, fellow, peace; stand aside: know you where you are?—For the other, Sir John:—let me see.—Simon Shadow!
Fal. Yea, marry, let me have him to sit under: he's like to be a cold soldier.
Shal. Where's Shadow?
Shad. Here, sir.
Fal. Shadow, whose son art thou?
Shad. My mother's son, sir.
Fal. Thy mother's son! like enough; and thy father's shadow: so the son of the female is the shadow of the male: it is often so, indeed; but not of the father's substance.
Shal. Do you like him, Sir John?
Fal. Shadow will serve for summer,—prick him; for we have a number of shadows to fill up the muster-book.
Shal. Thomas Wart!
Fal. Where's he?
Wart. Here, sir.
Fal. Is thy name Wart?
Wart. Yea, sir.
Fal. Thou art a very ragged wart.
Shal. Shall I prick him, Sir John?
Fal. It were superfluous; for his apparel is built upon his back, and the whole frame stands upon pins: prick him no more.
Shal. Ha, ha, ha!—you can do it, sir; you can do it: I commend you well.—Francis Feeble!
Fee. Here, sir.
Fal. What trade art thou, Feeble?
Fee. A woman's tailor, sir.
Shal. Shall I prick him, sir?
Fal. You may; but if he had been a man's tailor, he'd ha' pricked you.—Wilt thou make as many holes in an enemy's battle as thou hast done in a woman's petticoat?
Fee. I will do my good will, sir; you can have no more.
Fal. Well said, good woman's tailor! well said, courageous Feeble! Thou wilt be as valiant as the wrathful dove or most magnanimous mouse.—Prick the woman's tailor well, Master Shallow; deep, Master Shallow.
Fee. I would Wart might have gone, sir.
Fal. I would thou wert a man's tailor, that thou mightst mend him, and make him fit to go. I cannot put him to a private soldier, that is the leader of so many thousands: let that suffice, most forcible Feeble.
Fee. It shall suffice, sir.
Fal. I am bound to thee, reverend Feeble.—Who is next?

Shal.   Peter Bull-calf of the green!

Fal.   Yea, marry, let's see Bull-calf.

Bull.   Here, sir.

Fal.   'Fore God, a likely fellow!—Come, prick me Bull-calf till he roar again.

Bull.   O Lord! good my lord captain,—

Fal.   What, dost thou roar before thou art pricked?

Bull.   O Lord, sir, I am a diseased man.

Fal.   What disease hast thou?

Bull.   A whoreson cold, sir,—a cough, sir—which I caught with ringing in the king's affairs upon his coronation day, sir.

Fal.   Come, thou shalt go to the wars in a gown; we will have away thy cold; and I will take such order, that thy friends shall ring for thee.—Is here all?

Shal.   Here is two more called than your number; you must have but four here, sir:—and so, I pray you, go in with me to dinner.

Fal.   Come, I will go drink with you, but I cannot tarry dinner. I am glad to see you, by my troth, Master Shallow.

Shal.   O, Sir John, do you remember since we lay all night in the windmill in Saint George's field?

Fal.   No more of that, good Master Shallow, no more of that.

Shal.   Ha, 't was a merry night. And is Jane Night-work alive?

Fal.   She lives, Master Shallow.

Shal.   She never could away with me.

Fal.   Never, never: she would always say, she could not abide Master Shallow.

Shal.   By the mass, I could anger her to the heart. She was then a bona-roba. Doth she hold her own well?

Fal.   Old, old, Master Shallow.

Shal.   Nay, she must be old; she cannot choose but be old; certain she's old, and had Robin Night-work by old Night-work before I came to Clement's Inn.

Sil.   That's fifty-five years ago.

Shal.   Ha, cousin Silence, that thou hadst seen that, that this knight and I have seen!—Ha, Sir John, said I well?

Fal.   We have heard the chimes at midnight, Master Shallow.

Shal.   That we have, that we have, that we have; in faith, Sir John, we have: our watchword was, 'Hem, boys!'—Come, let's to dinner; come, let's to dinner.—Jesus! the days that we have seen!—Come, come.

             [*Exeunt Falstaff, Shallow, and Silence*

Bull.   Good Master corporate Bardolph, stand my friend, and here is four Harry ten shillings in French crowns for you. In very truth, sir, I had as lief be hanged, sir, as go;

and yet for mine own part, sir, I do not care; but rather, because I am unwilling, and, for mine own part, have a desire to stay with my friends: else, sir, I did not care for mine own part so much.

Bard. Go to; stand aside.

Moul. And good master corporal captain, for my old dame's sake, stand my friend: she has nobody to do anything about her, when I am gone; and she is old, and cannot help herself. You shall have forty, sir.

Bard. Go to; stand aside.

Fee. By my troth, I care not; a man can die but once;—we owe God a death. I'll ne'er bear a base mind:—an't be my destiny, so; an't be not, so. No man's too good to serve his prince; and let it go which way it will, he that dies this year is quit for the next.

Bard. Well said; thou'rt a good fellow.

Fee. 'Faith, I'll bear no base mind.

Re-enter FALSTAFF *and Justices*

Fal. Come, sir, which men shall I have?

Shal. Four of which you please.

Bard. Sir, a word with you.—I have three pound to free Mouldy and Bull-calf.

Fal. Go to; well.

Shal. Come, Sir John, which four will you have?

Fal. Do you choose for me.

Shal. Marry, then,—Mouldy, Bull-calf, Feeble, and Shadow.

Fal. Mouldy and Bull-calf: for you, Mouldy, stay at home till you are past service:—and, for your part, Bull-calf, grow till you come unto it: I will none of you.

Shal. Sir John, Sir John, do not yourself wrong: they are your likeliest men, and I would have you served with the best.

Fal. Will you tell me, Master Shallow, how to choose a man? Care I for the limb, the thews, the stature, bulk, and big assemblance of a man? Give me the spirit, Master Shallow.—Here's Wart;—you see what a ragged appearance it is: 'a shall charge you, and discharge you, with the motion of a pewterer's hammer; come off, and on, swifter than he that gibbets-on the brewer's bucket. And this same half-faced fellow, Shadow,—give me this man: he presents no mark to the enemy; the foeman may with as great aim level at the edge of a pen-knife. And, for a retreat,—how swiftly will this Feeble, the woman's tailor, run off! O, give me the spare men, and spare me the great ones.—Put me a caliver into Wart's hand, Bardolph.

Bard. Hold, Wart, traverse; thus, thus, thus.

Fal. Come, manage me your caliver. So:—very

well:—go to:—very good:—exceeding good.—O, give me always a little, lean, old, chapped, bald shot.—Well said, i' faith, Wart: thou'rt a good scab: hold, there's a tester for thee.

Shal. He is not his craft's master; he doth not do it right. I remember at Mile End Green,—when I lay at Clement's Inn,—I was then Sir Dagonet in Arthur's show, there was a little quiver fellow, and 'a would manage you his piece thus: and 'a would about, and about, and come you in: 'rah, tah, tah,' would 'a say; 'bounce,' would 'a say; and away again would 'a go, and again would 'a come.—I shall ne'er see such a fellow.

Fal. These fellows will do well, Master Shallow.—God keep you, Master Silence: I will not use many words with you.—Fare you well, gentlemen both: I thank you: I must a dozen mile to-night.—Bardolph, give the soldiers coats.

Shal. Sir John, the Lord bless you, and God prosper your affairs! God send us peace! As you return, visit my house; let our old acquaintance be renewed: peradventure, I will with you to the court.

Fal. 'Fore God, I would you would, Master Shallow.

Shal. Go to; I have spoke at a word. Fare you well.

Fal. Fare you well, gentle gentlemen. [*Exeunt Shallow and Silence*] On, Bardolph; lead the men away. [*Exeunt Bardolph, Recruits, etc.*] As I return, I will fetch off these justices: I do see the bottom of Justice Shallow. Lord, Lord, how subject we old men are to this vice of lying! This same starved justice hath done nothing but prate to me of the wildness of his youth, and the feats he hath done about Turnbull Street; and every third word a lie, duer paid to the hearer than the Turk's tribute. I do remember him at Clement's Inn, like a man made after supper of a cheese-paring: when he was naked, he was, for all the world, like a forked radish, with a head fantastically carved upon it with a knife; he was so forlorn, that his dimensions to any thick sight were invisible: 'a was the very genius of famine; yet lecherous as a monkey, and the whores called him mandrake. He came ever in the rearward of the fashion, and sung those tunes to the overscutched huswives that he heard the carmen whistle, and sware they were his Fancies, or his Good-nights. And now is this Vice's dagger become a squire, and talks as familiarly of John o' Gaunt as if he had been sworn brother to him; and I'll be sworn he never saw him but once in the Tilt-yard; and then he burst his head for crowding among the marshal's men. I saw it, and told John o' Gaunt he beat his own name; for you might have thrust him and all his apparel into an eel-skin: the case of a treble hautboy was a mansion for him, a court; and now has he land and beeves. Well, I'll be acquainted with him, if I return; and it shall go hard but I will make him a philosopher's two stones to me. If the young dace be a bait for the old pike, I see no reason in the law of nature but I may snap at him. Let time shape, and there an end. *[Exit*

ACT FOUR

SCENE I.—A Forest in Yorkshire

Enter the ARCHBISHOP OF YORK, MOWBRAY, HASTINGS, *and others*

Arch. What is this forest called?
Hast. 'T is Gaultree Forest, an 't shall please your grace.
Arch. Here stand, my lords, and send discoverers forth
To know the numbers of our enemies.
Hast. We have sent forth already.
Arch.   'T is well done.—
My friends and brethren in these great affairs,
I must acquaint you that I have received
New-dated letters from Northumberland;
Their cold intent, tenour, and substance, thus:—
Here doth he wish his person, with such powers
As might hold sortance with his quality,
The which he could not levy; whereupon
He is retired, to ripe his growing fortunes,
To Scotland; and concludes in hearty prayers
That your attempts may overlive the hazard
And fearful meeting of their opposite.
Mowb. Thus do the hopes we have in him touch ground,
And dash themselves to pieces.

Enter a Messenger

Hast.   Now, what news?
Mess. West of this forest, scarcely off a mile,
In goodly form comes on the enemy;
And, by the ground they hide, I judge their number
Upon or near the rate of thirty thousand.
Mowb. The just proportion that we gave them out.
Let us sway on and face them in the field.

Enter WESTMORELAND

Arch. What well-appointed leader fronts us here?
Mowb. I think it is my Lord of Westmoreland.
West. Health and fair greeting from our general,
The prince, Lord John and Duke of Lancaster.
Arch. Say on, my Lord of Westmoreland, in peace,
What doth concern your coming?

West.   Then, my lord,
Unto your grace do I in chief address
The substance of my speech.   If that rebellion
Came like itself, in base and abject routs,
Led on by heady youth, guarded with rags,
And countenanced by boys and beggary;
I say, if damned commotion so appeared
In his true, native, and most proper shape,
You, reverend father, and these noble lords,
Had not been here to dress the ugly form
Of base and bloody insurrection
With your fair honours.   You, lord archbishop,—
Whose see is by a civil peace maintained;
Whose beard the silver hand of peace hath touched;
Whose learning and good letters peace hath tutored;
Whose white investments figure innocence,
The dove and very blessèd spirit of peace,—
Wherefore do you so ill translate yourself,
Out of the speech of peace, that bears such grace,
Into the harsh and boisterous tongue of war;
Turning your books to graves, your ink to blood,
Your pens to lances, and your tongue divine
To a loud trumpet and a point of war?
    Arch.   Wherefore do I this?—so the question stands.
Briefly to this end:—we are all diseased;
And, with our surfeiting and wanton hours
Have brought ourselves into a burning fever,
And we must bleed for it: of which disease
Our late king, Richard, being infected, died.
But, my most noble Lord of Westmoreland,
I take not on me here as a physician;
Nor do I, as an enemy to peace,
Troop in the throngs of military men;
But, rather, show awhile like fearful war
To diet rank minds sick of happiness
And purge the obstructions which begin to stop
Our very veins of life.   Hear me more plainly.
I have in equal balance justly weighed
What wrongs our arms may do, what wrongs we suffer,
And find our griefs heavier than our offences.
We see which way the stream of time doth run,
And are enforced from our most quiet sphere
By the rough torrent of occasion;
And have the summary of all our griefs,
When time shall serve, to show in articles,
Which long ere this we offered to the king,
And might be no suit gain our audience.
When we are wronged, and would unfold our griefs,
We are denied access unto his person
Even by those men that most have done us wrong.

The dangers of the days but newly gone,
Whose memory is written on the earth
With yet-appearing blood, and the examples
Of every minute's instance, present now,
Have put us in these ill-beseeming arms;
Not to break peace, or any branch of it,
But to establish here a peace indeed,
Concurring both in name and quality.
    West.   When ever yet was your appeal denied?
Wherein have you been gallèd by the king?
What peer hath been suborned to grate on you,
That you should seal this lawless bloody book
Of forged rebellion with a seal divine,
And consecrate commotion's bitter edge?
    Arch.   My brother general, the commonwealth,
To brother born an household cruelty
I make my quarrel in particular.
    West.   There is no need of any such redress;
Or, if there were, it not belongs to you.
    Mowb.   Why not to him, in part, and to us all,
That feel the bruises of the days before,
And suffer the condition of these times
To lay a heavy and unequal hand
Upon our honours?
    West.   O, my good Lord Mowbray,
Construe the times to their necessities,
And you shall say indeed, it is the time
And not the king that doth you injuries.
Yet, for your part, it not appears to me,
Either from the king or in the present time,
That you should have an inch of any ground
To build a grief on.   Were you not restored
To all the Duke of Norfolk's signiories,
Your noble and right-well remembered father's?
    Mowb.   What thing, in honour, had my father lost,
That need to be revived and breathed in me?
The king, that loved him, as the state stood then,
Was force perforce, compelled to banish him:
And when that Harry Bolingbroke and he,
Being mounted and both rousèd in their seats,
Their neighing coursers daring of the spur,
Their armèd staves in charge, their beavers down,
Their eyes of fire sparkling through sights of steel,
And the loud trumpet blowing them together,
Then, then, when there was nothing could have stayed
My father from the breast of Bolingbroke,
O, then the king did throw his warder down:
His own life hung upon the staff he threw;
Then threw he down himself, and all their lives
That by indictment and by dint of sword

Have since miscarried under Bolingbroke.
   West. You speak, Lord Mowbray, now you know not what.
The Earl of Hereford was reputed then
In England the most valiant gentleman:
Who knows on whom fortune would then have smiled?
But if your father had been victor there,
He ne'er had borne it out of Coventry;
For all the country in a general voice
Cried hate upon him; and all their prayers and love
Were set on Hereford, whom they doted on,
And blessed, and graced, indeed, more than the king.
But this is mere digression from my purpose.—
Here come I from our princely general
To know your griefs; to tell you from his grace
That he will give you audience, and wherein
It shall appear that your demands are just,
You shall enjoy them,—everything set off
That might so much as think you enemies.
   Mowb. But he hath forced us to compel this offer,
And it proceeds from policy, not love.
   West. Mowbray, you overween to take it so.
This offer comes from mercy, not from fear;
For, lo, within a ken our army lies,
Upon mine honour, all too confident
To give admittance to a thought of fear.
Our battle is more full of names than yours,
Our men more perfect in the use of arms,
Our armour all as strong, our cause the best;
Then reason wills our hearts should be as good:
Say you not then, our offer is compelled.
   Mowb. Well, by my will, we shall admit no parley.
   West. That argues but the shame of your offence:
A rotten case abides no handling.
   Hast. Hath the Prince John a full commission,
In very ample virtue of his father,
To hear and absolutely to determine
Of what conditions we shall stand upon?
   West. That is intended in the general's name:
I muse you make so slight a question.
   Arch. Then take, my Lord of Westmoreland, this
        schedule,
For this contains our general grievances:
Each several article herein redressed,
All members of our cause, both here and hence,
That are insinewed to this action,
Acquitted by a true substantial form:
And present execution of our wills
To us and to our purposes consigned;
We come within our awful banks again,
And knit our powers to the arm of peace.

West.   This will I show the general.   Please you, lords,
In sight of both our battles we may meet:
And either end in peace, which God so frame,
Or to the place of difference call the swords
Which must decide it.
    Arch.   My lord, we will do so.
                                [Exit Westmoreland
    Mowb.   There is a thing within my bosom tells me
That no conditions of our peace can stand.
    Hast.   Fear you not that; if we can make our peace
Upon such large terms and so absolute
As our conditions shall consist upon,
Our peace shall stand as firm as rocky mountains.
    Mowb.   Ay, but our valuation shall be such,
That every slight and false-derivéd cause,
Yea, every idle, nice, and wanton reason,
Shall to the king taste of this action;
That, were our royal faiths martyrs in love,
We shall be winnowed with so rough a wind
That even our corn shall seem as light as chaff,
And good from bad find no partition.
    Arch.   No, no, my lord.   Note this,—the king is weary
Of dainty and such picking grievances;
For he hath found, to end one doubt by death
Revives two greater in the heirs of life;
And therefore will he wipe his tables clean,
And keep no tell-tale to his memory
That may repeat and history his loss
To new remembrance: for full well he knows
He cannot so precisely weed this land
As his misdoubts present occasion:
His foes are so enrooted with his friends,
That, plucking to unfix an enemy
He doth unfasten so and shake a friend.
So that this land, like an offensive wife
That hath enraged him on to offer strokes,
As he is striking holds his infant up
And hangs resolved correction in the arm
That was upreared to execution.
    Hast.   Besides, the king hath wasted all his rods
On late offenders, that he now doth lack
The very instruments of chastisement;
So that his power, like to a fangless lion,
May offer, but not hold.
    Arch.   'T is very true:
And therefore be assured, my good lord marshal,
If we do now make our atonement well,
Our peace will, like a broken limb united,
Grow stronger for the breaking.
    Mowb.   Be it so.

Here is returned my Lord of Westmoreland.

Re-enter WESTMORELAND

   West.   The prince is here at hand.   Pleaseth your lord-
      ship
To meet his grace just distance 'tween our armies?
   Mowb.   Your grace of York, in God's name, then, set
      forward.
   Arch.   Before, and greet his grace.—My lord, we come.
                                    [Exeunt

SCENE II.—Another Part of the Forest

Enter, from one side, MOWBRAY, *the* ARCHBISHOP, HASTINGS,
   and others : from the other side, PRINCE JOHN OF
   LANCASTER, WESTMORELAND, *Officers, and Attendants*

   P. John.   You are well encountered here, my cousin
      Mowbray.—
Good day to you, gentle lord árchbishop;—
And so to you, Lord Hastings,—and to all.—
My Lord of York, it better showed with you
When that your flock, assembled by the bell,
Encircled you to hear with reverence
Your exposition on the holy text,
Than now to see you here an iron man
Cheering a rout of rebels with your drum,
Turning the Word to sword, and life to death.
That man that sits within a monarch's heart
And ripens in the sunshine of his favour,
Would he abuse the countenance of the king,
Alack, what mischiefs might he set abroach
In shadow of such greatness!   With you, lord bishop,
It is even so.   Who hath not heard it spoken,
How deep you were within the books of God?
To us, the speaker in his parliament;
To us, the imagined voice of God himself,
The very opener and intelligencer
Between the grace, the sanctities of heaven
And our dull workings.   O, who shall believe
But you misuse the reverence of your place,
Employ the countenance and grace of Heaven
As a false favourite doth his prince's name
In deeds dishonourable?   You have ta'en up
Under the counterfeited seal of God
The subjects of His substitute, my father;
And both against the peace of Heaven and him
Have here up-swarmed them.
   Arch.   Good my Lord of Lancaster,

I am not here against your father's peace;
But, as I told my Lord of Westmoreland,
The time misordered doth, in common sense,
Crowd us and crush us to this monstrous form,
To hold our safety up. I sent your grace
The parcels and particulars of our grief,—
The which hath been with scorn shoved from the court,—
Whereon this Hydra son of war is born;
Whose dangerous eyes may well be charmed asleep
With grant of our most just and right desires,
And true obedience, of this madness cured,
Stood tamely to the foot of majesty.
    Mowb. If not, we ready are to try our fortunes
To the last man.
    Hast.   And though we here fall down,
We have supplies to second our attempt;
If they miscarry, theirs shall second them;
And so success of mischief shall be born,
And heir from heir shall hold this quarrel up
While England shall have generation.
    P. John. You are too shallow, Hastings, much too
          shallow,
To sound the bottom of the after-times.
    West. Pleaseth your grace to answer them directly,
How far forth you do like their articles?
    P. John. I like them all, and do allow them well;
And swear here, by the honour of my blood,
My father's purposes have been mistook;
And some about him have too lavishly
Wrested his meaning and authority.—
My lord, these griefs shall be with speed redressed;
Upon my soul, they shall. If these may please you,
Discharge your powers unto their several counties,
As we will ours: and here, between the armies,
Let's drink together friendly and embrace,
That all their eyes may bear those tokens home,
Of our restoréd love and amity.
    Arch. I take your princely word for these redresses.
    P. John. I give it you, and will maintain my word:
And thereupon I drink unto your grace.   [*Drinks*
    Hast. [*To an Officer*] Go, captain, and deliver to the
          army
This news of peace: let them have pay, and part.
I know, it will well please them: hie thee, captain.
                      [*Exit Officer*
    Arch. To you, my noble Lord of Westmoreland.
                      [*Drinks*
    West. I pledge your grace: [*Drinks*] and if you knew
          what pains
I have bestowed to breed this present peace,

You would drink freely; but my love to you
Shall show itself more openly hereafter.
    Arch.   I do not doubt you.
    West.   I am glad of it.—
Health to my Lord, and gentle cousin Mowbray.   [*Drinks*
    Mowb.   You wish me health in very happy season;
For I am, on the sudden, something ill.
    Arch.   Against ill chances men are ever merry,
But heaviness foreruns the good event.
    West.   Therefore be merry, coz; since sudden sorrow
Serves to say thus, 'Some good thing comes to-morrow.'
    Arch.   Believe me, I am passing light in spirit.
    Mowb.   So much the worse, if your own rule be true.
                                    [*Shouts within*
    P. John.   The word of peace is rendered: hark, how
        they shout!
    Mowb.   This had been cheerful after victory.
    Arch.   A peace is of the nature of a conquest;
For then both parties nobly are subdued,
And neither party loser.
    P. John.   Go, my lord,
And let our army be dischargéd too.— [*Exit Westmoreland*
And, good my lord, so please you, let your trains
March by us, that we may peruse the men
We should have coped withal.
    Arch.   Go, good Lord Hastings,
And, ere they be dismissed, let them march by.
                                    [*Exit Hastings*
    P. John.   I trust, lords, we shall lie to-night together.

Re-enter WESTMORELAND

Now, cousin, wherefore stands our army still?
    West.   The leaders, having charge from you to stand,
Will not go off until they hear you speak.
    P. John.   They know their duties.

Re-enter HASTINGS

    Hast.   My lord, our army is dispersed already.
Like youthful steers unyoked, they take their courses
East, west, north, south; or, like a school broke up,
Each hurries toward his home and sporting-place.
    West.   Good tidings, my Lord Hastings; for the which
I do arrest thee, traitor, of high treason:—
And you, lord árchbishop,—and you, Lord Mowbray,—
Of capital treason I attach you both.
    Mowb.   Is this proceeding just and honourable?
    West.   Is your assembly so?
    Arch.   Will you thus break your faith?

P. John   I pawned thee none.
I promised you redress of these same grievances
Whereof you did complain; which, by mine honour,
I will perform with a most Christian care.
But, for you, rebels, look to taste the due
Meet for rebellion and such acts as yours.
Most shallowly did you these arms commence,
Fondly brought here, and foolishly sent hence.—
Strike up our drums! pursue the scattered stray;
God, and not we, hath safely fought to-day.—
Some guard these traitors to the block of death,
Treason's true bed, and yielder up of breath.   [*Exeunt*

SCENE III.—Another Part of the Forest

Alarums: Excursions. Enter FALSTAFF *and*
COLEVILLE, *meeting*

Fal. What's your name, sir? of what condition are
you, and of what place, I pray?
Cole. I am a knight, sir; and my name is Coleville of
the dale.
Fal. Well, then, Coleville is your name, a knight is your
degree, and your place, the dale: Coleville shall still be
your name, a traitor your degree, and the dungeon your
place,—a dale deep enough; so shall you be still Coleville
of the dale.
Cole. Are not you Sir John Falstaff?
Fal. As good a man as he, sir, whoe'er I am. Do ye
yield, sir, or shall I sweat for you? If I do sweat, they are
the drops of thy lovers, and they weep for thy death;
therefore, rouse up fear and trembling, and do observance
to my mercy.
Cole. I think you are Sir John Falstaff, and in that
thought yield me.
Fal. I have a whole school of tongues in this belly of
mine, and not a tongue of them all speaks any other word
but my name. An I had but a belly of any indifferency, I
were simply the most active fellow in Europe: my womb,
my womb, my womb undoes me.—Here comes our general.

Enter PRINCE JOHN OF LANCASTER, WESTMORELAND, *and
others*

P. John. The heat is past; follow no further now,—
Call in the powers, good cousin Westmoreland.—
                                    [*Exit Westmoreland*
Now, Falstaff, where have you been all this while?
When everything is ended, then you come:

These tardy tricks of yours will, on my life,
One time or other break some gallows' back.
    Fal. I would be sorry, my lord, but it should be thus:
I never knew yet but rebuke and check was the reward of
valour. Do you think me a swallow, an arrow, or a bullet?
have I, in my poor and old motion, the expedition of
thought? I have speeded hither with the very extremest
inch of possibility; I have foundered nine-score and odd
posts, and here, travel-tainted as I am, have, in my pure
and immaculate valour, taken Sir John Coleville of the
dale, a most furious knight, and valorous enemy. But
what of that? he saw me, and yielded; that I may justly
say with the hook-nosed fellow of Rome, I came, saw, and
overcame.
    P. John. It was more of his courtesy than your deserv-
ing.
    Fal. I know not:—here he is, and here I yield him, and
I beseech your grace, let it be booked with the rest of this
day's deeds; or, by the Lord, I will have it in a particular
ballad else, with mine own picture on the top of it, Coleville
kissing my foot: to the which course if I be enforced, if
you do not all show like gilt twopences to me, and I, in
the clear sky of fame, o'ershine you as much as the full
moon doth the cinders of the element, which show like
pins' heads to her, believe not the word of the noble:
therefore let me have right, and let desert mount.
    P. John. Thine's too heavy to mount.
    Fal. Let it shine then.
    P. John. Thine's too thick to shine.
    Fal. Let it do something, my good lord, that may do
me good, and call it what you will.
    P. John. Is thy name Coleville?
    Cole.   It is, my lord.
    P. John. A famous rebel art thou, Coleville.
    Fal. And a famous true subject took him.
    Cole. I am, my lord, but as my betters are
That led me hither: had they been ruled by me,
You should have won them dearer than you have.
    Fal. I know not how they sold themselves: but thou,
like a kind fellow, gavest thyself away gratis; and I thank
thee for thee.

          Re-enter WESTMORELAND

    P. John. Now, have you left pursuit?
    West. Retreat is made, and execution stayed.
    P. John. Send Coleville, with his confederates,
To York, to present execution.
Blunt, lead him hence, and see you guard him sure.
               [Exit Coleville, guarded
And now despatch we toward the court, my lords.

I hear, the king my father is sore sick:
Our news shall go before us to his majesty;
Which, cousin, you shall bear,—to comfort him;
And we with sober speed will follow you.

    Fal. My lord, beseech you, give me leave to go
Through Glostershire; and, when you come to court,
Stand my good lord, 'pray, in your good report.

    P. John. Fare you well, Falstaff: I, in my condition,
Shall better speak of you than you deserve.   [*Exit*

    Fal. I would you had but the wit: 't were better
than your dukedom.—Good faith, this same young sober-
blooded boy doth not love me, nor a man cannot make him
laugh;—but that's no marvel, he drinks no wine. There's
never any of these demure boys come to any proof; for
thin drink doth so over-cool their blood, and making many
fish-meals, that they fall into a kind of male green-sickness;
and then, when they marry, they get wenches. They are
generally fools and cowards, which some of us should be
too, but for inflammation. A good sherris-sack hath a
two-fold operation in it. It ascends me into the brain;
dries me there all the foolish, and dull, and crudy vapours
which environ it; makes it apprehensive, quick, forgetive,
full of nimble, fiery, and delectable shapes; which, delivered
o'er to the voice, the tongue, which is the birth, becomes
excellent wit. The second property of your excellent sherris
is, the warming of the blood; which, before cold and
settled, left the liver white and pale, which is the badge of
pusillanimity and cowardice; but the sherris warms it,
and makes it course from the inwards to the parts extreme:
it illumineth the face, which, as a beacon, gives warning
to all the rest of this little kingdom, man, to arm; and
then the vital commoners and inland petty spirits muster
me all to their captain, the heart, who, great, and puffed
up with this retinue, doth any deed of courage; and this
valour comes of sherris. So that skill in the weapon is
nothing without sack, for that sets it a-work; and learning,
a mere hoard of gold kept by a devil, till sack commences
it and sets it in act and use. Hereof comes it that Prince
Harry is valiant; for the cold blood he did naturally
inherit of his father, he hath, like lean, steril, and bare
land, manured, husbanded, and tilled, with excellent endeavour of drinking good and good store of fertile sherris,
that he is become very hot and valiant. If I had a thousand
sons, the first human principle I would teach them should
be—to forswear thin potations, and to addict themselves
to sack.

Enter BARDOLPH

How now, Bardolph?
    Bard. The army is dischargéd all, and gone.

Fal. Let them go. I'll through Glostershire; and there will I visit Master Robert Shallow, esquire: I have him already tempering between my finger and my thumb, and shortly will I seal with him. Come away.   [*Exeunt*

SCENE IV.—Westminster.   The Jerusalem Chamber

Enter KING HENRY, CLARENCE, PRINCE HUMPHREY, WARWICK, *and others*

K. Hen.   Now, lords, if God doth give successful end
To this debate that bleeedeth at our doors,
We will our youth lead on to higher fields,
And draw no swords but what are sanctified.
Our navy is addressed, our power collected,
Our substitutes in absence well invested,
And everything lies level to our wish:
Only, we want a little personal strength;
And pause us till these rebels now afoot
Come underneath the yoke of government.
War.   Both which we doubt not but your majesty
Shall soon enjoy.
K. Hen.   Humphrey, my son of Gloster,
Where is the prince your brother?
P. Humph.   I think he's gone to hunt, my lord, at
          Windsor.
K. Hen.   And how accompanied?
P. Humph.   I do not know, my lord.
K. Hen.   Is not his brother Thomas of Clarence with
          him?
P. Humph.   No, my good lord; he is in presence here.
Clar.   What would my lord and father?
K. Hen.   Nothing but well to thee, Thomas of Clarence.
How chance thou art not with the prince thy brother?
He loves thee, and thou dost neglect him, Thomas.
Thou hast a better place in his affection
Than all thy brothers; cherish it, my boy,
And noble offices thou may'st effect
Of mediation, after I am dead,
Between his greatness and thy other brethren:
Therefore, omit him not; blunt not his love,
Nor lose the good advantage of his grace,
By seeming cold, or careless of his will;
For he is gracious if he be observed;
He hath a tear for pity, and a hand
Open as day for melting charity;
Yet notwithstanding, being incensed, he's flint,
As humorous as winter, and as sudden
As flaws congealéd in the spring of day.

His temper, therefore, must be well observed:
Chide him for faults—and do it reverently—
When you perceive his blood inclined to mirth;
But, being moody, give him line and scope
Till that his passions, like a whale on ground,
Confound themselves with working. Learn this, Thomas,
And thou shalt prove a shelter to thy friends,
A hoop of gold to bind thy brothers in,
That the united vessel of their blood
Mingled with venom of suggestion—
As, force perforce, the age will pour it in—
Shall never leak, though it do work as strong
As aconitum or rash gunpowder.
    Clar. I shall observe him with all care and love.
    K. Hen. Why art thou not at Windsor with him,
        Thomas?
    Clar. He is not there to-day: he dines in London.
    K. Hen. And how accompanied? canst thou tell that?
    Clar. With Poins, and other his continual followers.
    K. Hen. Most subject is the fattest soil to weeds;
And he, the noble image of my youth,
Is overspread with them; therefore, my grief
Stretches itself beyond the hour of death.
The blood weeps from my heart when I do shape
In forms imaginary the unguided days
And rotten times that you shall look upon
When I am sleeping with my ancestors.
For when his headstrong riot hath no curb,
When rage and hot blood are his counsellors,
When means and lavish manners meet together,
O, with what wings shall his affections fly
Towards fronting peril and opposed decay!
    War. My gracious lord, you look beyond him quite.
The prince but studies his companions
Like a strange tongue: wherein, to gain the language,
'T is needful that the most immodest word
Be looked upon and learned; which once attained,
Your highness knows, comes to no further use
But to be known and hated. So, like gross terms,
The prince will in the perfectness of time
Cast off his followers; and their memory
Shall as a pattern or a measure live
By which his grace must mete the lives of others,
Turning past evils to advantages.
    K. Hen. 'T is seldom when the bee doth leave her comb
In the dead carrion.

        Enter WESTMORELAND

                Who's here? Westmoreland?
    West. Health to my sovereign, and new happiness

Added to that that I am to deliver!
Prince John, your son, doth kiss your grace's hand:
Mowbray, the Bishop Scroop, Hastings, and all,
Are brought to the correction of your law.
There is not now a rebel's sword unsheathed,
But Peace puts forth her olive everywhere.
The manner how this action hath been borne,
Here at more leisure may your highness read,
With every course in his particular.   [*Giving packet*
    K. Hen. O Westmoreland, thou art a summer bird,
Which ever in the haunch of winter sings
The lifting up of day.

Enter HARCOURT

                    Look! here's more news.
    Har. From enemies Heaven keep your majesty;
And when they stand against you may they fall
As those that I am come to tell you of.
The Earl of Northumberland and the Lord Bardolph
With a great power of English and of Scots,
Are by the sheriff of Yorkshire overthrown.
The manner and true order of the fight,
This packet, please it you, contains at large.
                              [*Giving packet*
    K. Hen. And wherefore should these good news make
          me sick?
Will Fortune never come with both hands full,
But write her fair words still in foulest letters?
She either gives a stomach and no food,—
Such are the poor, in health; or else a feast,
And takes away the stomach,—such are the rich
That have abundance, and enjoy it not.
I should rejoice now at this happy news;
And now my sight fails, and my brain is giddy:—
O me! come near me; now I am much ill.   [*Swoons*
    P. Humph. Comfort, your majesty!
    Clar.   O my royal father!
    West. My sovereign lord, cheer up yourself, look up!
    War. Be patient, princes; you do know, these fits
Are with his highness very ordinary.
Stand from him, give him air; he'll straight be well.
    Clar. No, no, he cannot long hold out these pangs
The incessant care and labour of his mind
Hath wrought the mure that should confine it in
So thin, that life looks through and will break out.
    P. Humph. The people fear me; for they do observe
Unfathered heirs and loathly births of nature:
The seasons change their manners, as the year
Had found some months asleep, and leaped them over.

Clar. The river hath thrice flowed, no ebb between;
And the old folk, time's doting chronicles,
Say, it did so a little time before
That our great-grandsire Edward sicked and died.
  War. Speak lower, princes, for the king recovers.
  P. Humph. This apoplexy will certain be his end.
  K. Hen. I pray you, take me up, and bear me hence
Into some other chamber: softly, pray.
                [*They place the King on a bed in an inner part of
                                        the room*
Let there be no noise made, my gentle friends;
Unless some dull and favourable hand
Will whisper music to my wearied spirit.
  War. Call for the music in the other room.
  K. Hen. Set me the crown upon my pillow here.
  Clar. His eye is hollow, and he changes much.
  War. Less noise, less noise!

                Enter PRINCE HENRY

  P. Hen. Who saw the Duke of Clarence?
  Clar. I am here, brother, full of heaviness.
  P. Hen. How now! rain within doors, and none abroad!
How doth the king?
  P. Humph.   Exceeding ill.
  P. Hen. Heard he the good news yet?
Tell it him.
  P. Humph. He altered much upon the hearing it.
  P. Hen. If he be sick with joy,
He will recover without physic.
  War. Not so much noise, my lords.—Sweet prince,
        speak low;
The king your father is disposed to sleep.
  Clar. Let us withdraw into the other room.
  War. Will 't please your grace to go along with us?
  P. Hen. No; I will sit and watch here by the king.
                        [*Exeunt all but Prince Henry*
Why doth the crown lie there upon his pillow,
Being so troublesome a bedfellow?
O polished perturbation! golden care!
That keep'st the ports of slumber open wide
To many a watchful night!—sleep with it now,
Yet not so sound and half so deeply sweet
As he whose brow with homely biggin bound
Snores out the watch of night. O majesty,
When thou dost pinch thy bearer, thou dost sit
Like a rich armour worn in heat of day,
That scalds with safety! By his gates of breath
There lies a downy feather, which stirs not:
Did he suspire, that light and weightless down

Perforce must move.—My gracious lord! my father!—
This sleep is sound indeed: this is a sleep
That from this golden rigol hath divorced
So many English kings. Thy due from me
Is tears and heavy sorrows of the blood,
Which nature, love, and filial tenderness,
Shall, O dear father, pay thee plenteously:
My due from thee is this imperial crown,
Which, as immediate from thy place and blood
Derives itself to me. Lo, here it sits,—

                  [*Putting it on his head*

Which Heaven shall guard; and put the world's whole
      strength
Into one giant arm, it shall not force
This lineal honour from me. This from thee
Will I to mine leave as't is left to me.   [*Exit*
   K. Hen. Warwick! Gloster! Clarence!

Re-enter WARWICK *and the rest*

   Clar.   Doth the king call?
   War. What would your majesty? how fares your
      grace?
   K. Hen. Why did you leave me here alone, my lords?
   Clar. We left the prince, my brother here, my liege,
Who undertook to sit and watch by you.
   K. Hen. The Prince of Wales? where is he? let me
      see him:
He is not here.
   War. This door is open; he is gone this way.
   P. Humph. He came not through the chamber where
      we stayed.
   K. Hen. Where is the crown? who took it from my
      pillow?—
   War. When we withdrew, my liege, we left it here.
   K. Hen. The prince hath ta'en it hence:—go, seek him
      out.
Is he so hasty, that he doth suppose
My sleep my death?—
Find him, my Lord of Warwick; chide him hither.

                      [*Exit Warwick*

This part of his conjoins with my disease,
And helps to end me.—See, sons, what things you are!
How quickly Nature falls into revolt
When gold becomes her object!
For this the foolish over-careful fathers
Have broke their sleeps with thought,—their brains with
      care,
Their bones with industry; for this they have
Engrosséd and piled up the cankered heaps

Of strange-achievéd gold; for this they have
Been thoughtful to invest their sons with arts,
And martial exercise: when, like the bee,
Culling from every flower the virtuous sweets,
Our thighs packed with wax, our mouths with honey,
We bring it to the hive, and, like the bees,
Are murdered for our pains.   This bitter taste
Yield his engrossments to the ending father.

Re-enter WARWICK

Now, where is he that will not stay so long
Till his friend sickness hath determined me?
     War.   My Lord, I found the prince in the next room,
Washing with kindly tears his gentle cheeks;
With such a deep demeanour in great sorrow,
That tyranny which never quaffed but blood
Would, by beholding him, have washed his knife
With gentle eye-drops.   He is coming hither.
     K. Hen.   But wherefore did he take away the crown?

Re-enter PRINCE HENRY

Lo, where he comes.—Come hither to me, Harry.—
Depart the chamber, leave us here alone.
          [*Exeunt Clarence, Prince Humphrey, Lords, etc.*
     P. Hen.   I never thought to hear you speak again.
     K. Hen.   Thy wish was father, Harry, to that thought:
I stay too long by thee, I weary thee.
Dost thou so hunger for mine empty chair
That thou wilt needs invest thee with mine honours
Before thy hour be ripe?   O foolish youth,
Thou seek'st the greatness that will overwhelm thee.
Stay but a little; for my cloud of dignity
Is held from falling with so weak a wind
That it will quickly drop: my day is dim.
Thou hast stolen that, which, after some few hours,
Were thine without offence; and at my death
Thou hast sealed up my expectation:
Thy life did manifest thou lov'dst me not,
And thou wilt have me die assured of it.
Thou hid'st a thousand daggers in thy thoughts,
Which thou hast whetted on thy stony heart
To stab at half an hour of my life.
What, canst thou not forbear me half an hour?
Then get thee gone, and dig my grave thyself,
And bid the merry bells ring to thine ear
That thou art crownéd, not that I am dead,
Let all the tears that should bedew my hearse
Be drops of balm to sanctify thy head:
Only compound me with forgotten dust;

141

Give that which gave thee life unto the worms.
Pluck down my officers, break my decrees;
For now a time is come to mock at form:
Harry the Fifth is crowned!—Up, vanity!
Down, royal state! all you sage counsellors, hence!
And to the English court assemble now
From every region apes of idleness!
Now, neighbour confines, purge you of your scum.
Have you a ruffian that will swear, drink, dance,
Revel the night, rob, murder, and commit
The oldest sins the newest kind of ways,
Be happy, he will trouble you no more:
England shall double gild his treble guilt,
England shall give him office, honour, might;
For the fifth Harry from curbed license plucks
The muzzle of restraint, and the wild dog
Shall flesh his tooth in every innocent.
O my poor kingdom, sick with civil blows,
When that my care could not withhold thy riots,
What wilt thou do when riot is thy care?
O, thou wilt be a wilderness again,
Peopled with wolves, thy old inhabitants!
    P. Hen.   [*Kneeling*]   O, pardon me, my liege! but for
        my tears,
The moist impediments unto my speech,
I had forestalled this dear and deep rebuke
Ere you with grief had spoke and I had heard
The course of it so far. There is your crown:
And He that wears the crown immortally
Long guard it yours! If I affect it more
Than as your honour and as your renown,
Let me no more from this obedience rise,
Which my most true and inward duteous spirit
Teacheth, this prostrate and exterior bending.
God witness with me, when I here came in
And found no course of breath within your majesty,
How cold it struck my heart! if I do feign,
O, let me in my present wildness die,
And never live to show the incredulous world
The noble change that I have purposéd!
Coming to look on you, thinking you dead,
And dead almost, my liege, to think you were,
I spake unto the crown as having sense,
And thus upbraided it: 'The care on thee depending
Hath fed upon the body of my father;
Therefore thou, best of gold, art worst of gold,
Other less fine in carat is more precious,
Preserving life in medicine potable:
But thou, most fine, most honoured, most renowned,
Hast eat thy bearer up.' Thus, my most royal liege,

Accusing it, I put it on my head,
To try with it, as with an enemy
That had before my face murdered my father,
The quarrel of a true inheritor.
But if it did infect my blood with joy,
Or swell my thoughts to any strain of pride;
If any rebel or vain spirit of mine
Did with the least affection of a welcome
Give entertainment to the might of it,
Let God for ever keep it from my head,
And make me as the poorest vassal is
That doth with awe and terror kneel to it!
    K. Hen.   O my son,
God put it in thy mind to take it hence,
That thou might'st win the more thy father's love,
Pleading so wisely in excuse of it.
Come hither, Harry: sit thou by my bed,
And hear, I think, the very latest counsel
That ever I shall breathe.   God knows, my son,
By what by-paths and indirect crook'd ways
I met this crown; and I myself know well
How troublesome it sat upon my head:
To thee it shall descend with better quiet,
Better opinion, better confirmation;
For all the soil of the achievement goes
With me into the earth.   It seemed in me
But as an honour snatched with boisterous hand,
And I had many living to upbraid
My gain of it by their assistances;
Which daily grew to quarrel and to bloodshed,
Wounding supposéd peace.   All these bold fears
Thou seest with peril I have answeréd;
For all my reign hath been but as a scene
Acting that argument: and now my death
Changes the mode; for what in me was purchased,
Falls upon thee in a more fairer sort;
So thou the garland wear'st successively.
Yet, though thou stand'st more sure than I could do,
Thou art not firm enough; since griefs are green,
And all my foes, which thou must make thy friends,
Have but their strings and teeth newly ta'en out;
By whose fell working I was first advanced,
And by whose power I might well lodge a fear
To be again displaced: which to avoid,
I cut some off, and had a purpose now
To lead out many to the Holy Land,
Lest rest and lying still might make them look
Too near unto my state.   Therefore, my Harry,
Be it thy course to busy giddy minds
With foreign quarrels, that action hence borne out

May waste the memory of the former days.
More would I, but my lungs are wasted so,
That strength of speech is utterly denied me.
How I came by the crown, O God forgive;
And grant it may with thee in true peace live!
   P. Hen. My gracious liege,
You won it, wore it, kept it, gave it me;
Then plain and right must my possession be:
Which I with more than with a common pain
'Gainst all the world will rightfully maintain.

Enter PRINCE JOHN OF LANCASTER, WARWICK, Lords, *and*
others

   K. Hen. Look, look, here comes my John of Lancaster.
   P. John. Health, peace, and happiness to my royal
      father!
   K. Hen. Thou bring'st me happiness and peace, son
      John;
But health, alack, with youthful wings is flown
From this bare withered trunk: upon thy sight,
My worldly business makes a period.—
Where is my Lord of Warwick?
   P. Hen.   My Lord of Warwick!
   K. Hen. Doth any name particular belong
Unto the lodging where I first did swoon?
   War. 'T is called Jerusalem, my noble lord.
   K. Hen. Laud be to God!—even there my life must
      end.
It hath been prophesied to me many years,
I should not die but in Jerusalem,
Which vainly I supposed the Holy Land.—
But, bear me to that chamber; there I'll lie;
In that Jerusalem shall Harry die.   [*Exeunt*

ACT FIVE

SCENE I.—Glostershire. A Hall in SHALLOW's House

Enter SHALLOW, FALSTAFF, BARDOLPH, *and Page*

   Shal. By cock and pie, sir, you shall not away to-night.
—What, Davy, I say!
   Fal. You must excuse me, Master Robert Shallow.
   Shal. I will not excuse you; you shall not be excused;
excuses shall not be admitted; there is no excuse shall
serve; you shall not be excused.—Why, Davy!

Enter DAVY

Davy. Here, sir.

Shal. Davy, Davy, Davy,—let me see, Davy; let me see:—yea, marry, William cook, bid him come hither—Sir John, you shall not be excused.

Davy. Marry, sir thus; those precepts cannot be served: and, again, sir,—shall we sow the headland with wheat?

Shal. With red wheat, Davy. But for William cook:—are there no young pigeons?

Davy. Yes, sir.—Here is now the smith's note for shoeing and plough-irons.

Shal. Let it be cast, and paid.—Sir John, you shall not be excused.

Davy. Now, sir, a new link to the bucket must needs be had:—and, sir, do you mean to stop any of William's wages, about the sack he lost the other day at Hinckley fair?

Shal. 'A shall answer it.—Some pigeons, Davy; a couple of short-legged hens, a joint of mutton, and any pretty little tiny kickshaws, tell William cook.

Davy. Doth the man of war stay all night, sir?

Shal. Yea, Davy. I will use him well. A friend i' the court is better than a penny in purse. Use his men well, Davy, for they are arrant knaves, and will backbite.

Davy. No worse than they are backbitten, sir; for they have marvellous foul linen.

Shal. Well conceited, Davy. About thy business, Davy.

Davy. I beseech you, sir, to countenance William Visor of Wincot against Clement Perkes of the hill.

Shal. There are many complaints, Davy, against that Visor: that Visor is an arrant knave, on my knowledge.

Davy. I grant your worship that he is a knave, sir; but yet, God forbid, sir, but a knave should have some countenance at his friend's request. An honest man, sir; is able to speak for himself, when a knave is not. I have served your worship, truly, sir, these eight years; and if I cannot once or twice in a quarter bear out a knave against an honest man, I have but a very little credit with your worship. The knave is mine honest friend, sir; therefore, I beseech your worship, let him be countenanced.

Shal. Go to; I say, he shall have no wrong. Look about, Davy. [*Exit Davy*] Where are you, Sir John! Come, come, come; off with your boots.—Give me your hand, Master Bardolph.

Bard. I am glad to see your worship.

Shal. I thank thee with all my heart, kind Master Bardolph:—[*to the Page*] and welcome, my tall fellow. —Come, Sir John.

Fal. I'll follow you, good Master Robert Shallow. [*Exit Shallow*] Bardolph, look to our horses. [*Exeunt Bardolph and Page*] If I were sawed into quantities, I should make four dozen of such bearded hermits' staves as Master Shallow. It is a wonderful thing, to see the semblable coherence of his men's spirits and his: they, by observing of him, do bear themselves like foolish justices; he, by conversing with them, is turned into a justice-like serving-man. Their spirits are so married in conjunction with the participation of society, that they flock together in consent, like so many wild-geese. If I had a suit to Master Shallow, I would humour his men with the imputation of being near their master: if to his men, I would curry with Master Shallow, that no man could better command his servants. It is certain that either wise bearing or ignorant carriage is caught, as men take diseases, one of another: therefore, let men take heed of their company. I will devise matter enough out of this Shallow, to keep Prince Harry in continual laughter the wearing-out of six fashions, which is four terms, or two actions, and 'a shall laugh without *intervallums*. O, it is much, that a lie with a slight oath, and a jest with a sad brow, will do with a fellow that never had the ache in his shoulders! O, you shall see him laugh, till his face be like a wet cloak ill laid up.

Shal. [*Within*] Sir John!

Fal. I come, Master Shallow; I come, Master Shallow.
                                                          [*Exit*

Scene II.—Westminster. A Room in the Palace

Enter, severally, Warwick *and the Lord Chief-Justice*

War. How now, my lord chief-justice? whither away?

Ch. Just. How doth the king?

War. Exceeding well: his cares are now all ended.

Ch. Just. I hope, not dead.

War.   He's walked the way of nature,
And, to our purposes, he lives no more.

Ch. Just. I would his majesty had called me with him:
The service that I truly did his life,
Hath left me open to all injuries.

War. Indeed, I think the young king loves you not.

Ch. Just. I know he doth not, and do arm myself
To welcome the condition of the time;
Which cannot look more hideously upon me
Than I have drawn it in my fantasy.

War. Here come the heavy issue of dead Harry:
O, that the living Harry had the temper
Of him the worst of these three gentlemen!

146

How many nobles then should hold their places
That must strike sail to spirits of vile sort!
    Ch. Just. O God, I fear, all will be overturned!

Enter PRINCE JOHN, PRINCE HUMPHREY, CLARENCE,
    WESTMORELAND, *and others*

    P. John. Good morrow, cousin Warwick, good morrow.
    P. Humph., Clar. Good morrow, cousin.
    P. John. We meet like men that had forgot to speak.
    War. We do remember; but our argument
Is all too heavy to admit much talk.
    P. John. Well, peace be with him that hath made us
        heavy!
    Ch. Just. Peace be with us, lest we be heavier!
    P. Humph. O, good my lord, you have lost a friend,
        indeed;
And I dare swear, you borrow not that face
Of seeming sorrow,—it is, sure, your own.
    P. John. Though no man be assured what grace to find,
You stand in coldest expectation:
I am the sorrier; 'would 't were otherwise.
    Clar. Well, you must now speak Sir John Falstaff fair;
Which swims against your stream of quality.
    Ch. Just. Sweet princes, what I did, I did in honour,
Led by the impartial conduct of my soul;
And never shall you see that I will beg
A ragged and forestalled remission.
If truth and upright innocency fail me,
I'll to the king my master that is dead
And tell him who hath sent me after him.
    War. Here comes the prince.

Enter KING HENRY THE FIFTH, *attended*

    Ch. Just. Good morrow, and God save your majesty!
    King. This new and gorgeous garment, majesty,
Sits not so easy on me as you think.—
Brothers, you mix your sadness with some fear:
This is the English, not the Turkish court;
Not Amurath an Amurath succeeds,
But Harry Harry. Yet be sad, good brothers,
For, to speak truth, it very well becomes you:
Sorrow so royally in you appears,
That I will deeply put the fashion on
And wear it in my heart. Why then, be sad;
But entertain no more of it, good brothers,
Than a joint burden laid upon us all.
For me, by Heaven, I bid you be assured
I'll be your father and your brother too;

Let me but bear your love, I'll bear your cares:
Yet weep that Harry's dead, and so will I;
But Harry lives, that shall convert those tears,
By number, into hours of happiness.
    P. John, etc.   We hope no other from your majesty.
    King.   You all look strangely on me:—[*to the Chief-
    Justice*] and you most;
You are, I think, assured I love you not.
    Ch. Just.   I am assured, if I be measured rightly,
Your majesty hath no just cause to hate me.
    King.   No!
How might a prince of my great hopes forget
So great indignities you laid upon me?
What! rate, rebuke, and roughly send to prison
The immediate heir of England! Was this easy?
May this be washed in Lethe, and forgotten?
    Ch. Just.   I then did use the person of your father;
The image of his power lay then in me:
And, in the administration of his law,
Whiles I was busy for the commonwealth
Your highness pleaséd to forget my place,
The majesty and power of law and justice,
The image of the king whom I presented,
And struck me in my very seat of judgment;
Whereon, as an offender to your father,
I gave bold way to my authority
And did commit you. If the deed were ill,
Be you contented, wearing now the garland,
To have a son set your decrees at naught,
To pluck down justice from your awful bench,
To trip the course of law, and blunt the sword
That guards the peace and safety of your person,
Nay, more; to spurn at your most royal image,
And mock your workings in a second body.
Question your royal thoughts, make the case yours,
Be now the father, and propose a son;
Hear your own dignity so much profaned,
See your most dreadful laws so loosely slighted,
Behold yourself so by a son disdained,
And then imagine me taking your part,
And, in your power, so silencing your son:
After this cold considerance, sentence me;
And, as you are a king, speak in your state
What I have done that misbecame my place,
My person, or my liege's sovereignty.
    King.   You are right, justice, and you weigh this well;
Therefore still bear the balance and the sword:
And I do wish your honours may increase
Till you do live to see a son of mine
Offend you, and obey you, as I did.

So shall I live to speak my father's words:—
'Happy am I, that have a man so bold
That dares do justice on my proper son;
And not less happy, having such a son;
That would deliver up his greatness so
Into the hands of justice.'—You did commit me
For which, I do commit into your hand
The unstained sword that you have use to bear;
With this remembrance,—that you use the same
With the like bold, just, and impartial spirit
As you have done 'gainst me. There is my hand.
You shall be as a father to my youth:
My voice shall sound as you do prompt mine ear
And I will stoop and humble my intents
To your well-practised, wise directions.—
And, princes all, believe me, I beseech you;
My father is gone wild into his grave;
For in his tomb lie my affections;
And with his spirit sadly I survive
To mock the expectation of the world,
To frustrate prophecies, and to raze out
Rotten opinion, who hath writ me down
After my seeming. The tide of blood in me
Hath proudly flowed in vanity till now:
Now doth it turn, and ebb back to the sea,
Where it shall mingle with the state of floods
And flow henceforth in formal majesty.
Now call we our high court of parliament:
And let us choose such limbs of noble counsel
That the great body of our state may go
In equal rank with the best governed nation;
That war, or peace, or both at once, may be
As things acquainted and familiar to us;
[*To the Lord Chief-Justice*] In which you, father, shall have
           foremost hand.—
Our coronation done, we will accite,
As I before remembered, all our state:
And, God consigning to my good intents,
No prince nor peer shall have just cause to say,
God shorten Harry's happy life one day.   [*Exeunt*

SCENE III.—Glostershire. The Garden of SHALLOW'S
House

Enter FALSTAFF, SHALLOW, SILENCE, BARDOLPH, *the
Page,* and DAVY

Shal. Nay, you shall see mine orchard, where, in an
arbour, we will eat a last year's pippin of my own graffing,

with a dish of caraways, and so forth:—come, cousin
Silence;—and then to bed.
Fal. 'Fore God, you have here a goodly dwelling, and a
rich.
Sha. Barren, barren, barren; beggars all, beggars all,
Sir John: marry, good air.—Spread, Davy; spread, Davy;
well said, Davy.
Fal. This Davy serves you for good uses; he is your
serving-man, and your husband.
Shal. A good varlet, a good varlet, a very good varlet
Sir John:—by the mass, I have drunk too much sack at
supper:—a good varlet. Now sit down, now sit down:—
come, cousin.
Sil. Ah, sirrah! quoth-a,—we shall

[*Singing*] *Do nothing but eat, and make good cheer,*
And praise heaven for the merry year;
When flesh is cheap and females dear,
And lusty lads roam here and there,
So merrily
And ever among so merrily.

Fal. There's a merry heart!—Good Master Silence, I'll
give you a health for that anon.
Shal. Give Master Bardolph some wine, Davy.
Davy. Sweet sir, sit; I'll be with you anon;—most
sweet sir, sit.—Master page, good master page, sit: [*Bardolph and Page sit at another table*] Profane! What you
want in meat, we'll have in drink. But you must bear:—
the heart's all.   [*Exit*
Shal. Be merry, Master Bardolph;—and my little
soldier there, be merry.

Sil. [*Singing*] *Be merry, be merry, my wife has all;*
For women are shrews, both short and tall:
'T is merry in hall when beards wag all,
And welcome merry shrove-tide.
Be merry, be merry, etc.

Fal. I did not think Master Silence had been a man of
this metal.
Sil. Who, I? I have been merry twice and once,
ere now.

Re-enter DAVY

Davy. There's a dish of leather-coats for you.
                          [*Setting them before Bardolph*
Shal. Davy,—
Davy. Your worship?—I'll be with you straight.—A
cup of wine, sir?

Sil.   [*Singing*]   *A cup of wine that's brisk and fine,*
     And drink unto the leman mine ;
     And a merry heart lives long-a.

Fal.   Well said, Master Silence.
Sil.   An we shall be merry, now comes in the sweet of the night.
Fal.   Health and long life to you, Master Silence.

Sil.   [*Singing*]   *Fill the cup and let it come ;*
     I'll pledge you a mile to the bottom.

Shal.   Honest Bardolph, welcome, if thou wantest anything, and wilt not call, beshrew thy heart.—Welcome, my little tiny thief, and welcome, indeed, too.—I'll drink to Master Bardolph, and to all the cavaleroes about London.
Davy.   I hope to see London once ere I die.
Bard.   If I might see you there, Davy,—
Shal.   By the mass, you'll crack a quart together,—ah! will you not, Master Bardolph?
Bard.   Yea, sir, in a pottle-pot.
Shal.   By God's liggens, I thank thee:—the knave will stick by thee, I can assure thee that: 'a will not out; he is true bred.
Bard.   And I'll stick by him, sir.
Shal.   Why, there spoke a king. Lack nothing: be merry. [*Knocking heard*] Look, who's at door there, ho! Who knocks?
Fal.   [*To Silence, who drinks a bumper*]
Why, now you have done me right.

Sil.   [*Singing*]   *Do me right,*
     And dub me knight,
     Samingo.

Is't not so?
Fal.   'T is so.
Sil.   Is 't so? Why, then say, an old man can do somewhat.

Re-enter DAVY

Davy.   If it please your worship, there's one Pistol come from the court with news.
Fal.   From the court! let him come in.—

Enter PISTOL

How now, Pistol?
Pist.   Sir John, God save you!
Fal.   What wind blew you hither, Pistol?
Pist.   Not the ill wind which blows no man to good —
Sweet knight, thou art now one of the greatest men in the realm.

Sil. By'r lady, I think he be, but goodman Puff of Barson.

Pist. Puff!

Puff in thy teeth, most recreant coward base!—
Sir John, I am thy Pistol, and thy friend,
And helter-skelter have I rode to thee;
And tidings do I bring, and lucky joys,
And golden times, and happy news of price.

Fal. I pr'ythee now, deliver them like a man of this world.

Pist. A foutra for the world, and worldlings base!
I speak of Africa, and golden joys.

Fal. O base Assyrian knight, what is thy news?
Let King Cophetua know the truth thereof.

Sil. [*Sings*] *And Robin Hood, Scarlet, and John.*

Pist. Shall Dunghill curs confront the Helicons?
And shall good news be baffled?
Then, Pistol, lay thy head in Furies' lap.

Shal. Honest gentleman, I know not your breeding.

Pist. Why, then, lament therefore.

Shal. Give me pardon, sir:—if, sir, you come with news from the court, I take it, there's but two ways, either to utter them, or to conceal them. I am, sir, under the king, in some authority.

Pist. Under which king, bezonian? speak, or die.

Shal. Under King Harry.

Pist.   Harry the Fourth? or Fifth?

Shal. Harry the Fourth.

Pist.   A foutra for thine office!—
Sir John, thy tender lambkin now is king;
Harry the Fifth's the man. I speak the truth:
When Pistol lies, do this; and fig me, like
The bragging Spaniard.

Fal. What! is the old king dead?

Pist. As nail in door: the things I speak are just.

Fal. Away, Bardolph! saddle my horse.—Master Robert Shallow, choose what office thou wilt in the land, 't is thine.—Pistol, I will double-charge thee with dignities.

Bard. O joyful day!—I would not take a knighthood for my fortune.

Pist. What! I do bring good news?

Fal. Carry Master Silence to bed.—Master Shallow, my Lord Shallow, be what thou wilt, I am Fortune's steward. Get on thy boots: we'll ride all night.—O sweet Pistol!—Away, Bardolph. [*Exit Bardolph*]—Come, Pistol, utter more to me; and, withal, devise something to do thyself good. Boot, boot, Master Shallow: I know the young king is sick for me. Let us take any man's horses; the laws of England are at my commandment. Happy are they which have been my friends; and woe to my lord chief-justice!

Pist. Let vultures vile seize on his lungs also!
'Where is the life that late I led?' say they;
Why, here it is;—welcome this pleasant day!   [*Exeunt*.

SCENE IV.—London. A Street

Enter Beadles, dragging in HOSTESS QUICKLY *and*
DOLL TEAR-SHEET

Host. No, thou arrant knave; I would to God I might
die, that I might have thee hanged: thou hast drawn my
shoulder out of joint.
First. Bead. The constables have delivered her over to
me, and she shall have whipping-cheer enough, I warrant
her. There hath been a man or two lately killed about her.
Doll. Nuthook, nuthook, you lie! Come on; I'll tell
thee what, thou damned tripe-visaged rascal. An the
child I now go with do miscarry, thou hadst better thou
hadst struck thy mother, thou paper-faced villain.
Host. O the Lord, that Sir John were come! he would
make this a bloody day to somebody. But I pray God
the fruit of her womb miscarry!   .
First Bead. If it do, you shall have a dozen of cushions
again; you have but eleven now. Come, I charge you
both go with me; for the man is dead that you and Pistol
beat among you.
Doll. I'll tell thee what, thou thin man in a censer, I
will have you as soundly swinged for this,—you blue-bottle
rogue! you filthy famished correctioner! if you be not
swinged, I'll forswear half-kirtles.
First Bead. Come, come, you she knight-errant, come.
Host. O God, that right should thus overcome might!
Well, of sufferance comes ease.
Doll. Come, you rogue, come; bring me to a justice.
Host. Ay; come, you starved blood-hound.
Doll. Goodman death! goodman bones!
Host. Thou atomy, thou!
Doll. Come, you thin thing; come, you rascal!
First Bead. Very well.   [*Exeunt*

SCENE V.—A Public Place near Westminster Abbey

Enter three Grooms, strewing rushes

First Groom. More rushes, more rushes!
Sec. Groom. The trumpets have sounded twice.
Third Groom. It will be two o'clock ere they come from
the coronation.

First Groom.   Despatch, despatch.   [*Exeunt Grooms*

Enter FALSTAFF, SHALLOW, PISTOL, BARDOLPH, *and the Page*

Fal.   Stand here by me, Master Robert Shallow; I will make the king do your grace.   I will leer upon him as 'a comes by, and do but mark the countenance that he will give me.
Pist.   God bless thy lungs, good knight.
Fal.   Come here, Pistol; stand behind me.—[*To Shallow*]   O, if I had had time to have made new liveries, I would have bestowed the thousand pound I borrowed of you.   But 't is no matter; this poor show doth better: this doth infer the zeal I had to see him,—
Shal.   It doth so.
Fal.   It shows my earnestness of affection,—
Shal.   It doth so.
Fal.   My devotion,—
Shal.   It doth, it doth, it doth.
Fal.   As it were, to ride day and night; and not to deliberate, not to remember, not to have patience to shift me,—
Shal.   It is most certain.
Fal.   But to stand stained with travel, and sweating with desire to see him; thinking of nothing else, putting all affairs else in oblivion, as if there were nothing else to be done but to see him.
Pist.   'T is *semper idem,* for *absque hoc nihil est :* 't is all in every part.
Shal.   'T is so, indeed.
Pist.   My knight, I will inflame thy noble liver,
And make thee rage.
Thy Doll, and Helen of thy noble thoughts,
Is in base durance, and contagious prison;
Hauled thither
By most mechanical and dirty hand:—
Rouse up revenge from ebon den with fell Alecto's snake,
For Doll is in.   Pistol speaks nought but truth.
Fal.   I will deliver her.
                    [*Shouts within, and the trumpets sound*
Pist.   There roared the sea, and trumpet-clangor sounds.

Enter KING *and his Train, the Chief-Justice among them*

Fal.   God save thy grace, King Hal! my royal Hal!
Pist.   The heavens thee guard and keep, most royal imp of fame!
Fal.   God save thee, my sweet boy!
King.   My lord chief-justice, speak to that vain man.

Ch. Just. Have you your wits? know you what 't is you speak?

Fal. My king! my Jove? I speak to thee, my heart!

King. I know thee not, old man: fall to thy prayers;
How ill white hairs become a fool and jester!
I have long dreamed of such a kind of man,
So surfeit-swelled, so old, and so profane;
But, being awake, I do despise my dream.
Make less thy body hence, and more thy grace;
Leave gormandising; know, the grave doth gape
For thee thrice wider than for other men.—
Reply not to me with a fool-born jest:
Presume not that I am the thing I was;
For God doth know, so shall the world perceive,
That I have turned away my former self;
So will I those that kept me company.
When thou dost hear I am as I have been,
Approach me, and thou shalt be as thou wast,
The tutor and the feeder of my riots:
Till then, I banish thee, on pain of death,
As I have done the rest of my misleaders,
Not to come near our person by ten mile.
For competence of life I will allow you,
That lack of means enforce you not to evil:
And as we hear you do reform yourselves,
We will, according to your strength and qualities,
Give you advancement.—Be 't your charge, my lord,
To see performed the tenor of our word.—
Set on.   *[Exeunt King and his Train*

Fal. Master Shallow, I owe you a thousand pound.

Shal. Ay, marry, Sir John; which I beseech you to let me have home with me.

Fal. That can hardly be, Master Shallow. Do not you grieve at this; I shall be sent for in private to him: look you, he must seem thus to the world: fear not your advancement: I will be the man yet that shall make you great.

Shal. I cannot conceive how, unless you should give me your doublet, and stuff me out with straw. I beseech you, Good Sir John, let me have five hundred of my thousand.

Fal. Sir, I will be as good as my word: this that you heard was but a colour.

Shal. A colour, I fear, that you will die in, Sir John.

Fal. Fear no colours: go with me to dinner:—come, Lieutenant Pistol;—come, Bardolph: I shall be sent for soon at night.

Re-enter PRINCE JOHN, *the Chief-Justice, Officers, etc.*

Ch. Just. Go, carry Sir John Falstaff to the Fleet;

Take all his company along with him.
   Fal. My lord! my lord!—
   Ch. Just. I cannot now speak: I will hear you soon.—
Take them away.
   Pist. *Si fortune me tormenta, sperato me contenta.*
          [*Exeunt Falstaff, Shallow, Pistol, Bardolph, Page,*
                                           and Officers
   P. John. I like this fair proceeding of the king's:
He hath intent his wonted followers
Shall all be very well provided for;
But all are banished till their conversations
Appear more wise and modest to the world.
   Ch. Just. And so they are.
   P. John. The king hath called his parliament, my lord.
   Ch. Just. He hath.
   P. John I will lay odds, that, ere this year expire,
We bear our civil swords and native fire
As far as France. I heard a bird so sing,
Whose music, to my thinking, pleased the king.
Come, will you hence?   [*Exeunt*

EPILOGUE

Spoken by a Dancer

FIRST my fear; then my court'sy; last my speech. My fear
is, your displeasure; my court'sy, my duty; and my
speech, to beg your pardons. If you look for a good speech
now, you undo me: for what I have to say is of mine own
making; and what indeed I should say will, I doubt,
prove mine own marring. But to the purpose, and so to
the venture.—Be it known to you—as it is very well—I
was lately here in the end of a displeasing play, to pray
your patience for it, and to promise you a better. I did
mean, indeed, to pay you with this; which, if, like an ill
venture, it come unluckily home, I break, and you, my
gentle creditors, lose. Here I promised you I would be,
and here I commit my body to your mercies; bate me some,
and I will pay you some, and, as most debtors do, promise
you infinitely.

   If my tongue cannot entreat you to acquit me, will you
command me to use my legs? and yet that were but light
payment,—to dance out of your debt. But a good conscience will make any possible satisfaction, and so will I.
All the gentlewomen here have forgiven me: if the gentlemen will not, then the gentlemen do not agree with the
gentlewomen, which was never seen before in such an
assembly.

One word more, I beseech you. If you be not too much cloyed with fat meat, our humble author will continue the story, with Sir John in it, and make you merry with fair Katharine of France: where, for anything I know, Falstaff shall die of sweat, unless already 'a be killed, with your hard opinions; for Oldcastle died a martyr, and this is not the man. My tongue is weary; when my legs are too, I will bid you good night; and so kneel down before you; but, indeed, to pray for the queen.

THE LIFE OF

KING HENRY THE FIFTH

DRAMATIS PERSONÆ

KING HENRY THE FIFTH
DUKE OF GLOUCESTER } *brothers to the King*
DUKE OF BEDFORD
DUKE OF EXETER, *uncle to the King*
DUKE OF YORK, *cousin to the King*
EARLS OF SALISBURY, WESTMORELAND, *and* WARWICK
ARCHBISHOP OF CANTERBURY
BISHOP OF ELY
EARL OF CAMBRIDGE
LORD SCROOP
SIR THOMAS GREY
SIR THOMAS ERPINGHAM, GOWER, FLUELLEN, MACMORRIS, JAMY, *officers in King Henry's army*
BATES, COURT, WILLIAMS, *soldiers in the same*
PISTOL, NYM, BARDOLPH
Boy
A Herald
CHARLES THE SIXTH, *King of France*
LEWIS, *the Dauphin*
DUKES OF BURGUNDY, ORLEANS, *and* BOURBON
The Constable of France
RAMBURES *and* GRANDPRÉ, *French lords*
MONTJOY, *a French herald*
Governor of Harfleur
Ambassadors to the King of England

ISABEL, *Queen of France*
KATHARINE, *daughter to Charles and Isabel*
ALICE, *a lady attending on her*
Hostess of a tavern in Eastcheap, formerly Mistress Quickly, and now married to Pistol

Lords, Ladies, Officers, Soldiers, Citizens, Messengers, and Attendants, Chorus

SCENE—*In England and in France*

THE LIFE OF

KING HENRY THE FIFTH

PROLOGUE

Enter Chorus

Chor.   O for a Muse of fire, that would ascend
The brightest heaven of invention,—
A kingdom for a stage, princes to act,
And monarchs to behold the swelling scene!
Then should the warlike Harry, like himself,
Assume the port of Mars; and at his heels,
Leashed in like hounds, should famine, sword, and fire,
Crouch for employment.   Pardon, gentles all,
The flat unraiséd spirits that have dared
On this unworthy scaffold to bring forth
So great an object: can this cockpit hold
The vasty fields of France? or may we cram
Within this wooden O the very casques
That did affright the air at Agincourt?
O, pardon, since a crookéd figure may
Attest in little place a million;
And let us, ciphers to this great accompt,
On your imaginary forces work.
Suppose within the girdle of these walls
Are now confined two mighty monarchies,
Whose high uprearéd and abutting fronts
The perilous narrow ocean parts asunder.
Piece out our imperfections with your thoughts;
Into a thousand parts divide one man,
And make imaginary puissance;
Think, when we talk of horses, that you see them
Printing their proud hoofs i' the receiving earth:—
For 't is your thoughts that now must deck our kings;
Carry them here and there; jumping o'er times,
Turning the accomplishment of many years
Into an hour-glass: for the which supply,
Admit me Chorus to this history;
Who prologue-like your humble patience pray,
Gently to hear, kindly to judge, our play.   [*Exit*

ACT ONE

Scene I.—London. An ante-chamber in the KING's
Palace

Enter the ARCHBISHOP OF CANTERBURY *and the*
BISHOP OF ELY

   Cant. My lord, I'll tell you,—that self bill is urged
Which in the eleventh year of the last king's reign
Was like, and had indeed against us passed,
But that the scrambling and unquiet time
Did push it out of farther question.
   Ely. But how, my lord, shall we resist it now?
   Cant. It must be thought on. If it pass against us,
We lose the better half of our possession:
For all the temporal lands which men devout
By testament have given to the church
Would they strip from us; being valued thus,—
As much as would maintain, to the king's honour,
Full fifteen earls and fifteen hundred knights,
Six thousand and two hundred good esquires;
And, to relief of lazars and weak age,
Of indigent faint souls past corporal toil,
A hundred almshouses right well supplied;
And to the coffers of the king, beside,
A thousand pounds by the year: thus runs the bill.
   Ely. This would drink deep.
   Cant.   'T would drink the cup and all
   Ely. But what prevention?
   Cant. The king is full of grace and fair regard.
   Ely. And a true lover of the holy church.
   Cant. The courses of his youth promised it not.
The breath no sooner left his father's body,
But that his wildness, mortified in him,
Seemed to die too; yea, at that very moment,
Consideration, like an angel, came
And whipped the offending Adam out of him,
Leaving his body as a paradise,
To envelope and contain celestial spirits.
Never was such a sudden scholar made;
Never came reformation in a flood,
With such a heady current, scouring faults;
Nor never Hydra-headed wilfulness
So soon did lose his seat, and all at once,
As in this king.
   Ely.   We are blesséd in the change.
   Cant. Hear him but reason in divinity,
And all admiring with an inward wish
You would desire the king were made a prelate:

162

Hear him debate of commonwealth affairs,
You would say it hath been all-in-all his study;
List his discourse of war, and you shall hear
A fearful battle rendered you in music:
Turn him to any cause of policy,
The Gordian knot of it he will unloose,
Familiar as his garter:—that, when he speaks,
The air, a chartered libertine, is still,
And the mute wonder lurketh in men's ears,
To steal his sweet and honeyed sentences:
So that the art and practic part of life
Must be the mistress to this theoric;
Which is a wonder how his grace should glean it,
Since his addiction was to courses vain:
His companies unlettered, rude and shallow,
His hours filled up with riots, banquets, sports;
And never noted in him any study,
Any retirement, any sequestration
From open haunts and popularity.
    Ely. The strawberry grows underneath the nettle,
And wholesome berries thrive and ripen best
Neighboured by fruit of baser quality:
And so the prince obscured his contemplation
Under the veil of wildness; which no doubt,
Grew like the summer grass, fastest by night,
Unseen, yet crescive in his faculty.
    Cant. It must be so; for miracles are ceased;
And therefore we must needs admit the means
How things are perfected.
    Ely   But, my good lord,
How now for mitigation of this bill
Urged by the commons?   Doth his majesty
Incline to it, or no?
    Cant.   He seems indifferent,
Or rather swaying more upon our part
Than cherishing the exhibiters against us;
For I have made an offer to his majesty,—
Upon our spiritual convocation
And in regard of causes now in hand,
Which I have opened to his grace at large,
As touching France,—to give a greater sum
Than ever at one time the clergy yet
Did to his predecessors part withal.
    Ely. How did this offer seem received, my lord?
    Cant. With good acceptance of his majesty;
Save that there was not time enough to hear—
As I perceived his grace would fain have done—
The severals and unhidden passages
Of his true titles to some certain dukedoms,
And, generally, to the crown and seat of France

163

Derived from Edward his great-grandfather.
  Ely.   What was the impediment that broke this off?
  Cant.   The French ambassador upon that instant
Craved audience; and the hour, I think, is come
To give him hearing; is it four o'clock?
  Ely.   It is.
  Cant.   Then go we in, to know his embassy;
Which I could, with a ready guess, declare
Before the Frenchman speak a word of it.
  Ely.   I'll wait upon you; and I long to hear it.
                              [*Exeunt*

SCENE II.—London. The Presence chamber in the
King's Palace

Enter KING HENRY, GLOUCESTER, BEDFORD, EXETER,
WARWICK, WESTMORELAND, *and Attendants*

  K. Hen.   Where is my gracious Lord of Canterbury?
  Exe.   Not here in presence.
  K. Hen.   Send for him, good uncle.
  West.   Shall we call in the ambassador, my liege?
  K. Hen.   Not yet, my cousin: we would be resolved,
Before we hear him, of some things of weight
That task our thoughts, concerning us and France.

Enter the ARCHBISHOP OF CANTERBURY, *and the*
BISHOP OF ELY

  Cant.   God and his angels guard your sacred throne,
And may you long become it!
  K. Hen.   Sure, we thank you.
My learned lord, we pray you to proceed,
And justly and religiously unfold
Why the law Salique, that they have in France,
Or should, or should not, bar us in our claim:
And God forbid, my dear and faithful lord,
That you should fashion, wrest, or bow your reading,
Or nicely charge your understanding soul
With opening titles miscreate, whose right
Suits not in native colours with the truth;
For God doth know how many, now in health,
Shall drop their blood in approbation
Of what your reverence shall incite us to.
Therefore take heed how you impawn our person,
How you awake our sleeping sword of war:
We charge you, in the name of God, take heed.
For never two such kingdoms did contend
Without much fall of blood; whose guiltless drops

Are every one a woe, a sore complaint
'Gainst him whose wrongs give edge unto the swords
That make such waste in brief mortality.
Under this conjuration speak, my lord;
For we will hear, note, and believe in heart
That what you speak is in your conscience washed
As pure as sin with baptism.
    Cant.   Then hear me, gracious sovereign, and you peers,
That owe yourselves, your lives, and services
To this imperial throne.—There is no bar
To make against your highness' claim to France
But this, which they produce from Pharamond,
In terram Salicam mulieres ne succedant,
'No woman shall succeed in Salique land:'
Which Salique land the French unjustly gloze
To be the realm of France, and Pharamond
The founder of this law and female bar.
Yet their own authors faithfully affirm
That the land Salique is in Germany,
Between the floods of Sala and of Elbe;
Where Charles the Great, having subdued the Saxons,
There left behind and settled certain French;
Who, holding in disdain the German women
For some dishonest manners of their life,
Established then this law,—to wit, no female
Should be inheritrix in Salique land:
Which Salique—as I said, 'twixt Elbe and Sala,—
Is at this day in Germany called Meisen.
Then doth it well appear the Salique law
Was not deviséd for the realm of France;
Nor did the French possess the Salique land
Until four hundred one and twenty years
After defunction of King Pharamond,
Idly supposed the founder of this law;
Who died within the year of our redemption
Four hundred twenty-six; and Charles the Great
Subdued the Saxons, and did seat the French
Beyond the river Sala, in the year
Eight hundred five.   Besides, their writers say,
King Pepin, which deposéd Childeric,
Did, as heir general, being descended
Of Blithild, which was daughter to Clothair,
Make claim and title to the crown of France.
Hugh Capet also,—who usurped the crown
Of Charles the duke of Lorraine, sole heir male
Of the true line and stock of Charles the Great,—
To fine his title with some show of truth,
Though, in pure truth, it was corrupt and naught,
Conveyed himself as heir to the Lady Lingare,
Daughter to Charlemain, who was the son

To Louis the emperor, and Louis the son
Of Charles the great.   Also King Louis the Tenth,
Who was sole heir to the usurper Capet,
Could not keep quiet in his conscience,
Wearing the crown of France, till satisfied
That fair Queen Isabel, his grandmother,
Was lineal of the Lady Ermengare,
Daughter to Charles the foresaid duke of Lorraine:
By the which marriage the line of Charles the Great
Was re-united to the crown of France.
So that, as clear as is the summer's sun,
King Pepin's title and Hugh Capet's claim,
King Louis his satisfaction, all appear
To hold in right and title of the female:
So do the kings of France unto this day,
Howbeit they would hold up this Salique law
To bar your highness claiming from the female,
And rather choose to hide them in a net
Than amply to imbar their crookéd titles
Usurped from you and your progenitors.
   K. Hen.   May I with right and conscience make this
       claim?
   Cant.   The sin upon my head, dread sovereign!
For in the book of Numbers is it writ,—
When the man dies, let the inheritance
Descend unto the daughter.   Gracious lord,
Stand for your own; unwind your bloody flag;
Look back into your mighty ancestors:
Go, my dread lord, to your great-grandsire's tomb,
From whom you claim; invoke his warlike spirit,
And your great-uncle's, Edward the Black Prince,
Who on the French ground played a tragedy,
Making defeat on the full power of France,
Whiles his most mighty father on a hill
Stood smiling to behold his lion's whelp
Forage in blood of French nobility.
O noble English, that could entertain
With half their forces the full pride of France
And let another half stand laughing by,
All out of work and cold for action!
   Ely.   Awake remembrance of these valiant dead,
And with your puissant arm renew their feats:
You are their heir; you sit upon their throne;
The blood and courage that renownéd them
Runs in your veins; and my thrice-puissant liege
Is in the very May-morn of his youth,
Ripe for exploits and mighty enterprises.
   Exe.   Your brother kings and monarchs of the earth
Do all expect that you should rouse yourself,
As did the former lions of your blood;

They know your grace hath cause and means and might.
    West. So hath your highness; never king of England
Had nobles richer and more loyal subjects,
Whose hearts have left their bodies here in England
And lie pavilioned in the fields of France.
    Cant. O, let their bodies follow, my dear liege,
With blood and sword and fire to win your right:
In aid whereof we of the spirituality
Will raise your highness such a mighty sum
As never did the clergy at one time
Bring in to any of your ancestors.
    K. Hen. We must not only arm to invade the French,
But lay down our proportions to defend
Against the Scot, who will make road upon us
With all advantages.
    Cant. They of those marches, gracious sovereign,
Shall be a wall sufficient to defend
Our inland from the pilfering borderers.
    K. Hen. We do not mean the coursing snatchers only,
But fear the main intendment of the Scot,
Who hath been still a giddy neighbour to us;
For you shall read that my great-grandfather
Never went with his forces into France,
But that the Scot on his unfurnished kingdom
Came pouring, like the tide into a breach,
With ample and brim fulness of his force,
Galling the gleanéd land with hot assays,
Girding with grievous siege castles and towns;
That England, being empty of defence,
Hath shook and trembled at the ill neighbourhood.
    Cant. She hath been then more feared than harmed,
         my liege;
For hear her but exampled by herself:—
When all her chivalry hath been in France
And she a mourning widow of her nobles,
She hath herself not only well defended,
But taken and impounded as a stray
The King of Scots; whom she did send to France,
To fill King Edward's fame with prisoner kings,
And make her chronicle as rich with praise
As is the ooze and bottom of the sea
With sunken wreck and sumless treasuries.
    West. But there's a saying, very old and true,—

        'If that you will France win,
          Then with Scotland first begin:'

For once the eagle England being in prey,
To her unguarded nest the weazel Scot
Comes sneaking, and so sucks her princely eggs,
Playing the mouse in absence of the cat,

To spoil and havoc more than she can eat.
   Exe. It follows then the cat must stay at home:
Yet that is but a crushed necessity,
Since we have locks to safeguard necessaries,
And pretty traps to catch the petty thieves.
While that the arméd hand doth fight abroad,
The advaséd head defends itself at home;
For government, though high, and low, and lower,
Put into parts, doth keep in one concent,
Congreeing in a full and natural close,
Like music.
   Cant.   True: therefore doth heaven divide
The state of man in divers functions,
Setting endeavour in continual motion;
To which is fixéd, as an aim or butt,
Obedience: for so work the honey-bees,
Creatures that by a rule in nature teach
The act of order to a peopled kingdom.
They have a king and officers of sorts;
Where some, like magistrates, correct at home,
Others, like merchants, venture trade abroad,
Others, like soldiers, arméd in their stings,
Make boot upon the summer's velvet buds,
Which pillage they with merry march bring home
To the tent-royal of their emperor:
Who, busied in his majesty, surveys
The singing masons building roofs of gold,
The civil citizens kneading up the honey,
The poor mechanic porters crowding in
Their heavy burdens at his narrow gate,
The sad-eyed justice, with his surly hum,
Delivering o'er to éxecutors pale
The lazy yawning drone.   I this infer,—
That many things, having full reference
To one concent, may work contrariously:
As many arrows, looséd several ways,
Fly to one mark;
As many several ways meet in one town;
As many fresh streams meet in one salt sea
As many lines close in the dial's centre;
So may a thousand actions, once afoot,
End in one purpose, and be all well borne
Without defeat.   There to France, my liege,
Divide your happy England into four;
Whereof take you one quarter into France,
And you withal shall make all Gallia shake.
If we, with thrice such powers left at home,
Cannot defend our own doors from the dog,
Let us be worried, and our nation lose
The name of hardiness and policy.

K. Hen.   Call in the messengers sent from the Dauphin.
                              [*Exeunt some Attendants*
Now are we well resolved; and, by God's help,
And yours, the noble sinews of our power,
France being ours, we'll bend it to our awe,
Or break it all to pieces: there we'll sit,
Ruling in large and ample empery
O'er France and all her almost kingly dukedoms,
Or lay these bones in an unworthy urn,
Tombless, with no remembrance over them:
Either our history shall with full mouth
Speak freely of our acts, or else our grave,
Like Turkish mute, shall have a tongueless mouth,
Not worshipped with a waxen epitaph.

Enter Ambassadors of France

Now are we well prepared to know the pleasure
Of our fair cousin Dauphin: for we hear
Your greeting is from him, not from the king.
    First Amb.   May't please your majesty to give us leave
Freely to render what we have in charge:
Or shall we sparingly show you far off
The Dauphin's meaning and our embassy?
    K. Hen.   We are no tyrant, but a Christian king;
Unto whose grace our passion is as subject
As are our wretches fettered in our prisons:
Therefore with frank and with uncurbéd plainness
Tell us the Dauphin's mind.
    First Amb.   Thus, then, in few.
Your highness, lately sending into France,
Did claim some certain dukedoms, in the right
Of your great predecessor, King Edward the Third.
In answer of which claim, the prince our master
Says, that you savour too much of your youth,
And bids you be advised there's naught in France
That can be with a nimble galliard won;
You cannot revel into dukedoms there.
He therefore sends you, meeter for your spirit,
This tun of treasure; and, in lieu of this,
Desires you let the dukedoms that you claim
Hear no more of you.   This the Dauphin speaks.
    K. Hen.   What treasure, uncle?
    Exe.   Tennis-balls, my liege.
    K. Hen.   We are glad the Dauphin is so pleasant with us;
His present and your pains we thank you for:
When we have matched our rackets to these balls,
We will, in France, by God's grace, play a set
Shall strike his father's crown into the hazard.
Tell him he hath made a match with such a wrangler

That all the courts of France will be disturbed
With chases. And we understand him well,
How he comes o'er us with our wilder days,
Not measuring what use we made of them.
We never valued this poor seat of England;
And therefore, living hence, did give ourself
To barbarous license; as 'tis ever common
That men are merriest when they are from home.
But tell the Dauphin I will keep my state,
Be like a king, and show my sail of greatness,
When I do rouse me in my throne of France:
For that I have laid by my majesty,
And plodded like a man for working-days;
But I will rise there with so full a glory
That I will dazzle all the eyes of France,
Yea, strike the Dauphin blind to look on us.
And tell the pleasant prince, this mock of his
Hath turned his balls to gun-stones; and his soul
Shall stand sore chargéd for the wasteful vengeance
That shall fly with them: for many a thousand widows
Shall this his mock mock out of their dear husbands;
Mock mothers from their sons, mock castles down;
And some are yet ungotten and unborn
That shall have cause to curse the Dauphin's scorn.
But this lies all within the will of God,
To whom I do appeal; and in whose name,
Tell you the Dauphin, I am coming on,
To venge me as I may, and to put forth
My rightful hand in a well-hallowed cause.
So get you hence in peace; and tell the Dauphin,
His jest will savour but of shallow wit,
When thousands weep, more than did laugh at it.
Convey them with safe conduct. Fare you well.
                                    [*Exeunt Ambassadors*
    Exe. This was a merry message.
    K. Hen. We hope to make the sender blush at it.
Therefore, my lords, omit no happy hour
That may give furtherance to our expedition;
For we have now no thought in us but France,
Save those to God that run before our business.
Therefore let our proportions for these wars
Be soon collected and all things thought upon
That may with reasonable swiftness add
More feathers to our wings; for, God before,
We 'll chide this Dauphin at his father's door.
Therefore let every man now task his thought,
That this fair action may on foot be brought.
                                    [*Exeunt. Flourish*

ACT TWO

Flourish.   Enter Chorus

Chor. Now all the youth of England are on fire,
And silken dalliance in the wardrobe lies:
Now thrive the armourers, and honour's thought
Reigns solely in the breast of every man:
They sell the pasture now to buy the horse;
Following the mirror of all Christian kings,
With wingéd heels, as English Mercuries.
For now sits expectation in the air,
And hides a sword from hilts unto the point
With crowns imperial, crowns and coronets,
Promised to Harry and his followers.
The French, advised by good intelligence
Of this most dreadful preparation,
Shake in their fear; and with pale policy
Seek to divert the English purposes.
O England,—model to thy inward greatness,
Like little body with a mighty heart,—
What mightst thou do that honour would thee do,
Were all thy children kind and natural!
But see thy fault!   France hath in thee found out
A nest of hollow bosoms, which he fills
With treacherous crowns; and three corrupted men,
One, Richard Earl of Cambridge; and the second,
Henry Lord Scroop of Masham; and the third,
Sir Thomas Grey, knight, of Northumberland,—
Have, for the gilt of France,—O guilt indeed!—
Confirmed conspiracy with fearful France;
And by their hands this grace of kings must die,
If hell and treason hold their promises,
Ere he take ship for France, and in Southampton;
Linger your patience on; and we'll digest
The abuse of distance; force a play.
The sum is paid; the traitors are agreed;
The king is set from London; and the scene
Is now transported, gentles, to Southampton;
There is the playhouse now, there must you sit:
And thence to France shall we convey you safe,
And bring you back, charming the narrow seas
To give you gentle pass; for, if we may,
We'll not offend one stomach with our play.
But, till the king come forth, and not till then,
Unto Southampton do we shift our scene.   [*Exit*

SCENE I.—London.   A Street

Enter CORPORAL NYM *and* LIEUTENANT BARDOLPH

Bard.   Well met, Corporal Nym.

Nym.   Good morrow, Lieutenant Bardolph.

Bard.   What, are Ancient Pistol and you friends yet?

Nym.   For my part, I care not: I say little; but when time shall serve, there shall be smites; but that shall be as it may.   I dare not fight; but I will wink and hold out mine iron: it is a simple one; but what though? it will toast cheese, and it will endure cold as another man's sword will: and there's an end.

Bard.   I will bestow a breakfast to make you friends; and we'll be all three sworn brothers in France: let it be so, good Corporal Nym.

Nym.   Faith, I will live so long as I may, that's the certain of it; and when I cannot live any longer, I will do as I may: that is my rest, that is the rendezvous of it.

Bard.   It is certain, corporal, that he is married to Nell Quickly: and certainly she did you wrong; for you were troth plight to her.

Nym.   I cannot tell: things must be as they may: men may sleep, and they may have their throats about them at that time; and some say knives have edges.   It must be as it may: though patience be a tired mare, yet she will plod.   There must be conclusions.   Well, I cannot tell.

Bard.   Here comes Ancient Pistol and his wife: good corporal, be patient here.

Enter PISTOL *and Hostess*

                              How now, mine host Pistol!

Pist.   Base tike, call'st thou me host?

Now, by this hand, I swear, I scorn the term;

Nor shall my Nell keep lodgers.

Host.   No, by my troth, not long; for we cannot lodge and board a dozen or fourteen gentlewomen that live honestly by the prick of their needles, but it will be thought we keep a bawdy house straight.   [*Nym draws his sword*] O well-a-day, Lady, if he be not drawn! [*Pistol also draws his sword*]   Now we shall see wilful adultery and murder committed.

Bard.   Good lieutenant,—good corporal,—offer nothing here.

Nym.   Pish!

Pist.   Pish for thee, Iceland dog! thou prick-ear'd cur of Iceland!

Host. Good Corporal Nym, show thy valour, and put up your sword.

Nym. Will you shog off?   I would have you solus.
                                    [*Sheathing his sword*

Pist. 'Solus,' egregious dog?   O viper vile!
The 'solus' in thy most mervailous face;
The 'solus' in thy teeth, and in thy throat,
And in thy hateful lungs, yea, in thy maw, perdy,
And, which is worse, within thy nasty mouth!
I do retort the 'solus' in thy bowels;
For I can take, and Pistol's cock is up,
And flashing fire will follow.

Nym. I am not Barbason; you cannot conjure me.
I have an humour to knock you indifferently well. If
you grow foul with me, Pistol, I will scour you with my
rapier, as I may, in fair terms: if you would walk off,
I would prick your guts a little, in good terms, as I may:
and that's the humour of it.

Pist. O braggart vile and damnéd furious wight!
The grave doth gape, and doting death is near:
Therefore exhale.   [*Nym draws his sword*

Bard. Hear me, hear me what I say: he that strikes
the first stroke, I'll run him up to the hilts, as I am a
soldier.   [*Draws his sword*

Pist. An oath of mickle might; and fury shall abate.
Give me thy fist, thy fore-foot to me give:
Thy spirits are most tall.   [*They sheathe their swords*

Nym. I will cut thy throat, one time or other, in fair
terms: that is the humour of it.

Pist. *Coupe la gorge!*
That is the word.   I thee defy again.
O hound of Crete, think'st thou my spouse to get?
No; to the spital go,
And from the powdering-tub of infamy
Fetch forth the lazar kite of Cressid's kind,
Doll Tear-sheet she by name, and her espouse:
I have, and I will hold, the *quondam* Quickly
For the only she; and—*pauca*, there's enough.
Go to.

Enter the Boy

Boy. Mine host Pistol, you must come to my master,—
and you, hostess:—he is very sick, and would to bed.—
Good Bardolph, put thy face between his sheets, and do
the office of a warming-pan.—Faith, he's very ill.

Bard. Away, you rogue!

Host. By my troth, he'll yield the crow a pudding one
of these days; the king has killed his heart.—Good husband,
come home presently.   [*Exeunt Hostess and Boy*

Bard. Come, shall I make you two friends?   We must

to France together: why the devil should we keep knives
to cut one another's throats?

Pist. Let floods o'erswell, and fiends for food howl on!

Nym. You 'll pay me the eight shillings I won of you
at betting?

Pist. Base is the slave that pays.

Nym. That now I will have: that's the humour of it.

Pist. As manhood shall compound: push home.

[*Pistol and Nym draw their swords*

Bard. By this sword, he that makes the first thrust,
I'll kill him; by this sword, I will.   [*Draws his sword*

Pist. Sword is an oath, and oaths must have their course.

Bard. Corporal Nym, an thou wilt be friends, be friends:
an thou wilt not, why, then, be enemies with me too.
Prithee, put up.

Nym. I shall have my eight shillings I won of you at
betting?

Pist. A noble shalt thou have, and present pay;
And liquor likewise will I give to thee,
And friendship shall combine, and brotherhood:
I'll live by Nym, and Nym shall live by me;
Is not this just? for I shall sutler be
Unto the camp, and profits will accrue.
Give me thy hand.   [*They sheathe their swords*

Nym. I shall have my noble?

Pist. In cash most justly paid.

Nym. Well, then, that's the humour of 't.

Re-enter Hostess

Host. As ever you came of women, come in quickly
to Sir John. Ah, poor heart! he is so shaked of a burning
quotidian tertian, that it is most lamentable to behold.
Sweet men, come to him.

Nym. The king hath run bad humours on the knight,
that's the even of it.

Pist. Nym, thou hast spoke the right;
His heart is fracted and corroborate.

Nym. The king is a good king: but it must be as it
may; he passes some humours and careers.

Pist. Let us condole the knight; for, lambkins, we will
live.

SCENE II.—Southampton. A council-chamber

Enter EXETER, BEDFORD, *and* WESTMORELAND

Bed. 'Fore God, his grace is bold, to trust these traitors.

Exe. They shall be apprehended by and by.

174

West. How smooth and even they do bear themselves!
As if allegiance in their bosoms sat,
Crownéd with faith and constant loyalty.
    Bed. The king hath note of all that they intend,
By interception which they dream not of.
    Exe. Nay, but the man that was his bedfellow,
Whom he hath dulled and cloyed with gracious favours,
That he should, for a foreign purse, so sell
His sovereign's life to death and treachery!

Trumpets sound.   Enter KING HENRY, CAMBRIDGE, SCROOP,
        GREY, *and Attendants*

    K. Hen. Now sits the wind fair, and we will aboard.
My Lord of Cambridge, my kind Lord of Masham,
And you, my gentle knight, give me your thoughts:
Think you not that the powers we bear with us
Will cut their passage through the force of France,
Doing the execution and the act
For which we have in head assembled them?
    Scroop. No doubt, my liege, if each man do his best.
    K. Hen. I doubt not that; since we are well persuaded
We carry not a heart with us from hence
That grows not in a fair consent with ours,
Nor leave not one behind that doth not wish
Success and conquest to attend on us.
    Cam. Never was monarch better feared and loved
Than is your majesty: there's not, I think, a subject
That sits in heart-grief and uneasiness
Under the sweet shade of your government.
    Grey. True: those that were your father's enemies
Have steeped their galls in honey, and do serve you
With hearts create of duty and of zeal.
    K. Hen. We therefore have great cause of thankfulness;
And shall forget the office of our hand,
Sooner than quittance of desert and merit
According to their weight and worthiness.
    Scroop. So service shall with steeléd sinews toil,
And labour shall refresh itself with hope,
To do your grace incessant services.
    K. Hen. We judge no less.—Uncle of Exeter,
Enlarge the man committed yesterday,
That railed against our person: we consider
It was excess of wine that set him on;
And on his more advice we pardon him.
    Scroop. That's mercy, but too much security:
Let him be punished, sovereign, lest example
Breed, by his sufferance, more of such a kind.
    K. Hen. O, let us yet be merciful.
    Cam. So may your highness, and yet punish too.

Grey. Sir,
You show great mercy, if you give him life
After the taste of much correction.
  K. Hen. Alas, your too much love and care of me
Are heavy orisons 'gainst this poor wretch!
If little faults, proceeding on distemper,
Shall not be winked at, how shall we stretch our eye
When capital crimes, chewed, swallowed, and digested,
Appear before us? We'll yet enlarge that man,
Though Cambridge, Scroop, and Grey, in their dear care
And tender preservation of our person,
Would have him punished.—And now to our French
                           causes:
Who are the late commissioners?
  Cam. I one, my lord:
Your highness bade me ask for it to-day.
  Scroop. So did you me, my liege.
  Grey. And me, my royal sovereign.
  K. Hen. Then, Richard Earl of Cambridge, there is
                           yours;
There yours, Lord Scroop of Masham; and, sir knight,
Grey of Northumberland, this same is yours:
Read them; and know, I know your worthiness.—
My Lord of Westmoreland, and uncle Exeter,
We will aboard to-night.—Why, how now, gentlemen!
What see you in those papers that you lose
So much complexion?—Look ye, how they change!
Their cheeks are paper.—Why, what read you there,
That hath so cowarded and chased your blood
Out of appearance?
  Cam.   I do confess my fault;
And do submit me to your highness' mercy.
  Grey.   }
  Scroop.   } To which we all appeal.
  K. Hen. The mercy that was quick in us but late,
By your own counsel is suppressed and killed:
You must not dare, for shame, to talk of mercy;
For your own reasons turn into your bosoms,
As dogs upon their masters, worrying you.—
See you, my princes and my noble peers,
These English monsters! My lord of Cambridge here,—
You know how apt our love was to accord
To furnish him with all appertinents
Belonging to his honour; and this man
Hath, for a few light crowns, lightly conspired
And sworn unto the practices of France,
To kill us here in Hampton: to the which
This knight, no less for bounty bound to us
Than Cambridge is, hath likewise sworn. But, O,
What shall I say to thee, Lord Scroop? thou cruel,

Ingrateful, savage and inhuman creature!
Thou that didst bear the key of all my counsels,
That knew'st the very bottom of my soul,
That almost mightst have coined me into gold,
Wouldst thou have practised on me for thy use,—
May it be possible, that foreign hire
Could out of thee extract one spark of evil
That might annoy my finger? 't is so strange,
That, though the truth of it stands off as gross
As black from white, my eye will scarcely see it.
Treason and murder ever kept together,
As two yoke-devils, sworn to either's purpose,
Working so grossly in a natural cause
That admiration did not whoop at them:
But thou, 'gainst all proportion, didst bring in
Wonder to wait on treason and on murder:
And whatsoever cunning fiend it was
That wrought upon thee so preposterously,
Hath got the voice in hell for excellence:
All other devils that suggest by treasons
Do botch and bungle up damnation
With patches, colours, and with forms being fetched
From glistering semblances of piety;
But he that tempered thee, bade thee stand up,
Gave thee no instance why thou shouldst do treason
Unless to dub thee with the name of traitor.
If that same demon that hath gulled thee thus
Should with his lion gait walk the whole world.
He might return to vasty Tartar back,
And tell the legions ' I can never win
A soul so easy as that Englishman's.'
O, how hast thou with jealousy infected
The sweetness of affiance!   Show men dutiful?
Why, so didst thou: seem they grave and learned?
Why, so didst thou: come they of noble family?
Why, so didst thou: seem they religious?
Why, so didst thou: or are they spare in diet,
Free from gross passion or of mirth or anger;
Constant in spirit, not swerving with the blood;
Garnished and decked in modest complement;
Not working with the eye without the ear,
And but in purgéd judgment trusting neither?
Such and so finely bolted didst thou seem:
And thus thy fall hath left a kind of blot,
To mark the full-fraught man and best indued
With some suspicion.   I will weep for thee;
For this revolt of thine, methinks, is like
Another fall of man.—Their faults are open:
Arrest them to the answer of the law;—
And God acquit them of their practices!

Exe. I arrest thee of high treason, by the name of
Richard Earl of Cambridge.

I arrest thee of high treason, by the name of Henry Lord
Scroop of Masham.

I arrest thee of high treason, by the name of Thomas
Grey, knight, of Northumberland.

Scroop. Our purposes God justly hath discovered;
And I repent my fault more than my death;
Which I beseech your highness to forgive,
Although my body pay the price of it.

Cam. For me,—the gold of France did not seduce:
Although I did admit it as a motive
The sooner to effect what I intended;
But God be thankéd for prevention;
Which I in sufferance heartily will rejoice,
Beseeching God and you to pardon me.

Grey. Never did faithful subject more rejoice
At the discovery of most dangerous treason
Than I do at this hour joy o'er myself,
Prevented from a damnéd enterprise:
My fault, but not my body, pardon, sovereign.

K. Hen. God quit you in his mercy! Hear your sentence.
You have conspired against our royal person,
Joined with an enemy proclaimed, from's coffers
Received the golden earnest of our death;
Wherein you would have sold your king to slaughter,
His princes and his peers to servitude,
His subjects to oppression and contempt,
And his whole kingdom into desolation.
Touching our person seek we no revenge;
But we our kingdom's safety must so tender,
Whose ruin you have sought, that to her laws
We do deliver you. Get you, therefore, hence,
Poor miserable wretches, to your death:
The taste whereof, God of his mercy give
You patience to endure, and true repentance
Of all your dear offences! Bear them hence.

> [*Exeunt Cambridge, Scroop, and Grey, guarded*

Now, lords, for France; the enterprise whereof
Shall be to you as us like glorious.
We doubt not of a fair and lucky war,
Since God so graciously hath brought to light
This dangerous treason, lurking in our way
To hinder our beginnings. We doubt not now
But every rub is smoothéd on our way.
Then forth, dear countrymen: let us deliver
Our puissance into the hand of God,
Putting it straight in expedition.
Cheerly to sea; the signs of war advance:
No king of England, if not king of France.   [*Exeunt*

SCENE III.—London. Before 'The Boar's Head'
Tavern, Eastcheap

Enter PISTOL, *Hostess*, NYM, BARDOLPH, *and Boy*

Host. Prithee, honey-sweet husband, let me bring thee
to Staines.

Pist. No; for my manly heart doth yearn.—
Bardolph, be blithe: Nym, rouse thy vaunting veins;—
Boy, bristle thy courage up;—for Falstaff he is dead,
And we must yearn therefore.

Bard. Would I were with him, wheresome'er he is,
either in heaven or in hell!

Host. Nay, sure, he's not in hell: he's in Arthur's
bosom, if ever man went to Arthur's bosom. 'A made a
finer end, and went away an it had been any christom
child; 'a parted even just between twelve and one, even
at the turning o' the tide: for after I saw him fumble with
the sheets, and play with flowers, and smile upon his
fingers' ends, I knew there was but one way; for his nose
was as sharp as a pen, and 'a babbled of green fields. 'How
now, Sir John!' quoth I: 'what, man! be o' good cheer.'
So 'a cried out 'God, God, God!' three or four times. Now
I, to comfort him, bid him 'a should not think of God; I
hoped there was no need to trouble himself with any such
thoughts yet. So 'a bade me lay more clothes on his
feet: I put my hand into the bed and felt them, and they
were as cold as any stone; then I felt to his knees, and they
were as cold as any stone; and so upward and upward
and all was as cold as any stone.

Nym. They say he cried out of sack.

Host. Ay, that 'a did.

Bard. And of women.

Host. Nay, that 'a did not.

Boy. Yes, that 'a did; and said they were devils in-
carnate.

Host. 'A could never abide carnation; 't was a colour
he never liked.

Boy. 'A said once, the devil would have him about
women.

Host. 'A did in some sort, indeed, handle women; but
then he was rheumatic, and talked of the whore of Babylon.

Boy. Do you not remember, 'a saw a flea stick upon
Bardolph's nose, and 'a said it was a black soul burning in
hell-fire?

Bard. Well, the fuel is gone that maintained that fire:
that's all the riches I got in his service.

Nym. Shall we shog? the king will be gone from
Southampton.

Pist.   Come, let's away.—My love, give me thy lips.
Look to my chattels and my movables:
Let senses rule; the word is 'Pitch and Pay;'
Trust none;
For oaths are straws, men's faiths are wafercakes,
And hold-fast is the only dog, my duck:
Therefore, Caveto be thy counsellor.
Go, clear thy crystals.—Yoke-fellows in arms,
Let us to France; like horse-leeches, my boys,
To suck, to suck, the very blood to suck!
 Boy. And that's but unwholesome food, they say.
 Pist. Touch her soft mouth, and march.
 Bard. Farewell, hostess.   [*Kissing her*
 Nym. I cannot kiss, that is the humour of it; but,
   adieu.
 Pist. Let housewifery appear; keep close, I thee com-
   mand.
 Host. Farewell; adieu.   [*Exeunt*

SCENE IV.—France. The King's Palace

Flourish.   Enter the FRENCH KING, *the* DAUPHIN, *the* DUKE
OF BURGUNDY, *the* CONSTABLE, *and others*

 Fr. King. Thus come the English with full power upon
   us;
And more than carefully it us concerns
To answer royally in our defences.
Therefore the Dukes of Berri and of Bretagne,
Of Brabant and of Orleans, shall make forth,—
And you, Prince Dauphin,—with all swift dispatch,
To line and new repair our towns of war
With men of courage and with means defendant;
For England his approaches makes as fierce
As waters to the sucking of a gulf.
It fits us, then, to be as provident
As fear may teach us, out of late examples
Left by the fatal and neglected English
Upon our fields.
 Dau.   My most redoubted father,
It is most meet we arm us 'gainst the foe;
For peace itself should not so dull a kingdom,
Though war nor no known quarrel were in question,
But that defences, musters, preparations,
Should be maintained, assembled and collected,
As were a war in expectation.
Therefore, I say 't is meet we all go forth
To view the sick and feeble parts of France:
And let us do it with no show of fear;

No, with no more than if we heard that England
Were busied with a Whitsun morris-dance:
For, my good liege, she is so idly kinged,
Her sceptre so fantastically borne
By a vain, giddy, shallow, humorous youth,
That fear attends her not.
   Con.   O peace, Prince Dauphin!
You are too much mistaken in this king:
Question your grace the late ambassadors,—
With what great state he heard their embassy,
How well supplied with noble counsellors,
How modest in exception, and withal
How terrible in constant resolution,—
And you shall find his vanities forespent
Were but the outside of the Roman Brutus,
Covering discretion with a coat of folly;
As gardeners do with ordure hide those roots
That shall first spring and be most delicate.
   Dau. Well, 't is not so, my lord high constable;
But though we think it so, it is no matter:
In cases of defence 't is best to weigh
The enemy more mighty than he seems:
So the proportions of defence are filled;
Which, of a weak and niggardly projection,
Doth, like a miser, spoil his coat with scanting
A little cloth.
   Fr. King. Think we King Harry strong:
And, princes, look you strongly arm to meet him.
The kindred of him hath been fleshed upon us;
And he is bred out of that bloody strain
That haunted us in our familiar paths:
Witness our too much memorable shame
When Cressy battle fatally was struck,
And all our princes captived, by the hand
Of that black name, Edward, Black Prince of Wales;
Whiles that his mountain sire,—on mountain standing,
Up in the air, crowned with the golden sun,—
Saw his heroical seed, and smiled to see him,
Mangle the work of nature and deface
The patterns that by God and by French fathers
Had twenty years been made.   This is a stem
Of that victorious stock; and let us fear
The native mightiness and fate of him.

               Enter a Messenger

   Mess. Ambassadors from Harry King of England
Do crave admittance to your majesty.
   Fr. King. We'll give them present audience.   Go, and
        bring them. [*Exeunt Messenger and certain Lords*

You see this chase is hotly followed, friends.
Dau. Turn head, and stop pursuit; for coward dogs
Most spend their mouths when what they seem to threaten
Runs far before them.   Good my sovereign,
Take up the English short, and let them know
Of what a monarchy you are the head:
Self-love, my liege, is not so vile a sin
As self-neglecting.

Re-enter Lords, with EXETER *and train*

Fr. King.   From our brother England?
Exe. From him; and thus he greets your majesty.
He wills you, in the name of God Almighty,
That you divest yourself, and lay apart
The borrowed glories that by gift of heaven,
By law of nature and of nations, 'long
To him and to his heirs; namely, the crown,
And all wide-stretchéd honours that pertain
By custom and the ordinance of times
Unto the crown, of France.   That you may know
'T is no sinister nor no awkward claim,
Picked from the worm-holes of long-vanished days,
Nor from the dust of old oblivion raked,
He sends you this most memorable line,   [*Gives a paper*
In every branch truly demonstrative;
Willing you overlook this pedigree:
And when you find him evenly derived
From his most famed of famous ancestors,
Edward the Third, he bids you then resign
Your crown and kingdom, indirectly held
From him the native and true challenger.
Fr. King. Or else what follows?
Exe. Bloody constraint; for if you hide the crown
Even in your hearts, there will he rake for it:
Therefore in fiery tempest is he coming,
In thunder and in earthquake, like a Jove,
That, if requiring fail, he will compel;
And bids you, in the bowels of the Lord,
Deliver up the crown; and to take mercy
On the poor souls for whom this hungry war
Opens his vasty jaws: and on your head
Turning the widows' tears, the orphans' cries,
The dead men's blood, the pining maidens' groans,
For husbands, fathers, and betrothéd lovers,
That shall be swallowed in this controversy.
This is his claim, his threatening, and my message;
Unless the Dauphin be in presence here,
To whom expressly I bring greeting too.
Fr. King. For us, we will consider of this further:

182

To-morrow shall you bear our full intent
Back to our brother England.
    Dau.   For the Dauphin,
I stand here for him: what to him from England!
    Exe.   Scorn and defiance; slight regard, contempt,
And any thing that may not misbecome
The mighty sender, doth he prize you at.
Thus says my king; an if your father's highness
Do not, in grant of all demands at large,
Sweeten the bitter mock you sent his majesty,
He 'll call you to so hot an answer of it,
That caves and womby vaultages of France
Shall chide your trespass, and return your mock
In second accent of his ordnance.
    Dau.   Say, if my father render fair return,
It is against my will; for I desire
Nothing but odds with England: to that end,
As matching to his youth and vanity,
I did present him with the Paris balls.
    Exe.   He 'll make your Paris Louvre shake **for it,**
Were it the mistress-court of mighty Europe:
And, be assured, you 'll find a difference,
As we his subjects have in wonder found,
Between the promise of his greener days
And these he masters now: now he weighs time
Even to the utmost grain:—that you shall read
In your own losses, if he stay in France.
    Fr. King.   To-morrow shall you know our mind at full.
    Exe.   Despatch us with all speed, lest that our king
Come here himself to question our delay;
For he is footed in this land already.
    Fr. King.   You shall be soon despatched with fair
           conditions:
A night is but small breath and little pause
To answer matters of this consequence.
                              [Flourish.   Exeunt

ACT THREE

Enter Chorus

    Chor.   Thus with imagined wing our swift scene flies
In motion of no less celerity
Than that of thought.   Suppose that you have seen
The well-appointed king at Hampton pier
Embark his royalty, and his brave fleet
With silken streamers the young Phœbus fanning:
Play with your fancies, and in them behold
Upon the hempen tackle ship-boys climbing;

Hear the shrill whistle which doth order give
To sounds confused; behold the threaden sails,
Borne with the invisible and creeping wind,
Draw the huge bottoms through the furrowed sea,
Breasting the lofty surge: O, do but think
You stand upon the rivage and behold
A city on the inconstant billows dancing;
For so appears this fleet majestical,
Holding due course to Harfleur.   Follow, follow:
Grapple your minds to sternage of this navy,
And leave your England, as dead midnight still,
Guarded with grandsires, babies, and old women,
Either past, or not arrived to, pith and puissance;
For who is he, whose chin is but enriched
With one appearing hair, that will not follow
These culled and choice-drawn cavaliers to France?
Work, work your thoughts, and therein see a siege;
Behold the ordnance on their carriages,
With fatal mouths gaping on girded Harfleur.
Suppose the ambassador from the French comes back;
Tells Harry that the king doth offer him
Katherine his daughter; and with her, to dowry,
Some petty and unprofitable dukedoms.
The offer likes not: and the nimble gunner
With linstock now the devilish cannon touches,
                    [*Alarum, and chambers go off, within*
And down goes all before them.   Still be kind,
And eke out our performance with your mind.   [*Exit*

SCENE I.—France.   Before Harfleur

Alarum.   Enter KING HENRY, EXETER, BEDFORD,
    GLOUCESTER, *and Soldiers, with scaling-ladders*

   K. Hen.   Once more unto the breach, dear friends, once
            more;
Or close the wall up with our English dead!
In peace there's nothing so becomes a man
As modest stillness and humility:
But when the blast of war blows in our ears,
Then imitate the action of the tiger;
Stiffen the sinews, summon up the blood,
Disguise fair nature with hard-favoured rage;
Then lend the eye a terrible aspéct;
Let it pry through the portage of the head
Like the brass cannon; let the brow o'erwhelm it
As fearfully as doth a galléd rock
O'erhang and jutty his confounded base,
Swilled with the wild and wasteful ocean.

Now set the teeth and stretch the nostril wide,
Hold hard the breath, and bend up every spirit
To his full height! On, on, you noblest English,
Whose blood is fet from fathers of war-proof!—
Fathers that, like so many Alexanders,
Have in these parts from morn till even fought
And sheathed their swords for lack of argument:—
Dishonour not your mothers; now attest
That those whom you called fathers did beget you.
Be copy now to men of grosser blood,
And teach them how to war! And you, good yeomen,
Whose limbs were made in England, show us here
The mettle of your pasture; let us swear
That you are worth your breeding; which I doubt not;
For there is none of you so mean and base,
That hath not noble lustre in your eyes.
I see you stand like greyhounds in the slips,
Straining upon the start. The game's afoot:
Follow your spirit; and, upon this charge,
Cry 'God for Harry, England, and Saint George!'
                    [*Exeunt. Alarum, and chambers go off*

SCENE II. The Same

Enter NYM, BARDOLPH, PISTOL, *and Boy*

Bard. On, on, on, on, on! to the breach! to the breach!
Nym. Pray thee, corporal, stay: the knocks are too
hot; and, for mine own part, I have not a case of lives:
the humour of it is too hot, that is the very plain-song of it.
Pist. The plain-song is most just; for humours do
      abound:
Knocks go and come; God's vassals drop and die;
            And sword and shield,
            In bloody field,
            Doth win immortal fame.
Boy. Would I were in an alehouse in London! I would
give all my fame for a pot of ale and safety.
Pist. And I:
            If wishes would prevail with me,
            My purpose should not fail with me,
                But thither would I hie.
Boy.   As duly, but not as truly,
            As bird doth sing on bough.

Enter FLUELLEN

Flu. Up to the breach, you dogs! avaunt, you cullions!
                    [*Driving them forward*

185

Pist. Be merciful, great duke, to men of mould.
Abate thy rage, abate thy manly rage,
Abate thy rage, great duke!
Good bawcock, bate thy rage! use lenity, sweet chuck!
Nym. These be good humours! your honour wins
bad humours.   [*Exeunt all but Boy*
Boy. As young as I am, I have observed these three
swashers. I am boy to them all three: but all they three,
though they would serve me, could not be man to me; for,
indeed, three such antics do not amount to a man. For
Bardolph, he is white-livered and red-faced; by the
means whereof 'a faces it out, but fights not. For Pistol,
he hath a killing tongue and a quiet sword; by the means
whereof 'a breaks words, and keeps whole weapons. For
Nym, he hath heard that men of few words are the best
men; and therefore he scorns to say his prayers, lest 'a
should be thought a coward: but his few bad words are
matched with as few good deeds: for 'a never broke any
man's head but his own, and that was against a post when
he was drunk. They will steal anything, and call it purchase. Bardolph stole a lute-case, bore it twelve leagues,
and sold it for three half-pence. Nym and Bardolph
are sworn brothers in filching, and in Calais they stole
a fire-shovel: I knew by that piece of service the men
would carry coals. They would have me as familiar with
men's pockets as their gloves or their handkerchers: which
makes much against my manhood, if I should take from
another's pocket to put into mine; for it is plain pocketing-
up of wrongs. I must leave them, and seek some better
service: their villainy goes against my weak stomach, and
therefore I must cast it up.   [*Exit*

Re-enter FLUELLEN, GOWER *following*

Gow. Captain Fluellen, you must come presently to
the mines; the Duke of Gloucester would speak with you.
Flu. To the mines! tell you the duke, it is not so good
to come to the mines; for, look you, the mines is not
according to the disciplines of the wars: the concavities
of it is not sufficient; for, look you, th' athversary,—you
may discuss unto the duke, look you,—is diggt himself
four yard under the countermines: by Cheshu, I think 'a
will plow up all, if there is not better directions.
Gow. The Duke of Gloucester, to whom the order of the
siege is given, is altogether directed by an Irishman,—
a very valiant gentleman, i' faith.
Flu. It is Captain Macmorris, is it not?
Gow. I think it be.
Flu. By Cheshu, he is an ass, as in the 'orld: I will
verify as much in his peard: he has no more directions in

the true disciplines of the wars, look you, of the Roman
disciplines, than is a puppy-dog.

Gow. Here 'a comes; and the Scots captain, Captain
Jamy, with him.

Flu. Captain Jamy is a marvellous falorous gentleman,
that is certain; and of great expedition and knowledge
in th' auncient wars, upon my particular knowledge of
his directions: by Cheshu, he will maintain his argument
as well as any military man in the 'orld, in the disciplines
of the pristine wars of the Romans.

Enter MACMORRIS *and* CAPTAIN JAMY

Jamy. I say gude-day, Captain Fluellen.

Flu. Got-den to your worship, goot Captain James.

Gow. How now, Captain Macmorris! have you quit
the mines? have the pioners given o'er?

Mac. By Chrish, la, tish ill done: the work ish give
over, the trompet sound the retreat. By my hand, I swear,
and my father's soul, the work ish ill done; it ish give
over: I would have blowed up the town, so Chrish save
me, la, in an hour: O, tish ill done, tish ill done; by my
hand, tish ill done!

Flu. Captain Macmorris, I peseech you now, will you
voutsafe me, look you, a few disputations with you, as
partly touching or concerning the disciplines of the wars,
the Roman wars, in the way of argument, look you, and
friendly communication; partly to satisfy my opinion,
and partly for the satisfaction, look you, of my mind,
as touching the direction of the military discipline; that
is the point.

Jamy. It sall be vary gude, gude feith, gude captains
baith: and I sall quit you with gude leve, as I may pick
occasion; that sall I, mary.

Mac. It is no time to discourse, so Chrish save me:
the day is hot, and the weather, and the wars, and the
king, and the dukes: it is no time to discourse. The
town is beseeched, and the trumpet call us to the breach;
and we talk, and, by Chrish, do nothing: 't is shame for
us all: so God sa' me, 't is shame to stand still; it is shame,
by my hand: and there is throats to be cut, and works
to be done; and there ish nothing done, so Chrish sa' me,
la!

Jamy. By the mess, ere theise eyes of mine take themselves to slomber, ai'll do gude service, or ai'll lig i' the
grund for it; ay, or go to death; and ai'll pay't as
valorously as I may, that sall I suerly do, that is the breff
and the long. Marry, I wad full fain heard some question
'tween you tway.

Flu. Captain Macmorris, I think, look you, under your
correction, there is not many of your nation—

Mac. Of my nation! What ish my nation? Ish a villain, and a bastard, and a knave, and a rascal—What ish my nation? Who talks of my nation?

Flu. Look you, if you take the matter otherwise than is meant, Captain Macmorris, peradventure I shall think you do not use me with that affability as in discretion you ought to use me, look you; being as good a man as yourself, both in the disciplines of war, and in the derivation of my birth, and in other particularities.

Mac. I do not know you so good a man as myself; so Chrish save me, I will cut off your head.

Gow. Gentlemen both, you will mistake each other.

Jamy. A! that's a foul fault.   [*A parley sounded*

Gow. The town sounds a parley.

Flu. Captain Macmorris, when there is more petter opportunity to be required, look you, I will be so pold as to tell you I know the disciplines of wars; and there is an end.   [*Exeunt*

SCENE III.—Harfleur. Before the gates

The GOVERNOR *and some Citizens on the walls ; the English forces below. Enter* KING HENRY *and his train*

K. Hen. How yet resolves the governor of the town?
This is the latest parle we will admit:
Therefore to our best mercy give yourselves,
Or, like to men proud of destruction,
Defy us to our worst: for, as I am a soldier,
A name that, in my thoughts, becomes me best,
If I begin the battery once again,
I will not leave the half-achieved Harfleur
Till in her ashes she lie buriéd.
The gates of mercy shall be all shut up,
And the fleshed soldier, rough and hard of heart,
In liberty of bloody hand shall range
With conscience wide as hell, mowing like grass
Your fresh-fair virgins and your flowering infants.
What is it then to me, if impious war,—
Arrayed in flames like to the prince of fiends,—
Do, with his smirched complexion, all fell feats
Enlinked to waste and desolation?
What is 't to me, when you yourself are cause,
If your pure maidens fall into the hand
Of hot and forcing violation?
What rein can hold licentious wickedness
When down the hill he holds his fierce career?
We may as bootless spend our vain command
Upon the enragéd soldiers in their spoil

As send precépts to the leviathan
To come ashore.   Therefore, you men of Harfleur,
Take pity of your town and of your people
Whiles yet my soldiers are in my command;
Whiles yet the cool and temperate wind of grace
O'erblows the filthy and contagious clouds
Of heady murder, spoil, and villainy.
If not, why, in a moment look to see
The blind and bloody soldier with foul hand
Defile the locks of your shrill-shrieking daughters;
Your fathers taken by the silver beards,
And their most reverend heads dashed to the walls;
Your naked infants spitted upon pikes,
Whiles the mad mothers with their howls confused
Do break the clouds, as did the wives of Jewry
At Herod's bloody-hunting slaughtermen.
What say you? will you yield, and this avoid?
Or, guilty in defence, be thus destroyed?
 Gov. Our expectation hath this day an end:
The Dauphin, whom of succours we entreated,
Returns us that his powers are yet not ready
To raise so great a siege.   Therefore, great king,
We yield our town and lives to thy soft mercy.
Enter our gates; dispose of us and ours;
For we no longer are defensible.
 K. Hen. Open your gates.—Come, uncle Exeter,
Go you and enter Harfleur; there remain,
And fortify it strongly 'gainst the French:
Use mercy to them all.   For us, dear uncle,—
The winter coming on and sickness growing
Upon our soldiers,—we will retire to Calais.
To-night in Harfleur we will be your guest;
To-morrow for the march are we addrest.
    [*Flourish.   The King and his train enter the town*

SCENE IV.—The French King's Palace

Enter KATHARINE *and* ALICE

 Kath. Alice, tu as été en Angleterre, et u parles bien le
langage.
 Alice. Un peu, madame.
 Kath. Je te prie, m'enseignez ; il faut que j'apprenne à
parler.   Comment appelez-vous la main en Anglois ?
 Alice. La main ? elle est appelée de hand.
 Kath. De hand.   Et les doigts ?
 Alice. Les doigts ? ma foi, j'oublie les doigts ; mais je
me souviendrai.   Les doigts ? je pense qu'ils sont appelés
de fingres; oui, de fingres.

Kath. La main, de hand; *les doigts*, de fingers. *Je pense que je suis le bon écolier ; j'ai gagné deux mots d'Anglois vitement. Comment appelez-vous les ongles ?*

Alice. Les ongles ? ,nous les appelons de nails.

Kath. De nails. *Écoutez ; dites-moi, si je parle bien.* de hand, de fingres, *et* de nails.

Alice. C'est bien dit, madame ; il est fort bon Anglois.

Kath. Dites-moi l'Anglois pour le bras.

Alice. De arm, *madame.*

Kath. Et le coude ?

Alice. De elbow.

Kath. De elbow. *Je m'en fais la répétition de tous les mots que vous m'avez appris dès à présent.*

Alice. Il est trop difficile, madame, comme je pense.

Kath. Excusez-moi, Alice ; écoutez : de hand, de fingres, de nails, de arma, de bilbow.

Alice. De elbow, *madame.*

Kath. O Seigneur Dieu, je m'en oublie ! de elbow. *Comment appelez-vous le col ?*

Alice. De neck, *madame.*

Kath. De nick. *Et le menton ?*

Alice. De chin.

Kath. De sin. *Le col,* de nick; *le menton,* de sin.

Alice. Oui. Sauf votre honneur, en vérité, vous prononcez les mots aussi droit que les natifs d'Angleterre.

Kath. Je ne doute point d'apprendre, par la grace de Dieu, et en peu de temps.

Alice. N'avez vous pas déjà oublié ce que je vous ai enseigné ?

Kath. Non, je reciterai à vous promptement : de hand, de fingres, de nails,—

Alice. De nails, *madame.*

Kath. De nails, de arm, de ilbow.

Alice. Sauf votre honneur, de elbow.

Kath. Ainsi dis-je ; de elbow, de nick, *et* de sin. *Comment appelez-vous le pied et la robe ?*

Alice. De foot, *madame :* et de coun.

Kath. De foot *et* de coun! *O Seigneur Dieu ! ce sont mots de son mauvais, corruptible, gros, et impudique, et non pour les dames d'honneur d'user : je ne voudrais prononcer ces mots devant les seigneurs de France pour tout le monde. Il faut* de foot *et* de coun *néanmoins. Je reciterai une autre fois ma leçon ensemble :* de hand, de fingres, de nails, de arm, de elbow, de nick, de sin, de foot, de coun.

Alice. Excellent, madame !

Kath. C'est assez pour une fois : allons-nous à diner.

[*Exeunt*

SCENE V.—Another Room in the French King's Palace

Enter the KING OF FRANCE, *the* DAUPHIN, *the* DUKE OF
  BOURBON, *the* CONSTABLE OF FRANCE, *and others*

Fr. King. 'T is certain he hath passed the river Somme.
  Con. And if he be not fought withal, my lord,
Let us not live in France; let us quit all,
And give our vineyards to a barbarous people.
  Dau. O *Dieu vivant !* shall a few sprays of us,
The emptying of our fathers' luxury,
Our scions, put in wild and savage stock,
Spirt up so suddenly into the clouds
And overlook their grafters?
  Bour. Normans,   but   bastard Normans,   Norman
            bastards!
Mort de mā vie ! if they march along
Unfought withal, but I will sell my dukedom,
To buy a slobbery and a dirty farm
In that nook-shotten isle of Albion.
  Con. *Dieu de batailles !* whence have they this mettle?
Is not their climate foggy, raw and dull;
On whom, as in despite, the sun looks pale,
Killing their fruit with frowns?   Can sodden water,
A drench for sur-reined jades, their barley-broth,
Decoct their cold blood to such valiant heat?
And shall our quick blood, spirited with wine,
Seem frosty?   O, for honour of our land,
Let us not hang like roping icicles
Upon our houses' thatch, whiles a more frosty people
Sweat drops of gallant youth in our rich fields,—
Poor we may call them in their native lords.
  Dau. By faith and honour,
Our madams mock at us, and plainly say
Our mettle is bred out, and they will give
Their bodies to the lust of English youth
To new-store France with bastard warriors.
  Bour. They bid us to the English dancing-schools,
And teach lavoltas high and swift corantos;
Saying our grace is only in our heels,
And that we are most lofty runaways.
  Fr. King. Where is Montjoy the herald? speed him
            hence;
Let him greet England with our sharp defiance.
Up, princes! and, with spirit of honour edged
More sharper than your swords, hie to the field:
Charles Delabret, high constable of France;
You Dukes of Orleans, Bourbon, and of Berri,
Alencon, Brabant, Bar, and Burgundy;

Jacques Chatillon, Rambures, Vaudemont,
Beaumont, Grandpré, Roussi, and Fauconberg,
Foix, Lestrale, Bouciqualt, and Charolois;
High dukes, great princes, barons, lords, and knights,
For your great seats, now quit you of great shames.
Bar Harry England, that sweeps through our land
With pennons painted in the blood of Harfleur:
Rush on his host, as doth the melted snow
Upon the valleys whose low vassal seat
The Alps doth spit and void his rheum upon:
Go down upon him,—you have power enough,—
And in a captive chariot into Rouen
Bring him our prisoner.
    Con.   This becomes the great.
Sorry am I his numbers are so few,
His soldiers sick, and famished in their march,
For I am sure, when he shall see our army,
He 'll drop his heart into the sink of fear,
And, for achievement, offer us his ransom.
    Fr. King.   Therefore, lord constable, haste on Montjoy;
And let him say to England, that we send
To know what willing ransom he will give.—
Prince Dauphin, you shall stay with us in Rouen.
    Dau.   Not so, I do beseech your majesty.
    Fr. King.   Be patient; for you shall remain with us.—
Now forth, lord constable, and princes all,
And quickly bring us word of England's fall.   [*Exeunt*

SCENE VI.—The English Camp in Picardy

Enter GOWER *and* FLUELLEN, *meeting*

    Gow.   How now, Captain Fluellen! come you from the
bridge?
    Flu.   I assure you, there is very excellent services
committed at the pridge.
    Gow.   Is the Duke of Exeter safe?
    Flu.   The Duke of Exeter is as magnanimous as Aga-
memnon; and a man that I love and honour with my
soul, and my heart, and my duty, and my life and my
living, and my uttermost power: he is not—Got be
praised and plessed!—any hurt in the orld; but keeps
the pridge most valiantly, with excellent discipline.   There
is an auncient lieutenant there at the pridge,—I think in
my very conscience he is as valiant a man as Mark Antony;
and he is a man of no estimation in the orld; but I did
see him do as gallant service.
    Gow.   What do you call him?
    Flu.   He is called Aunchient Pistol.
    Gow.   I know him not.

Enter PISTOL

Flu. Here is the man.
Pist. Captain, I thee beseech to do me favours:
The Duke of Exeter doth love thee well.
Flu. Ay, I praise Got; and I have merited some love
at his hands.
Pist. Bardolph, a soldier firm and sound of heart,
Of buxom valour, hath, by cruel fate,
And giddy Fortune's furious fickle wheel,—
That goddess blind,
That stands upon the rolling restless stone—
Flu. By your patience, Aunchient Pistol. Fortune is
painted blind, with a muffler afore her eyes, to signify to
you that Fortune is blind; and she is painted also with a
wheel, to signify to you, which is the moral of it, that she
is turning, and inconstant, and mutability, and variation:
and her foot, look you, is fixed upon a spherical stone,
which rolls, and rolls, and rolls:—in good truth, the poet
makes a most excellent description of it: Fortune is an
excellent moral.
Pist. Fortune is Bardolph's foe, and frowns on him;
For he hath stolen a pax, and hangéd must 'a be:
A damnéd death!
Let gallows gape for dog; let man go free,
And let not hemp his wind-pipe suffocate:
But Exeter hath given the doom of death
For pax of little price.
Therefore, go speak——the duke will hear thy voice;
And let not Bardolph's vital thread be cut
With edge of penny cord and vile reproach:
Speak, captain, for his life, and I will thee requite.
Flu. Aunchient Pistol, I do partly understand your
meaning.
Pist. Why then, rejoice therefore.
Flu. Certainly, aunchient, it is not a thing to rejoice at:
for if, look you, he were my prother, I would desire the
duke to use his good pleasure, and put him to execution;
for discipline ought to be used.
Pist. Die and be damned! and figo for thy friendship!
Flu. It is well.
Pist. The fig of Spain!   [*Exit*
Flu. Very good.
Gow. Why, this is an arrant counterfeit rascal; I
remember him now; a bawd, a cutpurse.
Flu. I'll assure you, 'a uttered as prave words at the
pridge as you shall see in a summer's day. But it is
very well; what he has spoke to me, that is well, I warrant
you, when time is serve.
Gow. Why, 't is a gull, a fool, a rogue, that now and

then goes to the wars, to grace himself, at his return into London, under the form of a soldier. And such fellows are perfect in the great commanders' names: and they will learn you by rote where services were done; at such and such a sconce, at such a breach, at such a convoy; who came off bravely, who was shot, who disgraced, what terms the enemy stood on; and this they con perfectly in the phrase of war, which they trick up with new-tuned oaths: and what a beard of the general's cut, and a horrid suit of the camp, will do among foaming bottles and ale-washed wits, is wonderful to be thought on. But you must learn to know such slanders of the age, or else you may be marvellously mistook.

Flu. I tell you what, Captain Gower;—I do perceive he is not the man that he would gladly make show to the orld he is: if I find a hole in his coat, I will tell him my mind. [*Drum within*] Hark you, the king is coming; and I must speak with him from the pridge.

Drum and Colours. Enter KING HENRY, GLOUCESTER, *and Soldiers*

Got pless your majesty!

K. Hen. How now, Fluellen! cam'st thou from the bridge?

Flu. Ay, so please your majesty. The Duke of Exeter had very gallantly maintained the pridge: the French is gone off, look you; and there is gallant and most prave passages; marry, th' athversary was have possession of the pridge; but he is enforced to retire, and the Duke of Exeter is master of the pridge: I can tell your majesty, the duke is a prave man.

K. Hen. What men have you lost, Fluellen?

Flu. The perdition of th' athversary hath been very great, reasonable great: marry, for my part, I think the duke hath lost never a man, but one that is like to be executed for robbing a church,—one Bardolph, if your majesty know the man: his face is all bubukles, and whelks, and knobs, and flames o' fire: and his lips plows at his nose, and it is like a coal of fire, sometimes plue and sometimes red; but his nose is executed, and his fire's out.

K. Hen. We would have all such offenders so cut off: —and we give express charge, that in our marches through the country, there be nothing compelled from the villages, nothing taken but paid for, none of the French upbraided or abused in disdainful language; for when lenity and cruelty play for a kingdom, the gentler gamester is the soonest winner.

Tucket.   Enter MONTJOY

Mont.   You know me by my habit.

K. Hen.   Well then I know thee: what shall I know of thee?

Mont.   My master's mind.

K. Hen.   Unfold it.

Mont.   Thus says my king:—Say thou to Harry of England: Though we seemed dead, we did but sleep; advantage is a better soldier than rashness.   Tell him we could have rebuked him at Harfleur, but that we thought not good to bruise an injury till it were full ripe: now we speak upon our cue, and our voice is imperial: England shall repent his folly, see his weakness, and amire our sufferance.   Bid him, therefore, consider of his ransom; which must proportion the losses we have borne, the subjects we have lost, the disgrace we have digested; which in weight to re-answer, his pettiness would bow under. For our losses, his exchequer is too poor; for the effusion of our blood, the muster of his kingdom too faint a number; and for our disgrace, his own person, kneeling at our feet, but a weak and worthless satisfaction.   To this add defiance: and tell him, for conclusion, he hath betrayed his followers, whose condemnation is pronounced.   So far my king and master; so much my office.

K. Hen.   What is thy name?   I know thy quality.

Mont.   Montjoy.

K. Hen.   Thou dost thy office fairly.   Turn thee back, And tell thy king I do not seek him now; But could be willing to march on to Calais Without impeachment: for, to say the sooth,— Though 't is no wisdom to confess so much Unto an enemy of craft and vantage,— My people are with sickness much enfeebled My numbers lessened, and those few I have Almost no better than so many French; Who when they were in health, I tell thee, herald, I thought upon one pair of English legs Did march three Frenchmen.—Yet, forgive me, God, That I do brag thus!—This your air of France Hath blown that vice in me; I must repent.— Go, therefore, tell thy master, here I am; My ransom is this frail and worthless trunk; My army but a weak and sickly guard: Yet, God before, tell him we will come on, Though France himself, and such another neighbour, Stand in our way.   There's for thy labour, Montjoy. Go, bid thy master well advise himself: If we may pass, we will; if we be hindered, We shall your tawny ground with your red blood

Discolour: and so, Montjoy, fare you well.
The sum of all our answer is but this:
We would not seek a battle, as we are;
Nor, as we are, we say we will not shun it:
So tell your master.
    Mont. I shall deliver so.   Thanks to your highness.
                                       [*Exit*

    Glou. I hope they will not come upon us now.
    K. Hen. We are in God's hand, brother, not in theirs.—
March to the bridge; it now draws toward night:—
Beyónd the river we'll encamp ourselves;
And on to-morrow bid them march away.   [*Exeunt*

    Scene VII.—The French Camp, near Agincourt

Enter the Constable of France, *the Lord* Rambures,
      Orleans, Dauphin, *with others*

    Con. Tut! I have the best armour of the world.—Would
it were day!
    Orl. You have an excellent armour; but let my horse
have his due.
    Con. It is the best horse of Europe.
    Orl. Will it never be morning?
    Dau. My Lord of Orleans, and my lord high constable;
you talk of horse and armour,—
    Orl. You are as well provided of both as any prince in
the world.
    Dau. What a long night is this!—I will not change my
horse with any that treads but on four pasterns. *Ca,
ha!* he bounds from the earth, as if his entrails were hairs;
le cheval volant, the Pegasus, *qui a les narines de feu!*
When I bestride him, I soar, I am a hawk: he trots the air;
the earth sings when he touches it; the basest horn of his
hoof is more musical than the pipe of Hermes.
    Orl. He's of the colour of the nutmeg.
    Dau. And of the heat of the ginger.   It is a beast for
Perseus: he is pure air and fire; and the dull elements of
earth and water never appear in him, but only in patient
stillness while his rider mounts him: he is indeed a horse;
and all other jades you may call beasts.
    Con. Indeed, my lord, it is a most absolute and excellent
horse.
    Dau. It is the prince of palfreys; his neigh is like the
bidding of a monarch, and his countenance enforces homage.
    Orl. No more, cousin.
    Dau. Nay, the man hath no wit that cannot, from the
rising of the lark to the lodging of the lamb, vary deserved
praise on my palfrey: it is a theme as fluent as the sea;

turn the sands into eloquent tongues, and my horse is argument for them all: 't is a subject for a sovereign to reason on, and for a sovereign's sovereign to ride on; and for the world, familiar to us and unknown, to lay apart their particular functions and wonder at him. I once writ a sonnet in his praise and began thus: 'Wonder of nature,'—

Orl. I have heard a sonnet begin so to one's mistress.

Dau. Then did they imitate that which I composed to my courser; for my horse is my mistress.

Orl. Your mistress bears well.

Dau. Me well; which is the prescript praise and perfection of a good and particular mistress.

Con. Ma foi, methought yesterday your mistress shrewdly shook your back.

Dau. So perhaps did yours.

Con. Mine was not bridled.

Dau. O then belike she was old and gentle; and you rode, like a kern of Ireland, your French hose off, and in your strait strossers.

Con. You have good judgment in horsemanship.

Dau. Be warned by me, then: they that ride so, and ride not warily, fall into foul bogs. I had rather have my horse to my mistress.

Con. I had as lief have my mistress a jade.

Dau. I tell thee, constable, my mistress wears her own hair.

Con. I could make as true a boast as that, if I had a sow to my mistress.

Dau. Le chien est retourné à son propre vomissement, et la truie lavée au bourbier : thou makest use of anything.

Con. Yet I do not use my horse for my mistress; or any such proverb, so little kin to the purpose.

Ram. My lord constable, the armour that I saw in your tent to-night,—are those stars or suns upon it?

Con. Stars, my lord.

Dau. Some of them will fall to-morrow, I hope.

Con. And yet my sky shall not want.

Dau. That may be, for you bear a many superfluously, and 't were more honour some were away.

Con. Even as your horse bears your praises; who would trot as well, were some of your brags dismounted.

Dau. Would I were able to load him with his desert!— Will it never be day?—I will trot to-morrow a mile, and my way shall be paved with English faces.

Con. I will not say so, for fear I should be faced out of my way:—but I would it were morning; for I would fain be about the ears of the English.

Ram. Who will go to hazard with me for twenty prisoners?

Con.   You must first go yourself to hazard, ere you have them.

Dau.   'T is midnight; I'll go arm myself.   [*Exit*

Orl.   The Dauphin longs for morning.

Ram.   He longs to eat the English.

Con.   I think he will eat all he kills.

Orl.   By the white hand of my lady, he's a gallant prince.

Con.   Swear by her foot, that she may tread out the oath.

Orl.   He is simply the most active gentleman of France.

Con.   Doing is activity; and he will still be doing.

Orl.   He never did harm, that I heard of.

Con.   Nor will do none to-morrow: he will keep that good name still.

Orl.   I know him to be valiant.

Con.   I was told that by one that knows him better than you.

Orl.   What's he?

Con.   Marry, he told me so himself; and he said he cared not who knew.

Orl.   He needs not; it is no hidden virtue in him.

Con.   By my faith, sir, but it is; never anybody saw it but his lackey: 't is a hooded valour; and when it appears, it will bate.

Orl.   Ill will never said well.

Con.   I will cap that proverb with—There is flattery in friendship.

Orl.   And I will take up that with—Give the devil his due.

Con.   Well placed: there stands your friend for the devil: have at the very eye of that proverb with—A pox of the devil.

Orl.   You are the better at proverbs, by how much—A fool's bolt is soon shot.

Con.   You have shot over.

Orl.   'T is not the first time you were overshot.

Enter a Messenger

Mess.   My lord high constable, the English lie within fifteen hundred paces of your tents.

Con.   Who hath measured the ground?

Mess.   The Lord Grandpré.

Con.   A valiant and most expert gentleman.—Would it were day!—Alas, poor Harry of England! he longs not for the dawning as we do.

Orl.   What a wretched and peevish fellow is this King of England, to mope with his fat-brained followers so far out of his knowledge!

Con. If the English had any apprehension, they would run away.

Orl. That they lack; for if their heads had any intellectual armour, they could never wear such heavy head-pieces.

Ram. That island of England breeds very valiant creatures; their mastiffs are of unmatchable courage.

Orl. Foolish curs, that run winking into the mouth of a Russian bear and have their heads crushed like rotten apples! You may as well say, that's a valiant flea that dare eat his breakfast on the lip of a lion.

Con. Just, just; and the men do sympathise with the mastiffs in robustious and rough coming-on, leaving their wits with their wives: and then give them great meals of beef, and iron and steel, they will eat like wolves, and fight like devils.

Orl. Ay, but these English are shrewdly out of beef.

Con. Then shall we find to-morrow they have only stomachs to eat and none to fight.—Now is it time to arm; come, shall we about it?

Orl. It is now two o'clock: but, let me see,—by ten We shall have each a hundred Englishmen.   [*Exeunt*

ACT FOUR

Enter Chorus

Chor.   Now entertain conjecture of a time
When creeping murmur and the poring dark
Fills the wide vessel of the universe.
From camp to camp, through the foul womb of night,
The hum of either army stilly sounds,
That the fixed sentinels almost receive.
The secret whispers of each other's watch:
Fire answers fire, and through their paly flames
Each battle sees the other's umbered face:
Steed threatens steed, in high and boastful neigh
Piercing the night's dull ear; and from the tents
The armourers, accomplishing the knights,
With busy hammers closing rivets up,
Give dreadful note of preparation:
The country cocks do crow, the clocks do toll,
And the third hour of drowsy morning name.
Proud of their numbers, and secure in soul,
The confident and over-lusty French
Do the low-rated English play at dice;

And chide the cripple tardy-gaited night
Who, like a foul and ugly witch, doth limp
So tediously away.   The poor condemnéd English.
Like sacrifices, by their watchful fires
Sit patiently and inly ruminate
The morning's danger; and their gesture sad,
Investing lank-lean cheeks and war-worn coats,
Presenteth them unto the gazing moon
So many horrid ghosts.   O, now, who will behold
The royal captain of this ruined band
Walking from watch to watch, from tent to tent,
Let him cry, 'Praise and glory on his head!'
For forth he goes and visits all his host;
Bids them good morrow with a modest smile,
And calls them brothers, friends, and countrymen.
Upon his royal face there is no note
How dread an army hath enrounded him;
Nor doth he dedicate one jot of colour
Unto the weary and all-watchéd night,
But freshly looks, and over-bears attaint
With cheerful semblance and sweet majesty;
That every wretch, pining and pale before,
Beholding him, plucks comfort from his looks:
A largess universal, like the sun,
His liberal eye doth give to every one,
Thawing cold fear, that mean and gentle all
Behold, as may unworthiness define,
A little touch of Harry in the night.
And so our scene must to the battle fly;
Where—O for pity!—we shall much disgrace
With four or five most vile and ragged foils,
Right ill-disposed, in brawl ridiculous,
The name of Agincourt.   Yet, sit and see;
Minding true things by what their mockeries be.   [*Exit*

SCENE I.—The English Camp at Agincourt

Enter KING HENRY, BEDFORD, *and* GLOUCESTER

   K. Hen.   Gloucester, 't is true that we are in great
        danger;
The greater therefore should our courage be.—
Good morrow, brother Bedford.—God Almighty!
There is some soul of goodness in things evil,
Would men observingly distil it out;
For our bad neighbour makes us early stirrers,
Which is both healthful and good husbandry:

Besides, they are our outward consciences,
And preachers to us all; admonishing
That we should dress us fairly for our end.
Thus may we gather honey from the weed,
And make a moral of the devil himself.

Enter ERPINGHAM

Good morrow, old Sir Thomas Erpingham:
A good soft pillow for that good white head
Were better than a churlish turf of France.
   Erp.   Not so, my liege: this lodging likes me better,
Since I may say 'Now lie I like a king.'
   K. Hen.   'T is good for men to love their present pains
Upon example; so the spirit is eased:
And when the mind is quickened, out of doubt,
The organs, though defunct and dead before,
Break up their drowsy grave, and newly move
With casted slough and fresh legerity.
Lend me thy cloak, Sir Thomas.—Brothers both,
Commend me to the princes in our camp;
Do my good morrow to them, and anon
Desire them all to my pavilion.
   Glou.   We shall, my liege.
   Erp.   Shall I attend your grace?
   K. Hen.   No, my good knight:
Go with my brothers to my lords of England:
I and my bosom must debate a while,
And then I would no other company,
   Erp.   The Lord in heaven bless thee, noble Harry!
             [*Exeunt Gloucester, Bedford, and Erpingham*
   K. Hen.   God-a-mercy, old heart! thou speak'st cheer-
      fully.

Enter PISTOL

   Pist.   Qui va là ?
   K. Hen.   A friend.
   Pist.   Discuss unto me; art thou officer?
Or art thou base, common, and popular?
   K. Hen.   I am a gentleman of a company.
   Pist.   Trail'st thou the puissant pike?
   K. Hen.   Even so.   Who are you?
   Pist.   As good a gentleman as the emperor.
   K. Hen.   Then you are a better than the king.
   Pist.   The king's a bawcock, and a heart of gold,
A lad of life, an imp of fame;
Of parents good, of fist most valiant:
I kiss his dirty shoe, and from heart-string
I love the lovely bully.   What is thy name?
   K. Hen.   Harry *le* Roi.

Pist. Le Roy! a Cornish name: art thou of Cornish crew?
K. Hen. No, I am a Welshman.
Pist. Know'st thou Fluellen?
K. Hen. Yes.
Pist. Tell him, I'll knock his leek about his pate Upon Saint Davy's day.
K. Hen. Do not you wear your dagger in your cap that day, lest he knock that about yours.
Pist. Art thou his friend?
K. Hen. And his kinsman too.
Pist. The figo for thee, then!
K. Hen. I thank you: God be with you!
Pist. My name is Pistol called.   [*Exit*
K. Hen. It sorts well with your fierceness.

Enter FLUELLEN *and* GOWER

Gow. Captain Fluellen!—
Flu. So!—in the name of Chesu Christ, speak lower.— It is the greatest admiration in the universal orld, when the true and auncient prerogatifs and laws of the wars is not kept: if you would take the pains but to examine the wars of Pompey the Great, you shall find, I warrant you, that there is no tiddle-taddle or pibble-pabble in Pompey's camp; I warrant you, you shall find the ceremonies of the wars, and the cares of it, and the forms of it, and the sobriety of it, and the modesty of it, to be otherwise.
Gow. Why, the enemy is loud; you hear him all night.
Flu. If the enemy is an ass and a fool and a prating coxcomb, is it meet, think you, that we should also, look you, be an ass and a fool and a prating coxcomb?—in your own conscience, now?
Gow. I will speak lower.
Flu. I pray you and peseech you that you will.
                    [*Exeunt Gower and Fluellen*
K. Hen. Though it appear a little out of fashion, There is much care and valour in this Welshman.

Enter three soldiers, JOHN BATES, ALEXANDER COURT, *and* MICHAEL WILLIAMS

Court. Brother John Bates, is not that the morning which breaks yonder?
Bates. I think it be: but we have no great cause to desire the approach of day.
Will. We see yonder the beginning of the day, but I think we shall never see the end of it.—Who goes there?
K. Hen. A friend.
Will. Under what captain serve you?
K. Hen. Under Sir Thomas Erpingham.

Will. A good old commander and a most kind gentleman: I pray you, what thinks he of our estate?

K. Hen. Even as men wrecked upon a sand, that look to be washed off the next tide.

Bates. He hath not told his thought to the king?

K. Hen. No; nor it is not meet he should. For, though I speak it to you, I think the king is but a man, as I am: the violet smells to him as it doth to me; the element shows to him as it doth to me; all his senses have but human conditions: his ceremonies laid by, in his nakedness he appears but a man; and though his affections are higher mounted than ours, yet, when they stoop, they stoop with the like wing. Therefore when he sees reason of fears, as we do, his fears out of doubt, be of the same relish as ours are: yet, in reason, no man should possess him with any appearance of fear, lest he, by showing it, should dishearten his army.

Bates. He may show what outward courage he will; but I believe, as cold a night as 't is, he could wish himself in Thames up to the neck;—and so I would he were, and I by him, at all adventures, so we were quit here.

K. Hen. By my troth, I will speak my conscience of the king: I think he would not wish himself anywhere but where he is.

Bates. Then I would he were here alone; so should he be sure to be ransomed, and a many poor men's lives saved.

K. Hen. I dare say you love him not so ill, to wish him here alone, howsoever you speak this to feel other men's minds: methinks I could not die anywhere so contented as in the king's company,—his cause being just and his quarrel honourable.

Will. That's more than we know.

Bates. Ay, or more than we should seek after; for we know enough, if we know we are the king's subjects: if his cause be wrong, our obedience to the king wipes the crime of it out of us.

Will. But if the cause be not good, the king himself hath a heavy reckoning to make, when all those legs and arms and heads, chopped off in a battle, shall join together at the latter day, and cry all, 'We died at such a place;' some swearing; some crying for a surgeon; some, upon their wives left poor behind them; some, upon the debts they owe; some, upon their children rawly left. I am afeard there are few die well that die in a battle; for how can they charitably dispose of anything, when blood is their argument? Now, if these men do not die well, it will be a black matter for the king that led them to it; whom to disobey were against all proportion of subjection.

K. Hen. So, if a son that is by his father sent about

merchandise do sinfully miscarry upon the sea, the imputation of his wickedness, by your rule, should be imposed
upon his father that sent him: or if a servant, under his
master's command transporting a sum of money, be
assailed by robbers and die in many irreconciled iniquities,
you may call the business of the master the author of the
servant's damnation;—but this is not so: the king is not
bound to answer the particular endings of his soldiers, the
father of his son, nor the master of his servant; for they
purpose not their death, when they purpose their services.
Besides, there is no king, be his cause never so spotless, if
it come to the arbitrement of swords, can try it out with all
unspotted soldiers: some peradventure have on them the
guilt of premeditated and contrived murder; some, of
beguiling virgins with the broken seals of perjury; some
making the wars their bulwark, that have before gored the
gentle bosom of peace with pillage and robbery. Now,
if these men have defeated the law and outrun native
punishment, though they can outstrip men, they have no
wings to fly from God: war is his beadle, war is his vengeance; so that here men are punished for before-breach
of the king's laws in now the king's quarrel: where they
feared the death, they have borne life away; and where
they would be safe, they perish: then if they die unpro-
vided, no more is the king guilty of their damnation
than he was before guilty of those impieties for the
which they are now visited. Every subject's duty is the
king's; but every subject's soul is his own. Therefore
should every soldier in the wars do as every sick man in
his bed, wash every mote out of his conscience: and dying
so, death is to him advantage; or not dying, the time was
blessedly lost wherein such preparation was gained: and
in him that escapes, it were not sin to think that, making
God so free an offer, He let him outlive that day to see
His greatness, and to teach others how they should
prepare.

Will. 'T is certain, every man that dies ill, the ill is
upon his own head, the king is not to answer it.

Bates. I do not desire he should answer for me; and yet
I determine to fight lustily for him.

K. Hen. I myself heard the king say he would not be
ransomed.

Will. Ay, he said so, to make us fight cheerfully: but
when our throats are cut, he may be ransomed, and we ne'er
the wiser.

K. Hen. If I live to see it, I will never trust his word
after.

Will. 'Mass, you'll pay him then. That's a perilous
shot out of an elder-gun, that a poor and a private displeasure can do against a monarch! you may as well go

about to turn the sun to ice with fanning in his face with
a peacock's feather. You'll never trust his word after!
come, 't is a foolish saying.

K. Hen. Your reproof is something too round: I should
be angry with you, if the time were convenient.

Will. Let it be a quarrel between us if you live.

K. Hen. I embrace it.

Will. How shall I know thee again?

K. Hen. Give me any gage of thine, and I will wear it in
my bonnet: then, if ever thou darest acknowledge it, I
will make it my quarrel.

Will. Here's my glove; give me another of thine.

K. Hen. There.

Will. This will I also wear in my cap: if ever thou
come to me and say, after to-morrow, 'This is my glove,'
by this hand, I will take thee a box on the ear.

K. Hen. If ever I live to see it, I will challenge it.

Will. Thou darest as well be hanged.

K. Hen. Well, I will do it, though I take thee in the
king's company.

Will. Keep thy word: fare thee well.

Bates. Be friends, you English fools, be friends: we
have French quarrels enow, if you could tell how to
reckon.

K. Hen. Indeed, the French may lay twenty French
crowns to one, they will beat us; for they bear them on
their shoulders: but it is no English treason to cut French
crowns; and to-morrow the king himself will be a clipper.

                                              [*Exeunt Soldiers*

Upon the king!—let us our lives, our souls,
Our debts, our careful wives,
Our children, and our sins, lay on the king!
We must bear all. O hard condition,
Twin-born with greatness, subject to the breath
Of every fool, whose sense no more can feel
But his own wringing! What infinite heart's-ease
Must kings neglect, that private men enjoy!
And what have kings, that privates have not too,
Save ceremony,—save general ceremony?
And what art thou, thou idol ceremony?
What kind of god art thou, that suffer'st more
Of mortal griefs than do thy worshippers?
What are thy rents? what are thy comings in?
O ceremony, show me but thy worth!
What is thy soul of adoration?
Art thou aught else but place, degree, and form,
Creating awe and fear in other men?
Wherein thou art less happy being feared
Than they in fearing.
What drink'st thou oft, instead of homage sweet

But poisoned flattery?   O, be sick, great greatness,
And bid thy ceremony give thee cure!
Think'st thou the fiery fever will go out
With titles blown from adulation?
Will it give place to flexure and low bending?
Canst thou, when thou command'st the beggar's knee,
Command the health of it?   No, thou proud dream,
That play'st so subtly with a king's repose:
I am a king that find thee; and I know
'T is not the balm, the sceptre, and the ball,
The sword, the mace, the crown imperial,
The intertissued robe of gold and pearl,
The farcéd title running 'fore the king,
The throne he sits on, nor the tide of pomp
That beats upon the high shore of this world,
No, not all these, thrice-gorgeous ceremony,
Not all these, laid in bed majestical,
Can sleep so soundly as the wretched slave,
Who with a body filled and vacant mind
Gets him to rest, crammed with distressful bread;
Never sees horrid night, the child of hell;
But, like a lackey, from the rise to set
Sweats in the eye of Phœbus, and all night
Sleeps in Elysium; next day, after dawn,
Doth rise and help Hyperion to his horse,
And follows so the ever-running year,
With profitable labour, to his grave:
And, but for ceremony, such a wretch,
Winding up days with toil and nights with sleep,
Had the fore-hand and vantage of a king.
The slave, a member of the country's peace,
Enjoys it; but in gross brain little wots
What watch the king keeps to maintain the peace,
Whose hours the peasant best advantages.

Enter ERPINGHAM

   Erp. My lord, your nobles, jealous of your absence,
Seek through your camp to find you.
   K. Hen.   Good old knight,
Collect them all together at my tent:
I'll be before thee.
   Erp.   I shall do't, my lord.   [*Exit*
   K. Hen. [*Kneeling*]   O God of battles! steel my
        soldiers' hearts;
Possess them not with fear; take from them now
The sense of reckoning, if the opposéd numbers
Pluck their hearts from them!   Not to-day, O Lord,
O, not to-day, think not upon the fault
My father made in compassing the crown!

I Richard's body have interréd new,
And on it have bestowed more contrite tears
Than from it issued forcéd drops of blood;
Five hundred poor I have in yearly pay,
Who twice a-day their withered hands hold up
Toward heaven, to pardon blood; and I have built
Two chantries, where the sad and solemn priests
Sing still for Richard's soul.   More will I do;
Though all that I can do is nothing worth,
Since that my penitence comes after all,
Imploring pardon.

Enter GLOUCESTER

  Glou.   My liege!
  K. Hen.   [*Afoot*]   My brother Gloucester's voice; Ay;
I know thy errand, I will go with thee:
The day, my friends, and all things stay for me.   [*Exeunt*

SCENE II.—The French Camp

Enter the DAUPHIN, ORLEANS, RAMBURES, *and others*

  Orl.   The sun doth gild our armour; up, my lords!
  Dau.   *Montez à cheval!*   My horse! *varlet! laquais!*
     ha!
  Orl.   O brave spirit!
  Dau.   *Via!—les eaux et la terre,—*
  Orl.   *Rein puis? l'air et le feu.*
  Dau.   *Ciel,* cousin Orleans.

Enter CONSTABLE

Now, my lord constable!
  Con.   Hark, how our steeds for present service neigh!
  Dau.   Mount them, and make incision in their hides,
That their hot blood may spin in English eyes,
And dout them with superfluous courage, ha?
  Ram.   What, will you have them weep our horses'
     blood!
How shall we, then, behold their natural tears?

Enter Messenger

  Mess.   The English are embattled, you French peers.
  Con.   To horse, you gallant princes: straight to horse!
Do but behold yon poor and starvéd band,
And your fair show shall suck away their souls,
Leaving them but the shales and husks of men.

There is not work enough for all our hands;
Scarce blood enough in all their sickly veins
To give each naked curtle-axe a stain,
That our French gallants shall to-day draw out,
And sheathe for lack of sport: let us but blow on them,
The vapour of our valour will o'erturn them.
'T is positive 'gainst all exceptions, lords,
That our superfluous lackeys and our peasants,—
Who in unnecessary action swarm
About our squares of battle,—were enow
To purge this field of such a hilding foe:
Though we upon this mountain's basis by
Took stand for idle speculation:
But that our honours must not.   What 's to say?
A very little little let us do,
And all is done.   Then let the trumpet sound
The tucket sonance and the note to mount;
For our approach shall so much dare the field,
That England shall couch down in fear, and yield.

Enter GRANDPRÉ

  Grand.   Why do you stay so long, my lords of France?
Yon island carrions, desperate of their bones,
Ill-favouredly become the morning field:
Their raggéd curtains poorly are let loose,
And our air shakes them passing scornfully:
Big Mars seems bankrupt in their beggared host
And faintly through a rusty beaver peeps:
The horsemen sit like fixéd candlesticks
With torch-staves in their hand; and their poor jades
Lob down their heads, dropping the hides and hips,
The gum down-roping from their pale-dead eyes,
And in their pale dull mouths the gimmal bit
Lies, foul with chewed grass, still and motionless;
And their exécutors, the knavish crows,
Fly o'er them, all impatient for their hour.
Description cannot suit itself in words
To demonstrate the life of such a battle
In life so lifeless as it shows itself.
  Con.   They have said their prayers, and they stay for
      death.
  Dau.   Shall we go send them dinners and fresh suits,
And give their fasting horses provender,
And after fight with them?
  Con.   I stay but for my guidon: to the field!
I will the banner from a trumpet take,
And use it for my haste.   Come, come, away
The sun is high, and we outwear the day.   [*Exeunt*

SCENE III.—The English Camp

Enter the English host ; GLOUCESTER, BEDFORD, EXETER, SALISBURY, *and* WESTMORELAND

Glou.   Where is the king?
Bed.   The king himself is rode to view their battle.
West.   Of fighting men they have full threescore thousand.
Exe.   There's five to one; besides, they all are fresh.
Sal.   God's arm strike with us! 't is a fearful odds.
God b' wi' you, princes all; I'll to my charge:
If we no more meet till we meet in heaven,
Then, joyfully,—my noble Lord of Bedford,—
My dear Lord Gloucester,—and my good Lord Exeter,—
And my kind kinsman,—warriors all, adieu!
Bed.   Farewell, good Salisbury; and good luck go with thee!
Exe.   Farewell, kind lord; fight valiantly to-day:
And yet I do thee wrong to mind thee of it,
For thou art framed of the firm truth of valour.
                                    [*Exit Salisbury*
Bed.   He is as full of valour as of kindness;
Princely in both.

Enter the KING

West.   O that we now had here
But one ten thousand of those men in England
That do no work to-day!
K. Hen.   What's he that wishes so?
My cousin Westmoreland? No, my fair cousin:
If we are marked to die, we are enow
To do our country loss; and if to live,
The fewer men, the greater share of honour.
God's will! I pray thee wish not one man more.
By Jove, I am not covetous for gold,
Nor care I who doth feed upon my cost;
It yearns me not if men my garments wear;
Such outward things dwell not in my desires:
But if it be a sin to covet honour,
I am the most offending soul alive.
No, faith, my coz, wish not a man from England:
God's peace! I would not lose so great an honour
As one man more, methinks, would share from me,
For the best hope I have. O, do not wish one more!
Rather proclaim it, Westmoreland, through my host,
That he which hath no stomach to this fight,
Let him depart; his passport shall be made
And crowns for convoy put into his purse:

We would not die in that man's company
That fears his fellowship to die with us.
This day is called the feast of Crispian:
He that outlives this day, and comes safe home,
Will stand a tip-toe when this day is named,
And rouse him at the name of Crispian.
He that shall live this day, and see old age,
Will yearly on the vigil feast his neighbours,
And say 'To-morrow is Saint Crispian:'
Then will he strip his sleeve and show his scars,
And say 'These wounds I had on Crispin's day.'
Old men forget; yet all shall be forgot,
But he'll remember with advantages
What feats he did that day; then shall our names,
Familiar in his mouth as household words,—
Harry the king, Bedford, and Exeter,
Warwick and Talbot, Salisbury and Gloucester,
Be in their flowing cups freshly remembered.
This story shall the good man teach his son;
And Crispin Crispian shall ne'er go by,
From this day to the ending of the world,
But we in it shall be rememberéd;
We few, we happy few, we band of brothers;
For he to-day that sheds his blood with me
Shall be my brother; be he ne'er so vile,
This day shall gentle his condition:
And gentlemen in England now a-bed
Shall think themselves accursed they were not here,
And hold their manhoods cheap whiles any speaks
That fought with us upon Saint Crispin's day.

Re-enter SALISBURY

Sal.   My sovereign lord, bestow yourself with speed:
The French are bravely in their battles set,
And will with all expedience charge on us.
   K. Hen.   All things are ready, if our minds be so.
   West.   Perish the man whose mind is backward now!
   K. Hen.   Thou dost not wish more help from England,
      coz?
   West.   God's will! my liege, would you and I alone,
Without more help, could fight this battle out!
   K. Hen.   Why, now thou hast unwished five thousand
      men;
Which likes me better than to wish us one.—
You know your places: God be with you all!

Tucket.   Enter MONTJOY

   Mont.   Once more I come to know of thee, King Harry,
If for thy ransom thou wilt now compound,

Before thy most assuréd overthrow:
For certainly thou art so near the gulf
Thou needs must be englutted.   Besides, in mercy,
The constable desires thee thou wilt mind
Thy followers of repentance; that their souls
May make a peaceful and a sweet retire
From off these fields, where, wretches, their poor bodies
Must lie and fester.
 K. Hen.   Who hath sent thee now?
 Mont. The Constable of France.
 K. Hen. I pray thee, bear my former answer back:
Bid them achieve me, and then sell my bones.
Good God! why should they mock poor fellows thus?
The man that once did sell the lion's skin
While the beast lived, was killed with hunting him.
A many of our bodies shall no doubt
Find native graves; upon the which, I trust,
Shall witness live in brass of this day's work:
And those that leave their valiant bones in France,
Dying like men, though buried in your dunghills,
They shall be famed; for there the sun shall greet them,
And draw their honours reeking up to heaven;
Leaving their earthly parts to choke your clime,
The smell whereof shall breed a plague in France.
Mark, then, abounding valour in our English,
That being dead, like to the bullet's grazing,
Break out into a second course of mischief,
Killing in rélapse of mortality.
Let me speak proudly:—tell the constable
We are but warriors for the working-day;
Our gayness and our gilt are all besmirched
With rainy marching in the painful field;
There's not a piece of feather in our host—
Good argument, I hope, we will not fly—
And time hath worn us into slovenry:
But, by the mass, our hearts are in the trim;
And my poor soldiers tell me, yet ere night
They'll be in fresher robes, or they will pluck
The gay new coats o'er the French soldiers' heads
And turn them out of service.   If they do this,—
As, if God please, they shall,—my ransom then
Will soon be levied.   Herald, save thou thy labour;
Come thou no more for ransom, gentle herald:
They shall have none, I swear, but these my joints,—
Which if they have as I will leave 'em them,
Shall yield them little, tell the constable.
 Mont. I shall, King Harry.   And so, fare thee well:
Thou never shalt hear herald any more.   [*Exit*
 K. Hen. I fear thou'lt once more come again for
  ransom.

Enter YORK

York. My lord, most humbly on my knee I beg
The leading of the vaward.
  K. Hen. Take it, brave York. Now, soldiers, march
                    away:
And how thou pleasest, God, dispose the day!   [*Exeunt*

SCENE IV.—The Field of Battle

Alarum. Excursions. Enter PISTOL, *French Soldier,
                    and Boy*

Pist. Yield, cur!
Fr. Sol. *Je pense que vou êtes le gentilhomme de bonne
qualité.*
Pist. Quality? Cality? Conster me. Art thou a
gentleman? what is thy name? discuss.
Fr. Sol. *O Seigneur Dieu!*
Pist. O, Signieur Dew should be a gentleman:
Perpend my words, O Signieur Dew, and mark;
O Signieur Dew, thou diest on point of fox,
Except, O signieur, thou do give to me
Egregious ransom.
Fr. Sol. *O, prenez miséricorde! ayez pitié de moi!*
Pist. Moy shall not serve; I will have forty moys;
Or I will fetch thy rim out at thy throat
In drops of crimson blood.
Fr. Sol. *Est-il impossible d'échapper la force de ton
bras?*
Pist. Brass, cur!
Thou damnéd and luxurious mountain goat,
Offer'st me brass?
Fr. Sol. *O pardonnez moi!*
Pist. Say'st thou me so? is that a ton of moys?
Come hither, boy: ask me this slave in French
What is his name.
Boy. *Écoutez: comment êtes-vous appelé?*
Fr. Sol. *Monsieur le Fer.*
Boy. He says his name is Master Fer.
Pist. Master Fer! I'll fer him, and firk him, and
ferret him: discuss the same in French unto him.
Boy. I do not know the French for fer, and ferret, and
firk.
Pist. Bid him prepare; for I will cut his throat.
Fr. Sol. *Que dit-il, monsieur?*
Boy. *Il me commande de vous dire que vous faites vous
prêt; car ce soldat ici est disposé tout à cette heure de couper
votre gorge.*

Pist.   Owy, cuppele gorge, permafoy,
Peasant, unless thou give me crowns, brave crowns;
Or mangled shalt thou be by this my sword.

Fr. Sol.   *O, je vous supplie, pour l'amour de Dieu, me pardonner ! Je suis gentilhomme de bonne maison : gardez, ma vie, et je vous donnerai deux cents écus.*

Pist.   What are his words?

Boy.   He prays you to save his life; he is a gentleman of a good house; and for his ransom he will give you two hundred crowns.

Pist.   Tell him my fury shall abate, and I
The crowns will take.

Fr. Sol.   *Petit monsieur, que dit-il ?*

Boy.   *Encore qu'il est contre son jurement de pardonner aucun prisonnier, néanmoins, pour les écus que vous l'avez promis, il est content de vous donner la liberté, le franchisement.*

Fr. Sol.   *Sur mes genoux je vous donne mille remercimens ; et je m'estime heureux que je suis tombé entre les mains d'un chevalier, je pense, le plus brave, vaillant, et très distingué seigneur d'Angleterre.*

Pist.   Expound unto me, boy.

Boy.   He gives you, upon his knees, a thousand thanks; and he esteems himself happy that he hath fallen into the hands of one, as he thinks, the most brave, valorous, and thrice-worthy signieur of England.

Pist.   As I suck blood, I will some mercy show.   Follow me!

Boy.   *Suivez-vous le grand capitaine.* [*Exeunt Pistol, and French Soldier*]   I did never know so full a voice issue from so empty a heart: but the saying is true, 'The empty vessel makes the greatest sound.'   Bardolph and Nym had ten times more valour than this roaring devil i' the old play, that every one may pare his nails with a wooden dagger; and they are both hanged; and so would this be, if he durst steal anything adventurously.   I must stay with the lackeys, with the luggage of our camp: the French might have a good prey of us, if he knew of it; for there is none to guard it but boys.

[*Exit*

SCENE V.—Another part of the Field

Enter CONSTABLE, ORLEANS, BOURBON, DAUPHIN,
RAMBURES, *and others*

Con.   *O Diable !*
Orl.   *O Seigneur !— le jour est perdu, tout est perdu !*
Dau.   *Mort de ma vie !* all is confounded, all!

213

Reproach and everlasting shame
Sit mocking in our plumes.   *O méchante fortune !*—
Do not run away.   [*A short alarum*
   Con.   Why, all our ranks are broke.
   Dau.   O perdurable shame!—let's stab ourselves.
Be these the wretches that we played at dice for?
   Orl.   Is this the king we sent to for his ransom?
   Bour.   Shame and eternal shame, nothing but shame!
Let's die in honour: once more back again:
And he that will not follow Bourbon now,
Let him go hence, and with his cap in hand,
Like a base pandar, hold the chamber-door
Whilst by a slave, no gentler than my dog,
His fairest daughter is contaminate.
   Con.   Disorder that has spoiled us, friend us now!
Let us on heaps go offer up our lives.
   Orl.   We are enow yet living in the field
To smother up the English in our throngs,
If any order might be thought upon.
   Bour.   The devil take order now!   I'll to the throng:
Let life be short; else shame will be too long.   [*Exeunt*

SCENE VI.—Another part of the Field

Alarums.   Enter KING HENRY *and forces,* EXETER,
and others

   K. Hen.   Well have we done, thrice valiant countrymen:
But all's not done; yet keep the French the field.
   Exe.   The Duke of York commends him to your majesty.
   K. Hen.   Lives he, good uncle? thrice within this hour
I saw him down; thrice up again, and fighting;
From helmet to the spur all blood he was.
   Exe.   In which array, brave soldier, doth he lie,
Larding the plain; and by his bloody side,
Yoke-fellow to his honour-owing wounds,
The noble Earl of Suffolk also lies.
Suffolk first died: and York, all haggled over,
Comes to him, where in gore he lay insteeped,
And takes him by the beard; kisses the gashes
That bloodily did yawn upon his face;
And cries aloud, 'Tarry, dear cousin Suffolk!
My soul shall thine keep company to heaven;
Tarry, sweet soul, for mine, then fly abreast,
As in this glorious and well-foughten field
We kept together in our chivalry!'
Upon these words I came and cheered him up:
He smiled me in the face, raught me his hand,

And, with a feeble gripe, says 'Dear my lord,
Commend my service to my sovereign.'
So did he turn and over Suffolk's neck
He threw his wounded arm and kissed his lips:
And so espoused to death, with blood he sealed
A testament of noble-ending love.
The pretty and sweet manner of it forced
Those waters from me which I would have stopped;
But I had not so much of man in me,
And all my mother came into mine eyes
And gave me up to tears.
    K. Hen.   I blame you not;
For hearing this, I must perforce compound
With mistful eyes, or they will issue too.—   [*Alarum*
But, hark! what new alarum is this same?—
The French have reinforced their scattered men:—
Then every soldier kill his prisoners;
Give the word through.   [*Exeunt*

SCENE VII.—Another part of the Field

Enter FLUELLEN *and* GOWER

    Flu. Kill the poys and the luggage! 't is expressly against the law of arms: 't is as arrant a piece of knavery, mark you now, as can be offert; in your conscience, now, is it not?
    Gow. 'T is certain there's not a boy left alive; and the cowardly rascals that ran from the battle ha' done this slaughter: besides, they have burned and carried away all that was in the king's tent; wherefore the king, most worthily, hath caused every soldier to cut his prisoner's throat. O, 't is a gallant king!
    Flu. Ay, he was porn at Monmouth, Captain Gower. What call you the town's name where Alexander the Pig was porn?
    Gow. Alexander the Great.
    Flu. Why, I pray you, is not pig great? the pig, or the great, or the mighty, or the huge, or the magnanimous, are all one reckonings, save the phrase is a little variations.
    Gow. I think Alexander the Great was born in Macedon: his father was called Philip of Macedon, as I take it.
    Flu. I think it is in Macedon where Alexander is porn. I tell you, captain, if you look in the maps of the 'orld, I warrant you shall find, in the comparisons between Macedon and Monmouth, that the situations, look you, is both alike. There is a river in Macedon; and there is also moreover a

river at Monmouth: it is called Wye at Monmouth: but
it is out of my prains what is the name of the other river;
but 't is all one, 't is alike as my fingers is to my fingers,
and there is salmons in both.   If you mark Alexander's life
well, Harry of Monmouth's life is come after it indifferent
well; for there is figures in all things.   Alexander,—Got
knows, and you know,—in his rages, and his furies, and his
wraths, and his cholers, and his moods, and his displeasures,
and his indignations, and also being a little intoxicates in
his prains, did, in his ales and his angers, look you, kill his
pest friend, Cleitus.

Gow.   Our king is not like him in that: he never killed
any of his friends.

Flu.   It is not well done, mark you now, to take the tales
out of my mouth, ere it is made and finished.   I speak but
in the figures and comparisons of it: as Alexander killed
his friend Cleitus, being in his ales and his cups; so also
Harry Monmouth, being in his right wits and his good
judgments, turned away the fat knight with the great pelly-
doublet: he was full of jests, and gipes, and knaveries, and
mocks: I have forgot his name.

Gow.   Sir John Falstaff.

Flu.   That is he: I'll tell you there is goot men porn at
Monmouth.

Gow.   Here comes his majesty.

Alarum.   Enter KING HENRY, *with a part of the English
forces ;* WARWICK, GLOUCESTER, EXETER, *and others*

K. Hen.   I was not angry since I came to France
Until this instant.   Take a trumpet, herald;
Ride thou unto the horsemen on yond hill;
If they will fight with us, bid them come down,
Or void the field; they do offend our sight:
If they'll do neither, we will come to them,
And make them skirr away, as swift as stones
Enforcéd from the old Assyrian slings:
Besides, we'll cut the throats of those we have
And not a man of them that we shall take
Shall taste our mercy:—Go, and tell them so.

Exe.   Here comes the herald of the French, my liege.

Glo.   His eyes are humbler than they used to be.

Enter MONTJOY

K. Hen.   How now! what means this, herald? know'st
        thou not
That I have fined these bones of mine for ransom?
Com'st thou again for ransom?

Mont.   No, great king:

216

I come to thee for charitable license,
That we may wander o'er this bloody field
To book our dead, and then to bury them;
To sort our nobles from our common men.
For many of our princes—woe the while!—
Lie drowned and soaked in mercenary blood;
So do our vulgar drench their peasant limbs
In blood of princes; and their wounded steeds
Fret fetlock deep in gore and with wild rage
Yerk out their arméd heels at their dead masters,
Killing them twice. O, give us leave, great king,
To view the field in safety and dispose
Of their dead bodies!
   K. Hen.   I tell thee truly, herald,
I know not if the day be ours or no;
For yet a many of your horsemen peer
And gallop o'er the field.
   Mont.   The days is yours.
   K. Hen.   Praiséd be God, and not our strength, for it!
What is this castle called that stands hard by?
   Mont.   They call it Agincourt.
   K. Hen.   Then call we this the field of Agincourt,
Fought on the day of Crispin Crispianus.
   Flu.   Your grandfather of famous memory, an't please
your majesty, and your great-uncle Edward the Black
Prince of Wales, as I have read in the chronicles, fought a
most prave pattle here in France.
   K. Hen.   They did, Fluellen.
   Flu.   Your majesty says very true: if your majesties
is remembered of it, the Welshmen did goot service in a
garden where leeks did grow, wearing leeks in their Monmouth caps; which, your majesty knows, to this hour is
an honourable badge of the service; and I do believe your
majesty takes no scorn to wear the leek upon Saint Tavy's
day.
   K. Hen.   I wear it for a memorable honour;
For I am Welsh, you know, good countryman.
   Flu.   All the waters in the Wye cannot wash your
majesty's Welsh plood out of your pody, I can tell you
that: Got pless it and preserve it, as long as it pleases his
grace, and his majesty too!
   K. Hen.   Thanks, good my countryman.
   Flu.   By Cheshu, I am your majesty's countryman, I
care not who know it; I will confess it to all the 'orld: I
need not to be ashamed of your majesty, praised be Got,
so long as your majesty is an honest man.
   K. Hen.   God keep me so!—Our heralds go with him:
Bring me just notice of the numbers dead
On both our parts.—Call yonder fellow hither.
       [Points to Williams. Exeunt Heralds with Montjoy

Exe. Soldier, you must come to the king.

K. Hen. Soldier, why wearest thou that glove in thy cap?

Will. An't please your majesty, 't is the gage of one that I should fight withal, if he be alive.

K. Hen. An Englishman?

Will. An't please your majesty, a rascal that swaggered with me last night; who, if alive and ever dare to challenge this glove, I have sworn to take him a box o' th' ear: or if I can see my glove in his cap, which he swore, as he was a soldier, he would wear if alive, I will strike it out soundly.

K. Hen. What think you, Captain Fluellen? is it fit this soldier keep his oath?

Flu. He is a craven and a villain else, an't please your majesty, in my conscience.

K. Hen. It may be his enemy is a gentleman of great sort, quite from the answer of his degree.

Flu. Though he be as goot a gentleman as the tevil is, as Lucifer and Belzepup himself, it is necessary, look your grace, that he keep his vow and his oath: if he be perjured, see you now, his reputation is as arrant a villain and a Jacksauce as ever his plack shoe trod upon Got's ground and his earth, in my conscience, la!

K. Hen. Then keep thy vow, sirrah, when thou meetest the fellow.

Will. So I will, my liege, as I live.

K. Hen. Who servest thou under?

Will. Under Captain Gower, my liege.

Flu. Gower is a goot captain, and is goot knowledge and literatured in the wars.

K. Hen. Call him hither to me, soldier.

Will. I will, my liege.   [*Exit*

K. Hen. Here, Fluellen; wear thou this favour for me, and stick it in thy cap; when Alençon and myself were down together, I plucked this glove from his helm: if any man challenge this, he is a friend to Alençon, and an enemy to our person; if thou encounter any such, apprehend him, an thou dost love me.

Flu. Your grace does me as great honours as can be desired in the hearts of his subjects: I would fain see the man, that has but two legs, that shall find himself aggriefed at this glove, that is all; but I would fain see it once, an please Got of his grace that I might see.

K. Hen. Knowest thou Gower?

Flu. He is my dear friend, an please you.

K. Hen. Pray thee, go seek him, and bring him to my tent.

Flu. I will fetch him.   [*Exit*

K. Hen. My Lord of Warwick, and my brother Gloucester,

Follow Fluellen closely at the heels:
The glove which I have given him for a favour
May haply purchase him a box o' th' ear;
It is the soldier's; I, by bargain, should
Wear it myself. Follow, good cousin Warwick:
If that the soldier strike him,—as I judge
By his blunt bearing he will keep his word,—
Some sudden mischief may arise of it;
For I do know Fluellen, valiant
And, touched with choler, hot as gunpowder,
And quickly will return an injury:
Follow, and see there be no harm between them.—
Go you with me, uncle of Exeter.   [*Exeunt*

SCENE VIII.—*Before* KING HENRY'S *pavilion*

Enter GOWER *and* WILLIAMS

Will.   I warrant it is to knight you, captain.

Enter FLUELLEN

Flu.   Got's will and his pleasure, captain, I peseech you now, come apace to the king: there is more good toward you peradventure than is in your knowledge to dream of.
Will.   Sir, know you this glove?
Flu.   Know the glove! I know the glove is a glove.
Will.   I know this; and thus I challenge it.
[*Strikes him*
Flu.   'Splood! an arrant traitor as any is in the universal 'orld, or in France, or in England!
Gow.   How now, sir! you villain!
Will.   Do you think I'll be forsworn?
Flu.   Stand away, Captain Gower; I will give treason his payment into plows, I warrant you.
Will.   I am no traitor.
Flu.   That's a lie in thy throat.—I charge you in his majesty's name, apprehend him: he's a friend of the Duke Alençon's.

Enter WARWICK *and* GLOUCESTER

War.   How now, how now! what's the matter?
Flu.   My Lord of Warwick, here is—praised be Got for it!—a most contagious treason come to light, look you, as you shall desire in a summer's day.—Here is his majesty.

Enter KING HENRY *and* EXETER

K. Hen.   How now! what's the matter?
Flu.   My liege, here is a villain and a traitor, that, look

your grace, has struck the glove which your majesty is take
out of the helmet of Alençon.

Will. My liege, this was my glove; here is the fellow
of it; and he that I gave it to in change promised to wear
it in his cap: I promised to strike him, if he did: I met
this man with my glove in his cap, and I have been as good
as my word.

Flu. Your majesty hear now, saving your majesty's
manhood, what an arrant, rascally, beggarly, lousy knave
it is: I hope your majesty is pear me testimony and witness,
and will avouchment, that this is the glove of Alençon,
that your majesty is give me; in your conscience, now.

K. Hen. Give me thy glove, soldier: look, here is the
fellow of it.
'T was I, indeed, thou promised'st to strike;
And thou hast given me most bitter terms.

Flu. And please your majesty, let his neck answer for
it, if there is any martial law in the 'orld.

K. Hen. How canst thou make me satisfaction?

Will. All offences, my liege, come from the heart:
never come any from mine that might offend your majesty.

K. Hen. It was ourself thou didst abuse.

Will. Your majesty came not like yourself: you
appeared to me but as a common man; witness the night,
your garment, your lowliness; and what your highness
suffered under that shape, I beseech you take it for your
own fault, and not mine; for had you been as I took you
for, I made no offence; therefore, I beseech your highness,
pardon me.

K. Hen. Here, uncle Exeter, fill this glove with crowns,
And give it to this fellow.—Keep it, fellow;
And wear it for an honour in thy cap
Till I do challenge it.—Give him the crowns:—
And, captain, you must needs be friends with him.

Flu. By this day and this light, the fellow has mettle
enough in his pelly. Hold, there is twelve pence for you;
and I pray you to serve Got, and keep you out of prawls,
and prabbles, and quarrels, and dissensions, and, I warrant
you, it is the petter for you.

Will. I will none of your money.

Flu. It is with a goot will; I can tell you, it will serve
you to mend your shoes: come, wherefore should you be
so pashful? your shoes is not so goot: 't is a good silling,
I warrant you, or I will change it.

Enter an English Herald

K. Hen. Now, herald,—are the dead numbered?
Her. Here is the number of the slaughtered French.
[*Delivers a paper*

K. Hen. What prisoners of good sort are taken, uncle?

Exe. Charles Duke of Orleans, nephew to the king;
John Duke of Bourbon, and Lord Bouciqualt:
Of other lords and barons, knights and squires,
Full fifteen hundred, besides common men.

K. Hen. This note doth tell me of ten thousand French
That in the field lie slain; of princes, in this number,
And nobles bearing banners, there lie dead
One hundred twenty-six: added to these,
Of knights, esquires, and gallant gentlemen,
Eight thousand and four hundred; of the which,
Five hundred were but yesterday dubbed knights:
So that, in these ten thousand they have lost,
There are but sixteen hundred mercenaries;
The rest are princes, barons, lords, knights, squires,
And gentlemen of blood and quality.
The names of those their nobles that lie dead:
Charles Delabret, high constable of France;
Jacques of Chatillon, admiral of France;
The master of the cross-bows, Lord Rambures;
Great master of France, the brave Sir Guiscard Dauphin;
John Duke of Alençon; Anthony Duke of Brabant,
The brother to the Duke of Burgundy;
And Edward Duke of Bar: of lusty earls,
Grandpré and Roussi, Fauconberg and Foix,
Beaumont and Marle, Vaudemont and Lestrale.
Here was a royal fellowship of death!
Where is the number of our English dead!
                              [*Herald presents another paper*
Edward the Duke of York, the Earl of Suffolk,
Sir Richard Ketly, Davy Gam, esquire;
None else of name; and of all other men
But five and twenty.—O God, thy arm was here;
And not to us, but to thy arm alone,
Ascribe we all!—When, without stratagem,
But in plain shock and even play of battle,
Was ever known so great and little loss
On one part and on the other?   Take it, God,
For it is only thine!

Exe.   'T is wonderful!

K. Hen. Come, go we in procession to the village:
And be it death proclaiméd through our host
To boast of this, or take that praise from God
Which is his only.

Flu. Is it not lawful, an please your majesty, to tell how many is killed?

K. Hen. Yes, captain; but with this acknowledgment
That God fought for us.

Flu. Yes, my conscience, he did us great goot.

K. Hen. Do we all holy rites:
Let there be sung *Non Nobis* and *Te Deum*.
The dead with charity enclosed in clay,
We'll then to Calais; and to England then;
Where ne'er from France arrived more happy men.

[*Exeunt*

ACT FIVE

Enter Chorus

Chor. Vouchsafe to those that have not read the story,
That I may prompt them: and of such as have,
I humbly pray them to admit the excuse
Of time, of numbers, and due course of things,
Which cannot in their huge and proper life
Be here presented. Now we bear the king
Toward Calais: grant him there; there seen,
Heave him away upon your wingéd thoughts
Athwart the sea. Behold, the English beach
Pales in the flood with men, with wives, and boys,
Whose shouts and claps out-voice the deep-mouthed sea,
Which like a mighty whiffler 'fore the king
Seems to prepare his way: so let him land,
And solemnly see him set on to London.
So swift a pace have thought, that even now
You may imagine him upon Blackheath;
Where that his lords desire him to have borne
His bruiséd helmet and his bended sword
Before him through the city: he forbids it,
Being free from vainness and self-glorious pride;
Giving full trophy, signal, and ostent
Quite from himself to God. But now behold,
In the quick forge and working-house of thought,
How London doth pour out her citizens!
The mayor, and all his brethren, in best sort,—
Like to the senators of th' antique Rome,
With the plebeians swarming at their heels,—
Go forth and fetch their conquering Cæsar in:
As, by a lower but loving likelihood,
Were now the general of our gracious empress,
As in good time he may, from Ireland coming,
Bringing rebellion broachéd on his sword,
How many would the peaceful city quit,
To welcome him! much more, and much more cause,
Did they this Harry. Now in London place him;—
As yet the lamentation of the French
Invites the King of England's stay at home;

The emperor's coming in behalf of France
To order peace between them, and omit
All the occurrences, whatever chanced,
Till Harry's back-return again to France
There must we bring him; and myself have played
The interim, by remembering you—'t is past.
Then brook abridgment, and your eyes advance,
After your thoughts, straight back again to France.   [*Exit*

SCENE I.—France.   An English Court of Guard

Enter FLUELLEN *and* GOWER

  Gow.   Nay, that's right; but why wear you your leek
to-day?   Saint Davy's day is past.
  Flu.   There is occasions and causes why and wherefore
in all things: I will tell you, as my friend, Captain Gower:
—the rascally, scald, beggarly, lousy, pragging knave,
Pistol,—which you and yourself and all the 'orld know to
be no petter than a fellow, look you now, of no merits,—
he is come to me and prings me pread and salt yesterday,
look you, and pid me eat my leek: it was in a place
where I could not preed no contention with him;
but I will be so pold as to wear it in my cap till I see
him once again, and then I will tell him a little piece of
my desires.
  Gow.   Why, here he comes, swelling like a turkey-cock.
  Flu.   'T is no matter for his swellings nor his turkey-
            cocks.

Enter PISTOL

Got pless you, Auncient Pistol! you scurvy, lousy knave,
Got pless you!
  Pist.   Ha! art thou bedlam? dost thou thirst, base
            Trojan,
To have me fold up Parca's fatal web?
Hence!   I am qualmish at the smell of leek.
  Flu.   I peseech you heartily, scurvy, lousy knave, at
my desires, and my requests, and my petitions, to eat,
look you, this leek: because, look you, you do not love
it, nor your affections and your appetites and your dis-
gestions doo's not agree with it, I would desire you to
eat it.
  Pist.   Not for Cadwallader and all his goats.
  Flu.   There is one goat for you. [*Strikes him*] Will
you be so goot, scald knave, as eat it?
  Pist.   Base Trojan, thou shalt die.

Flu. You say very true, scald knave, when Got's will is: I will desire you to live in the meantime, and eat your victuals: come, there is sauce for it. [*Strikes him*] You called me yesterday mountain-squire; but I will make you to-day a squire of low degree. I pray you, fall to: if you can mock a leek, you can eat a leek.

Gow. Enough, captain: you have astonished him.

Flu. I say, I will make him eat some part of my leek, or I will peat his pate four days.—Pite, I pray you; it is goot for your green wound and your ploody coxcomb.

Pis. Must I bite?

Flu. Yes, certainly, and out of doubt and out of question too, and ambiguities.

Pist. By this leek I'll most horribly revenge:
I eat and eat, I swear—

Flu. Eat, I pray you: will you have some more sauce to your leek? there is not enough leek to swear by.

Pist. Quiet thy cudgel; thou dost see I eat.

Flu. Much goot do you, scald knave, heartily. Nay, pray you, throw none away; the skin is goot for your proken coxcomb. When you take occasions to see leeks hereafter, I pray you, mock at 'em; that is all.

Pist. Good.

Flu. Ay, leeks is goot:—hold you, there is a groat to heal your pate.

Pist. Me a groat!

Flu. Yes, verily, and in truth, you shall take it; or I have another leek in my pocket, which you shall eat.

Pist. I take thy groat in earnest of revenge.

Flu. If I owe you anything, I will pay you in cudgels: you shall be a woodmonger, and buy nothing of me but cudgels. God b' wi' you, and keep you, and heal your pate. [*Exit*

Pist. All hell shall stir for this.

Gow. Go, go; you are a counterfeit cowardly knave. Will you mock at an ancient tradition,—begun upon an honourable respect, and worn as a memorable trophy of predeceased valour,—and dare not avouch in your deeds any of your words? I have seen you gleeking and galling at this gentleman twice or thrice. You thought, because he could not speak English in the native garb, he could not therefore handle an English cudgel: you find it otherwise; and henceforth let a Welsh correction teach you a good English condition. Fare ye well. [*Exit*

Pist. Doth Fortune play the huswife with me now?
News have I, that my Nell is dead i' the spital
Of malady of France;
And there my rendezvous is quite cut off.
Old I do wax; and from my weary limbs.

Honour is cudgelled.   Well, bawd will I turn,
And something lean to cutpurse of quick hand.
To England will I steal, and there I'll steal:
And patches will I get unto these scars,
And swear I got them in the Gallia wars.   [*Exit*

SCENE II.—Troyes in Champagne.   A Room in the French
King's Palace

Enter at one door, KING HENRY, EXETER, BEDFORD, GLOU-
CESTER, WARWICK, WESTMORELAND, *and other Lords ;
at another, the* FRENCH KING, QUEEN ISABEL, *the*
PRINCESS KATHARINE, ALICE. *and other ladies ; the*
DUKE OF BURGUNDY, *and his train*

K. Hen.   Peace to this meeting, wherefore we are met!
Unto our brother France, and to our sister,
Health and fair time of day;—joy and good wishes
To our most fair and princely cousin Katharine;—
And, as a branch and member of this royalty,
By whom this great assembly is contrived,
We do salute you, Duke of Burgundy;—
And, princes French, and peers, health to you all!
   Fr. King.   Right joyous are we to behold your face,
Most worthy brother England; fairly met:—
So are you, princes English, every one.
   Q. Isa.   So happy be the issue, brother England,
Of this good day and of this gracious meeting,
As we are now glad to behold your eyes;
Your eyes, which hitherto have borne in them
Against the French that met them in their bent
The fatal balls of murdering basilisks:
The venom of such looks, we fairly hope,
Have lost their quality, and that this day
Shall change all griefs and quarrels into love.
   K. Hen.   To cry amen to that, thus we appear.
   Q. Isa.   You English princes all, I do salute you.
   Bur.   My duty to you both, on equal love,
Great Kings of France and England!   That I have
         laboured,
With all my wits, my pains and strong endeavours
To bring your most imperial majesties
Unto this bar and royal interview,
Your mightiness' on both parts best can witness.
Since then my office hath so far prevailed
That, face to face and royal eye to eye,
You have congreeted, let it not disgrace me.

If I demand, before this royal view,
What rub or what impediment there is,
Why that the naked, poor and mangled Peace,
Dear nurse of arts, plenty, and joyful births,
Should not in this best garden of the world,
Our fertile France, put up her lovely visage?
Alas, she hath from France too long been chased,
And all her husbandry doth lie on heaps,
Corrupting in it own fertility.
Her vine, the merry cheerer of the heart,
Unprunéd dies; her hedges even-pleached,
Like prisoners wildly overgrown with hair,
Put forth disordered twigs; her fallow leas
The darnel, hemlock, and rank fumitory
Do root upon, while that the coulter rusts
That should deracinate such savagery;
The even mead, that erst brought sweetly forth
The freckled cowslip, burnet, and green clover,
Wanting the scythe, all uncorrected, rank,
Conceives by idleness, and nothing teems
But hateful docks, rough thistles, kecksies, burs,
Losing both beauty and utility.
And as our vineyards, fallows, meads, and hedges,
Defective in their natures, grow to wildness,
Even so our houses, and ourselves and children,
Have lost, or do not learn for want of time,
The sciences that should become our country;
But grow, like savages,—as soldiers will
That nothing do but meditate on blood,—
To swearing, and stern looks, diffused attire,
And everything that seems unnatural.
Which to reduce into our former favour,
You are assembled: and my speech entreats
That I may know the let, why gentle Peace
Should not expel these inconveniences
And bless us with her former qualities.
    K. Hen.   If, Duke of Burgundy, you would the peace,
Whose want gives growth to the imperfections
Which you have cited, you must buy that peace
With full accord to all our just demands;
Whose tenours and particular effects
You have, enscheduled briefly, in your hands.
    Bur.   The king hath heard them; to the which **as yet**
There is no answer made.
    K. Hen.   Well, then, the peace,
Which you before so urged, lies in his answer.
    Fr. King.   I have but with a cursorary eye
O'erglancéd the articles: pleaseth your grace
To appoint some of your council presently
To sit with us once more, with better heed

To re-survey them, we will suddenly
Pass our accept and peremptory answer.
    K. Hen.   Brother, we shall.—Go, uncle Exeter,—
And brother Clarence,—and you, brother Gloucester,—
Warwick,—and Huntingdon,—go with the king;
And take with you free power to ratify,
Augment, or alter, as your wisdoms best
Shall see advantageable for our dignity,
Anything in or out of our demands;
And we'll consign thereto.   Will you, fair sister,
Go with the princes, or stay with us?
    Q. Isa.   Our gracious brother, I will go with them:
Haply a woman's voice may do some good,
When articles too nicely urged be stood on.
    K. Hen.   Yet leave our cousin Katharine here with us:
She is our capital demand, comprised
Within the fore-rank of our articles.
    Q. Isa.   She hath good leave.
                   [*Exeunt all except Henry, Katharine, and Alice*
    K. Hen.   Fair Katharine, and most fair,
Will you vouchsafe to teach a soldier terms
Such as will enter at a lady's ear
And plead his love-suit to her gentle heart?
    Kath.   Your majesty shall mock at me; I cannot speak
your England.
    K. Hen.   O fair Katharine, if you will love me soundly
with your French heart, I will be glad to hear you confess
it brokenly with your English tongue.   Do you like me,
Kate?
    Kath.   *Pardonnez-moi*, I cannot tell vat is 'like me.'
    K. Hen.   An angel is like you, Kate, and you are like an
angel.
    Kath.   *Que dit-il? que je suis semblable à les anges?*
    Alice.   *Oui vraiment, sauf votre grace, ainsi dit-il.*
    K. Hen.   I said so, dear Katharine; and I must not
blush to affirm it.
    Kath.   *O bon Dieu ! les langues des hommes sont pleines
de tromperies.*
    K. Hen.   What says she, fair one? that the tongues of
men are full of deceits?
    Alice.   Oui, dat de tongues of de mans is be full of
deceits: dat is de princess.
    K. Hen.   The princess is the better English-woman.   I'
faith, Kate, my wooing is fit for thy understanding: I am
glad thou canst speak no better English; for, if thou
couldst, thou wouldst find me such a plain king that thou
wouldst think I had sold my farm to buy my crown.   I
know no ways to mince it in love, but directly to say 'I
love you:' then if you urge me farther than to say 'do
you in faith?' I wear out my suit.   Give me your answer;

i' faith, do; and so clap hands and a bargain: how say
you, lady?

Kath. *Sauf votre honneur*, me understand well.

K. Hen. Marry, if you would put me to verses or to
dance for your sake, Kate, why you undid me: for the one,
I have neither words nor measure, and for the other, I have
no strength in measure, yet a reasonable measure in strength.
If I could win a lady at leap-frog, or by vaulting into my
saddle with my armour on my back, under the correction
of bragging be it spoken, I should quickly leap into a
wife. Or if I might buffet for my love, or bound my horse
for her favours, I could lay on like a butcher, and sit like a
jack-an-apes, never off. But, before God, Kate, I cannot
look greenly, nor gasp out my eloquence, nor I have no
cunning in protestation; only downright oaths, which I
never use till urged, nor never break for urging. If thou
canst love a fellow of this temper, Kate, whose face is not
worth sun-burning, that never looks in his glass for love of
anything he sees there,—let thine eye be thy cook. I speak
to thee plain soldier: if thou canst love me for this, take me;
if not, to say to thee that I shall die, is true,—but for thy
love, by the Lord, no; yet I love thee too. And while,
thou livest, dear Kate, take a fellow of plain and uncoined
constancy; for he perforce must do thee right, because he
hath not the gift to woo in other places; for these fellows
of infinite tongue, that can rhyme themselves into ladies'
favours, they do always reason themselves out again.
What! a speaker is but a prater; a rhyme is but a ballad.
A good leg will fall; a straight back will stoop; a black
beard will turn white; a curled pate will grow bald; a fair
face will wither; a full eye will wax hollow; but a good
heart, Kate, is the sun and the moon; or rather the sun
and not the moon;—for it shines bright and never changes,
but keeps his course truly. If thou would have such a one,
take me; and take me, take a soldier; take a soldier, take
a king. And what sayest thou then to my love? speak,
my fair, and fairly, I pray thee.

Kath. Is it possible dat I sould love de enemy of
France?

K. Hen. No; it is not possible you should love the
enemy of France, Kate; but, in loving me, you should love
the friend of France; for I love France so well that I will
not part with a village of it; I will have it all mine: and,
Kate, when France is mine and I am yours, then yours is
France and you are mine.

Kath. I cannot tell vat is dat.

K. Hen. No, Kate? I will tell thee in French; which
I am sure will hang upon my tongue like a new-married wife
about her husband's neck, hardly to be shook off. *Quand
j'ai le possession de France et quand vous avez le possession*

de moi,—let me see, what then?   Saint Denis be my speed!
—*donc votre est France et vous êtes mienne.*   It is as easy for
me, Kate, to conquer the kingdom as to speak so much
more French: I shall never move thee in French, unless it
be to laugh at me.

    Kath.   *Sauf votre honneur, le François que vous parlez,
il est meilleur que l'Anglois lequel je parle.*

    K. Hen.   No, faith, is't not Kate: but thy speaking of
my tongue, and I thine, most truly-falsely, must needs be
granted to be much at one.   But, Kate, dost thou understand thus much English—Canst thou love me?

    Kath.   I cannot tell.

    K. Hen.   Can any of your neighbours tell, Kate?   I'll
ask them.   Come, I know thou lovest me: and at night,
when you come into your closet, you'll question this gentlewoman about me; and I know, Kate, you will to her dispraise those parts in me that you love with your heart:
but, good Kate, mock me mercifully; the rather, gentle
princess, because I love thee cruelly.   If ever thou beest
mine, Kate—as I have a saving faith within me tells me
thou shalt—I get thee with scambling, and thou must therefore needs prove a good soldier-breeder: shall not thou and
I, between Saint Denis and Saint George, compound a boy,
half French, half English, that shall go to Constantinople
and take the Turk by the beard? shall we not? what sayest
thou, my fair flower-de-luce?

    Kath.   I do not know dat.

    K. Hen.   No; 't is hereafter to know, but now to
promise: do but now promise, Kate, you will endeavour for
your French part of such a boy; and for my English moiety
take the word of a king and a bachelor.   How answer you,
*la plus belle Katharine du monde, mon très cher et devin
déesse?*

    Kath.   Your *majesté* ave *fausse* French enough to deceive
de most *sage demoiselle* dat is *en France.*

    K. Hen.   Now, fie upon my false French!   By mine
honour, in true English, I love thee, Kate: by which
honour I dare not swear thou lovest me; yet my blood
begins to flatter me that thou dost, notwithstanding the
poor and untempering effect of my visage.   Now, beshrew
my father's ambition! he was thinking of civil wars when he
got me: therefore was I created with a stubborn outside,
with an aspect of iron, that, when I come to woo ladies, I
fright them.   But, in faith, Kate, the elder I wax, the better
I shall appear: my comfort is, that old age, that ill layer up
of beauty, can do no more spoil upon my face: thou hast
me, if thou hast me, at the worst; and thou shalt wear me,
if thou wear me, better and better:—and therefore tell
me, most fair Katharine, will you have me?   Put off your
maiden blushes; avouch the thoughts of your heart with

the looks of an empress; take me by the hand, and say
'Harry of England, I am thine:' which word thou shalt no
sooner bless mine ear withal, but I will tell thee aloud
'England is thine, Ireland is thine, France is thine, and
Henry Plantagenet is thine;' who, though I speak it before
his face, if he be not fellow with the best king, thou shalt
find the best king of good fellows. Come, your answer
in broken music—for thy voice is music and thy English
broken; therefore, queen of all, Katharine, break thy mind
to me in broken English—wilt thou have me?

Kath. Dat is as it sall please de *roi mon père.*

K. Hen. Nay, it will please him well, Kate; it shall
please him, Kate.

Kath. Den it sall also content me.

K. Hen. Upon that I kiss your hand, and I call you my
queen.

*Kath. Laissez, mon seigneur, laissez, laissez: ma foi, je
ne veux point que vous abaissiez votre grandeur en baisant la
main d'une de votre seigneurie indigne serviteur; excusez-
moi, je vous supplie, mon très-puissant seigneur.*

K. Hen. Then I will kiss your lips, Kate.

*Kath. Les dames et demoiselles pour être baisées devant
leur noces, il n'est pas la coutume de France.*

K. Hen. Madame my interpreter, what says she?

Alice. Dat is not be de fashion *pour les* ladies of France,
—I cannot tell vat is *baiser* en Anglish.

K. Hen. To kiss.

Alice. Your majesty *intendre* bettre *que moi.*

K. Hen. It is not a fashion for the maids in France to
kiss before they are married, would she say?

Alice. Oui, vraiment.

K. Hen. O Kate, nice customs court'sy to great kings.
Dear Kate, you and I cannot be confined within the weak
list of a country's fashion: we are the makers of manners,
Kate; and the liberty that follows our places stops the
mouth of all find-faults,—as I will do yours, for upholding
the nice fashion of your country in denying me a kiss:
therefore, patiently and yielding. [*Kissing her*] You have
witchcraft in your lips, Kate: there is more eloquence in a
sugar touch of them than in the tongues of the French
council; and they should sooner persuade Harry of England
than a general petition of monarchs. Here comes your
father.

Re-enter the FRENCH KING *and* QUEEN, BURGUNDY, BED-
FORD, GLOUCESTER, EXETER, WARWICK, WESTMORE-
LAND, *and other Lords*

Bur. God save your majesty! my royal cousin, teach
you our princess English?

K. Hen.   I would have her learn, my fair cousin, how perfectly I love her; and that is good English.

Bur.   Is she not apt?

K. Hen.   Our tongue is rough, coz, and my condition is not smooth; so that, having neither the voice nor the heart of flattery about me, I cannot so conjure up the spirit of love in her, that he will appear in his true likeness.

Bur.   Pardon the frankness of my mirth, if I answer you for that. If you would conjure in her, you must make a circle; if conjure up love in her in his true likeness, he must appear naked and blind. Can you blame her, then, being a maid yet rosed over with the virgin crimson of modesty, if she deny the appearance of a naked blind boy in her naked seeing self? It were, my lord, a hard condition for a maid to consign to.

K. Hen.   Yet they do wink and yield—as love is blind and enforces.

Bur.   They are then excused, my lord, when they see not what they do.

K. Hen.   Then, good my lord, teach your cousin to consent to winking.

Bur.   I will wink on her to consent, my lord, if you will teach her to know my meaning: for maids, well summered and warm kept, are like flies at Bartholomew-tide, blind, though they have their eyes; and then they will endure handling, which before would not abide looking on.

K. Hen.   This moral ties me over to time and a hot summer; and so I shall catch the fly, your cousin, in the latter end, and she must be blind too.

Bur.   As love is, my lord, before it loves.

K. Hen.   It is so: and you may, some of you, thank love for my blindness, who cannot see many a fair French city for one fair French maid that stands in my way.

Fr. King.   Yes, my lord, you see them perspectively, the cities turned into a maid; for they are all girdled with maiden walls that war hath never entered.

K. Hen.   Shall Kate be my wife?

Fr. King.   So please you.

K. Hen.   I am content; so the maiden cities you talk of may wait on her; so the maid that stood in the way for my wish shall show me the way to my will.

Fr. King.   We have consented to all terms of reason.

K. Hen.   Is't so, my lords of England?

West.   The king hath granted every article:—
His daughter first; and then, in sequel, all,
According to their firm proposéd natures.

Exe.   Only he hath not yet subscribéd this:
Where your majesty demands, that the King of France having any occasion to write for matter of grant, shall

name your highness in this form and with this addition, in
French, *Notre très-cher fils Henri, Roi d'Angleterre, Héritier
de France;* and thus in Latin, *Præclarissimus filius noster
Henricus Rex Angliæ et Hæres Franciæ.*

Fr. King. Not this I have not, brother, so denied,
But your request shall make me let it pass.

K. Hen. I pray you, then, in love and dear alliance,
Let that one article rank with the rest;
And thereupon give me your daughter.

Fr. King. Take her, fair son, and from her blood raise up
Issue to me; that the contending kingdoms
Of France and England, whose very shores look pale
With envy of each other's happiness,
May cease their hatred; and this dear conjunction
Plant neighbourhood and Christian-like accord
In their sweet bosoms, that ne'er war advance
His bleeding sword 'twixt England and fair France.

All. Amen!

K. Hen. Now, welcome, Kate;—and bear me witness all,
That here I kiss her as my sovereign queen.   [*Flourish*

Q. Isa. God, the best maker of all marriages,
Combine your hearts in one, your realms in one!
As man and wife, being two, are one in love,
So be there 'twixt your kingdoms such a spousal,
That never may ill office, or fell jealousy,
Which troubles oft the bed of blessèd marriage,
Thrust in between the paction of these kingdoms,
To make divorce of their incorporate league;
That English may as French, French Englishmen,
Receive each other. God speak this Amen!

All. Amen!

K. Hen. Prepare we for our marriage:—on which day,
My Lord of Burgundy, we'll take your oath,
And all the peers', for surety of our league.
Then shall I swear to Kate, and you to me;
And may our oaths well kept and prosperous be!

[*Sennet.   Exeunt*

EPILOGUE

Enter Chorus

Chor. Thus far, with rough and all-unable pen,
  Our bending author hath pursued the story,
In little room confining mighty men,
  Mangling by starts the full course of their glory.
Small time, but in that small most greatly lived
  This star of England: Fortune made his sword;

By which the world's best garden he achieved,
   And of it left his son imperial lord.
Henry the Sixth, in infant bands crowned King
   Of France and England, did this king succeed;
Whose state so many had the managing,
   That they lost France and made his England bleed.
Which oft our stage hath shown; and, for their sake,
In your fair minds let this acceptance take.   [*Exit*

KING HENRY THE SIXTH

FIRST PART

DRAMATIS PERSONÆ

KING HENRY THE SIXTH
DUKE OF GLOSTER, *uncle to the King, and Protector*
DUKE OF BEDFORD, *uncle to the King, and Regent of France*
THOMAS BEAUFORT, *Duke of Exeter, great-uncle to the King*
HENRY BEAUFORT, *great-uncle to the King, Bishop of Winchester, and afterwards Cardinal*
JOHN BEAUFORT, *Earl, afterwards Duke, of Somerset*
RICHARD PLANTAGENET, *son of Richard late Earl of Cambridge, afterwards Duke of York*
EARL OF WARWICK
EARL OF SALISBURY
EARL OF SUFFOLK
LORD TALBOT, *afterwards Earl of Shrewsbury*
JOHN TALBOT, *his son*
EDMUND MORTIMER, *Earl of March*
SIR JOHN FASTOLFE
SIR WILLIAM LUCY
SIR WILLIAM GLANSDALE
SIR THOMAS GARGRAVE
Mayor of London
WOODVILLE, *Lieutenant of the Tower*
VERNON, *of the White-rose or York faction*
BASSET, *of the Red-rose or Lancaster faction*
A *lawyer. Mortimer's keepers*

CHARLES, *Dauphin, and afterwards King, of France*
REIGNIER, *Duke of Anjou, and titular King of Naples*
DUKE OF BURGUNDY
DUKE OF ALENCON
BASTARD OF ORLEANS
Governor of Paris
Master-gunner of Orleans, and his son
General of the French Forces in Bordeaux
A *French sergeant.   A porter*
An old shepherd, father to Joan la Pucelle

MARGARET, *daughter to Reignier, afterwards married to King Henry*
COUNTESS OF AUVERGNE
JOAN LA PUCELLE, *commonly called Joan of Arc*

Lords, Warders of the Tower, Heralds, Officers, Soldiers, Messengers, and Attendants

Fiends appearing to La Pucelle

SCENE—*Partly in England, and partly in France*

236

THE FIRST PART OF

KING HENRY VI

ACT ONE

Scene I.—Westminister Abbey

Dead March. Enter the funeral of King Henry V., *attended on by the* Duke of Bedford, *Regent of France; the* Duke of Gloster, *Protector; the* Duke of Exeter, *the* Earl of Warwick, *the* Bishop of Winchester, *Heralds, etc.*

    Bed. Hung be the heavens with black, yield day to
           night!
Comets, importing change of times and states,
Brandish your crystal tresses in the sky,
And with them scourge the bad revolting stars
That have consented unto Henry's death!
King Henry the Fifth, too famous to live long!
England ne'er lost a king of so much worth.
    Glo. England ne'er had a king until his time.
Virtue he had, deserving to command;
His brandished sword did blind men with his beams;
His arms spread wider than a dragon's wings;
His sparkling eyes, replete with wrathful fire,
More dazzled and drove back his enemies
Than mid-day sun fierce bent against their faces.
What should I say? his deeds exceed all speech;
He ne'er lift up his hand but conqueréd.
    Exe. We mourn in black: why mourn we not in blood?
Henry is dead and never shall revive;
Upon a wooden coffin we attend,
And death's dishonourable victory
We with our stately presence glorify,
Like captives bound to a triumphant car.
What! shall we curse the planets of mishap
That plotted thus our glory's overthrow?
Or shall we think the subtle-witted French
Conjurers and sorcerers, that, afraid of him,
By magic verses have contrived his end?

Win. He was a king blessed of the King of kings.
Unto the French the dreadful judgment-day
So dreadful will not be as was his sight.
The battles of the Lord of hosts he fought;
The church's prayers made him so prosperous.
    Glo. The church! where is it? Had not churchmen
          prayed,
His dread of life had not so soon decayed;
None do you like but an effeminate prince,
Whom, like a school-boy, you may overawe.
    Win. Gloster, whate'er we like, thou art Protector
And lookest to command the prince and realm.
Thy wife is proud; she holdeth thee in awe,
More than God or religious churchmen may.
    Glo. Name not religion, for thou lov'st the flesh,
And ne'er throughout the year to church thou go'st,
Except it be to pray against thy foes.
    Bed. Cease, cease these jars and rest your minds in
          peace!
Let's to the altar.—Herald, wait on us.—
Instead of gold, we'll offer up our arms;
Since arms avail not now that Henry's dead.
Posterity, await for wretched years,
When at their mothers' moist eyes babes shall suck,
Our isle be made a marish of salt tears,
And none but women left to wail the dead.
Henry the Fifth, thy ghost I invocate!
Prosper this realm, keep it from civil broils,
Combat with adverse planets in the heavens!
A far more glorious star thy soul will make
Than Julius Cæsar or bright—

Enter a Messenger

    Mess. My honourable lords, health to you all!
Sad tidings bring I to you out of France,
Of loss, of slaughter, and discomfiture;
Guienne, Champagne, Rheims, Orleans,
Paris, Guysors, Poictiers, are all quite lost.
    Bed. What say'st thou, man, before dead Henry's
          corse?
Speak softly, or the loss of those great towns
Will make him burst his lead and rise from death.
    Glo. Is Paris lost? is Rouen yielded up?
If Henry were recalled to life again,
These news would cause him once more yield the ghost.
    Exe. How were they lost? what treachery was used?
    Mess. No treachery; but want of men and money.
Amongst the soldiers this is mutteréd,—
That here you maintain several factions,

And whilst a field should be dispatched and fought,
You are disputing of your generals.
One would have lingering wars with little cost;
Another would fly swift, but wanteth wings;
A third thinks, that without expense at all,
By guileful fair words peace may be obtained.
Awake, awake, English nobility!
Let not sloth dim your honours new-begot:
Cropped are the flower-de-luces in your arms,
Of England's coat one half is cut away.
    Exe. Were our tears wanting to this funeral,
These tidings would call forth their flowing tides.
    Bed. Me they concern; Regent I am of France.—
Give me my steeléd coat. I'll fight for France.—
Away with these disgraceful wailing robes!
Wounds will I lend the French instead of eyes,
To weep their intermissive miseries.

Enter another Messenger

    Mess. Lords, view these letters full of bad mischance.
France is revolted from the English quite,
Except some petty towns of no import.
The Dauphin Charles is crownéd king in Rheims:
The Bastard of Orleans with him is joined;
Reignier, Duke of Anjou, doth take his part;
The Duke of Alençon flieth to his side.
    Exe. The Dauphin crownéd king! all fly to him!
O, whither shall we fly from this reproach?
    Glo. We will not fly, but to our enemies' throats.—
Bedford, if thou be slack, I'll fight it out.
    Bed. Gloster, why doubt'st thou of my forwardness?
An army have I mustered in my thoughts
Wherewith already France is overrun.

Enter another Messenger

    Mess. My gracious lords, to add to your laments,
Wherewith you now bedew King Henry's hearse,
I must inform you of a dismal fight
Betwixt the stout Lord Talbot and the French.
    Win. What! wherein Talbot overcame? is't so?
    Mess. O, no; wherein Lord Talbot was o'er-thrown:
The circumstance I'll tell you more at large.
The tenth of August last this dreadful lord,
Retiring from the siege of Orleans,
Having full scarce six thousand in his troop,
By three and twenty thousand of the French
Was round encompasséd and set upon.
No leisure had he to enrank his men;
He wanted pikes to set before his archers;

Instead whereof sharp stakes plucked out of hedges
They pitchéd in the ground confusedly,
To keep the horsemen off from breaking in.
More than three hours the flight continuéd;
Where valiant Talbot above human thought
Enacted wonders with his sword and lance.
Hundreds he sent to hell, and none durst stand him;
Here, there, and everywhere, enraged he flew.
The French exclaimed, the devil was in arms;
All the whole army stood agazed on him.
His soldiers, spying his undaunted spirit,
A Talbot! a Talbot! cried out amain,
And rushed into the bowels of the battle.
Here had the conquest fully been sealed up,
If Sir John Fastolfe had not played the coward.
He, being in the vaward placed behind
With purpose to relieve and follow them,
Cowardly fled, not having struck one stroke.
Hence grew the general wrack and massacre;
Encloséd were they with their enemies:
A base Walloon, to win the Dauphin's grace,
Thrust Talbot with a spear into the back,
Whom all France with their chief assembled strength
Durst not presume to look once in the face.
    Bed. Is Talbot slain? then I will slay myself
For living idly here in pomp and ease
Whilst such a worthy leader, wanting aid,
Unto his dastard foemen is betrayed.
    Mess. O no, he lives, but is took prisoner,
And Lord Scales with him, and Lord Hungerford;
Most of the rest slaughtered or took likewise.
    Bed. His ransom there is none but I shall pay.
I'll hale the Dauphin headlong from his throne;
His crown shall be the ransom of my friend;
Four of their lords I'll change for one of ours.—
Farewell, my masters; to my task will I;
Bonfires in France forthwith I am to make,
To keep our great Saint George's feast withal.
Ten thousand soldiers with me I will take,
Whose bloody deeds shall make all Europe quake.
    Mess. So you had need, for Orleans is besieged;
The English army is grown weak and faint:
The Earl of Salisbury craveth supply,
And hardly keeps his men from mutiny,
Since they, so few, watch such a multitude.
    Exe. Remember, lords, your oaths to Henry sworn,
Either to quell the Dauphin utterly,
Or bring him in obedience to your yoke.
    Bed. I do remember't; and here take my leave,
To go about my preparation.   [*Exit*

Glo. I'll to the Tower with all the haste I can,
To view the artillery and munition;
And then I will proclaim young Henry king.   [*Exit*
  Exe.   To Eltham will I, where the young king is,
Being ordained his special governor,
And for his safety there I'll best devise.   [*Exit*
  Win.   Each hath his place and function to attend:
I am left out; for me nothing remains.
But long I will not be Jack out of office:
The king from Eltham I intend to steal
And sit at chiefest stern of public weal.   [*Exeunt*

SCENE II.—France.   Before Orleans

Flourish.   Enter CHARLES, ALENÇON, *and* REIGNIER,
    marching with drum and Soldiers

  Char.   Mars his true moving, even as in the heavens
So in the earth, to this day is not known.
Late did he shine upon the English side;
Now we are victors, upon us he smiles.
What towns of any moment but we have?
At pleasure here we lie near Orleans;
Otherwhiles the famished English, like pale ghosts,
Faintly beseige us one hour in a month.
  Alen.   They want their porridge and their fat bull-
          beeves;
Either they must be dieted like mules
And have their provender tied to their mouths,
Or piteous they will look like drownéd mice.
  Reig.   Let's raise the siege; why live we idly here?
Talbot is taken, whom we wont to fear:
Remaineth none but mad-brained Salisbury,
And he may well in fretting spend his gall;
Nor men nor money hath he to make war.
  Char.   Sound, sound alarum! we will rush on them.
Now for the honour of the forlorn French!
Him I forgive my death that killeth me
When he sees me go back one foot or fly.   [*Exeunt*
     [*Alarum; they are beaten back by the English with
                                    great loss*

Re-enter CHARLES, ALENÇON, *and* REIGNIER

  Char.   Who ever saw the like? what men have I!
Dogs! cowards! dastards! I would ne'er have fled,
But that they left me midst my enemies.
  Reig.   Salisbury is a desperate homicide;
He fighteth as one weary of his life.
The other lords, like lions wanting food,

Do rush upon us as their hungry prey.
   Alen. Froissart, a countryman of ours, records,
England all Olivers and Rowlands bred
During the time Edward the Third did reign.
More truly now may this be verified;
For none but Samsons and Goliases
It sendeth forth to skirmish.   One to ten!
Lean raw-boned rascals! who would e'er suppose
They had such courage and audacity?
   Char. Let's leave this town; for they are hare-brained
       slaves,
And hunger will enforce them be more eager.
Of old I know them; rather with their teeth
The walls they'll tear down than forsake the siege.
   Reig. I think, by some odd gimmers or device
Their arms are set like clocks, still to strike on;
Else ne'er could they hold out so as they do.
By my consent, we'll even let them alone.
   Alen. Be it so.

Enter the BASTARD OF ORLEANS

   Bast. Where's the Prince Dauphin?   I have news for
       him.
   Char. Bastard of Orleans, thrice welcome to us.
   Bast. Methinks your looks are sad, your cheer appalled.
Hath the late overthrow wrought this offence?
Be not dismayed, for succour is at hand;
A holy maid hither with me I bring,
Which by a vision sent to her from heaven
Ordainéd is to raise this tedious siege
And drive the English forth the bounds of France.
The spirit of deep prophecy she hath,
Exceeding the nine sibyls of old Rome;
What's past and what's to come she can descry.
Speak, shall I call her in?   Believe my words,
For they are certain and infallible.
   Char. Go, call her in.—[*Exit Bastard*]   But first, to
       try her skill,
Reignier, stand thou as Dauphin in my place;
Question her proudly, let thy looks be stern.
By this means shall we sound what skill she hath.

Re-enter the BASTARD OF ORLEANS, *with* JOAN LA PUCELLE

   Reig. Fair maid, is't thou wilt do these wondrous feats?
   Puc. Reignier, is't thou that thinkest to beguile me?
Where is the Dauphin?   Come, come from behind;
I know thee well, though never seen before.
Be not amazed, there's nothing hid from me;
In private will I talk with thee apart.—

Stand back, you lords, and give us leave awhile.
    Reig.   She takes upon her bravely at first dash.
    Puc.   Dauphin, I am by birth a shepherd's daughter,
My wit untrained in any kind of art.
Heaven and our Lady gracious hath it pleased
To shine on my contemptible estate.
Lo, whilst I waited on my tender lambs,
And to sun's parching heat displayed my cheeks,
God's mother deignéd to appear to me,
And in a vision full of majesty
Willed me to leave my base vocation
And free my country from calamity.
Her aid she promised and assured success;
In complete glory she revealed herself;
And, whereas I was black and swart before,
With those clear rays which she infused on me
That beauty am I blessed with which you see.
Ask me what question thou canst possible,
And I will answer unpremeditated;
My courage try by combat, if thou dar'st,
And thou shalt find that I exceed my sex.
Resolve on this, thou shalt be fortunate
If thou receive me for thy warlike mate.
    Char.   Thou hast astonished me with thy high terms.
Only this proof I'll of thy valour make:
In single combat thou shalt buckle with me,
And if thou vanquishest, thy words are true;
Otherwise I renounce all confidence.
    Puc.   I am prepared. Here is my keen-edged sword,
Decked with five flower-de-luces on each side;
The which at Touraine, in St. Katherine's church-yard,
Out of a great deal of old iron I chose forth.
    Char.   Then come on, o' God's name; I fear no woman.
    Puc.   And while I live, I'll ne'er fly from a man.
              [*Here they fight, and Joan la Pucelle overcomes*
    Char.   Stay, stay thy hands! thou art an Amazon,
And fightest with the sword of Deborah.
    Puc.   Christ's mother helps me, else I were too weak.
    Char.   Whoe'er helps thee, 't is thou that must help me.
Impatiently I burn with thy desire;
My heart and hands thou hast at once subdued
Excellent Pucelle, if thy name be so,
Let me thy servant and not sovereign be;
'T is the French Dauphin sueth to thee thus.
    Puc.   I must not yield to any rites of love,
For my profession's sacred from above.
When I have chaséd all thy foes from hence,
Then will I think upon a recompense.
    Char.   Meantime look gracious on thy prostrate thrall.
    Reig.   My lord, methinks, is very long in talk.

Alen. Doubtless he shrives this woman to her smock;
Else ne'er could he so long protract his speech.
    Reig. Shall we disturb him, since he keeps no mean?
    Alen. He may mean more than we poor men do know;
These women are shrewd tempters with their tongues.
    Reig. My lord, where are you? what devise you on?
Shall we give over Orleans, or no?
    Puc. Why, no, I say, distrustful recreants!
Fight till the last gasp; I will be your guard.
    Char. What she says I'll confirm; we'll fight it out.
    Puc. Assigned am I to be the English scourge.
This night the siege assuredly I'll raise;
Expect Saint Martin's summer, halcyon days,
Since I have enteréd into these wars.
Glory is like a circle in the water,
Which never ceaseth to enlarge itself
Till by broad spreading it disperse to nought.
With Henry's death the English circle ends;
Disperséd are the glories it included.
Now am I like that proud insulting ship
Which Cæsar and his fortune bare at once.
    Char. Was Mahomet inspiréd with a dove?
Thou with an eagle art inspiréd then.
Helen, the mother of great Constantine,
Nor yet Saint Philip's daughters, were like thee.
Bright star of Venus, fallen down on the earth,
How may I reverently worship thee enough?
    Alen. Leave off delays, and let us raise the siege.
    Reig. Woman, do what thou canst to save our honours;
Drive them from Orleans and be immortalised.
    Char. Presently we'll try.—Come, let's away about it;
No prophet will I trust, if she prove false.   [*Exeunt*

SCENE III.—London. Before the Tower

Enter the DUKE OF GLOSTER, *with his Serving-men,
in blue coats*

    Glo. I am come to survey the Tower this day;
Since Henry's death, I fear, there is conveyance.—
Where be these warders, that they wait not here?
Open the gates; it is Gloster that calls.
    First Ward. [*Within*] Who's there that knocks so
        imperiously?
    First Serv. It is the noble Duke of Gloster.
    Sec. Ward. [*Within*] Whoe'er he be, you may not be
        let in.
    First Serv. Villains, answer you so the lord Protector?
    First Ward. [*Within*] The Lord protect him! so we
        answer him;

We do no otherwise than we are willed.
   Glo. Who willéd you? or whose will stands but mine?
There's none Protector of the realm but I.
Break up the gates, I'll be your warrantize.
Shall I be flouted thus by dunghill grooms?
      [*Gloster's men rush at the Tower Gates, and Woodvile,*
                   the Lieutenant, speaks within
   Wood. What noise is this? what traitors have we here?
   Glo. Lieutenant, is it you whose voice I hear?
Open the gates; here's Gloster that would enter.
   Wood. Have patience, noble duke, I may not open;
The Cardinal of Winchester forbids:
From him I have express commandément
That thou nor none of thine shall be let in.
   Glo. Faint-hearted Woodvile, prizest him fore me?
Arrogant Winchester, that haughty prelate,
Whom Henry, our late sovereign, ne'er could brook?
Thou art no friend to God or to the king.
Open the gates or I'll shut thee out shortly.
   Serv. Open the gates unto the lord Protector,
Or we'll burst them open, if that you come not quickly.

Enter to the Protector at the Tower Gates WINCHESTER
and his men, in tawny coats

   Win. How now, ambitious Humphrey! what means
     this?
   Glo. Peeled priest, dost thou command me to be shut
     out?
   Win. I do, thou most usurping proditor,
And not protector, of the king or realm.
   Glo. Stand back, thou manifest conspirator,
Thou that contriv'dst to murther our dead lord,
Thou that giv'st whores indulgences to sin
I'll canvass thee in thy broad cardinal's hat,
If thou proceed in this thy insolence.
   Win. Nay, stand thou back; I will not budge a foot:
This be Damascus, be thou curséd Cain,
To slay thy brother Abel, if thou wilt.
   Glo. I will not slay thee, but I'll drive thee back;
Thy scarlet robes as a child's bearing-cloth
I'll use to carry thee out of this place.
   Win. Do what thou dar'st; I beard thee to thy face.
   Glo. What! am I dared and bearded to my face?—
Draw, men, for all this privilegéd place;
Blue coats to tawny coats!—Priest, beware your beard;
I mean to tug it and to cuff you soundly.
Under my feet I stamp thy cardinal's hat,
In spite of pope or dignities of church,
Here by the cheeks I'll drag thee up and down.

Win. Gloster, thou'lt answer this before the pope.
Glo. Winchester goose, I cry, a rope! a rope!—
Now beat them hence; why do you let them stay?—
Thee I'll chase hence, thou wolf in sheep's array.—
Out, tawny coats!—out, scarlet hypocrite!

*Here Gloster's men beat out the Cardinal's men: and
enter in the hurly-burly the* MAYOR OF LONDON *and his
Officers*

May. Fie, lords! that you being supreme magistrates,
Thus contumeliously should break the peace!
Glo. Peace, mayor! thou knowest little of my wrongs.
Here's Beaufort, that regards nor God nor king
Hath here distrained the Tower to his use.
Win. Here's Gloster, here's a foe to citizens;
One that still motions war and never peace,
O'ercharging your free purses with large fines,
That seeks to overthrow religion,
Because he is Protector of the realm,
And would have armour here out of the Tower,
To crown himself King and suppress the Prince.
Glo. I will not answer thee with words, but blows.
                              [*Here they skirmish again*
May. Nought rests for me in this tumultuous strife
But to make open proclamation.—
Come, officer; as loud as e'er thou canst.
Off. All manner of men assembled here in arms this day
against God's peace and the king's, we charge and com-
mand you, in his highness' name, to repair to your several
dwelling-places; and not to wear, handle, or use any sword,
weapon, or dagger, henceforward, upon pain of death.
Glo. Cardinal, I'll be no breaker of the law;
But we shall meet, and break our minds at large.
Win. Gloster, we will meet, to thy cost, be sure;
Thy heart-blood I will have for this day's work.
May. I'll call for clubs, if you will not away.—
This cardinal's more haughty than the devil.
Glo. Mayor, farewell; thou dost but what thou may'st.
Win. Abominable Gloster, guard thy head;
For I intend to have it ere long.
                    [*Exeunt, severally, Gloster and Winchester with their
                                                          Serving-men*
May. See the coast cleared, and then we will depart.—
Good God, that nobles should such stomachs bear!
I myself fight not once in forty year.   [*Exeunt*

SCENE IV.—Before Orleans

Enter, on the walls, a Master-Gunner and his Boy

M. Gun.   Sirrah, thou know'st how Orleans is besieged,
And how the English have the suburbs won.
    Boy.   Father, I know; and oft have shot at them,
Howe'er unfortunate I missed my aim.
    M. Gun.   But now thou shalt not.   Be thou ruled by
      me.
Chief master-gunner am I of this town;
Something I must do to procure me grace.
The prince's espials have informéd me
How the English, in the suburbs close intrenched,
Wont, through a secret grate of iron bars
In yonder tower to overpeer the city
And thence discover how with most advantage
They may vex us with shot or with assault.
To intercept this inconvenience,
A piece of ordnance 'gainst it I have placed;
And even these three days have I watched,
If I could see them.
Now do thou watch, for I can stay no longer.
If thou spyest any, run and bring me word,
And thou shalt find me at the governor's.   [*Exit*
    Boy.   Father, I warrant you; take you no care;
I'll never trouble you, if I may spy them.   [*Exit*

Enter, on the turrets, the LORDS SALISBURY *and* TALBOT, SIR
    WILLIAM GLANSDALE, SIR THOMAS GARGRAVE, *and
    others*

    Sal.   Talbot, my life, my joy, again returned!
How wert thou handled being prisoner?
Or by what means got'st thou to be released?
Discourse, I prithee, on this turret's top.
    Tal.   The Duke of Bedford had a prisoner
Calléd the brave Lord Ponton de Santrailles;
For him was I exchanged and ransoméd.
But with a baser man of arms by far
Once in contempt they would have bartered me;
Which I disdaining scorned, and cravéd death
Rather than I would be so vile esteemed.
In fine, redeemed I was as I desired.
But, O, the treacherous Fastolfe wounds my heart,
Whom with my bare fists I would execute,
If I now had him brought into my power.
    Sal.   Yet tell'st thou not how thou wert entertained.
    Tal.   With scoffs and scorns and contumelious taunts.

In open market-place produced they me
To be a public spectacle to all:
Here, said they, is the terror of the French,
The scarecrow that affrights our children so.
Then broke I from the officers that led me,
And with my nails digged stones out of the ground
To hurl at the beholders of my shame.
My grisly countenance made others fly;
None durst come near for fear of sudden death.
In iron walls they deemed me not secure;
So great fear of my name 'mongst them was spread
That they supposed I could rend bars of steel
And spurn in pieces posts of adamant:
Wherefore a guard of chosen shot I had
That walked about me every minute while,
And if I did but stir out of my bed,
Ready they were to shoot me to the heart.

Enter the boy with a linstock

   Sal. I grieve to hear what torments you endured,
But we will be revenged sufficiently.
Now it is supper-time in Orleans;
Here, through this grate, I count each one
And view the Frenchmen how they fortify.
Let us look in; the sight will much delight thee.
Sir Thomas Gargrave, and Sir William Glansdale,
Let me have your express opinions
Where is best place to make our battery next.
   Gar. I think, at the north gate; for there stand lords.
   Glan. And I, here, at the bulwark of the bridge.
   Tal. For aught I see, this city must be famished,
Or with light skirmishes enfeebléd.
           [Here they shoot. Salisbury and Gargrave fall
   Sal. O Lord, have mercy on us, wretched sinners!
   Gar. O Lord, have mercy on me, woful man!
   Tal. What chance is this that suddenly hath crossed
us?—
Speak, Salisbury; at least, if thou canst speak:
How far'st thou, mirror of all martial men?
One of thy eyes and thy cheek's side struck off!—
Accurséd tower! accurséd fatal hand
That hath contrived this woful tragedy!
In thirteen battles Salisbury o'ercame;
Henry the Fifth he first trained to the wars;
Whilst any trump did sound, or drum struck up,
His sword did ne'er leave striking in the field.—
Yet liv'st thou, Salisbury? though thy speech doth fail,
One eye thou hast, to look to heaven for grace;
The sun with one eye vieweth all the world.—

Heaven, be thou gracious to none alive,
If Salisbury wants mercy at thy hands!—
Bear hence his body; I will help to bury it.—
Sir Thomas Gargrave, hast thou any life?
Speak unto Talbot; nay, look up to him.—
Salisbury, cheer thy spirit with this comfort:
Thou shalt not die whiles—
He beckons with his hand and smiles on me,
As who should say 'When I am dead and gone,
Remember to avenge me on the French.'—
Plantagenet, I will; and like thee, Nero,
Play on the lute, beholding the towns burn.
Wretched shall France be only in my name.—
        [*Here an alarum, and it thunders and lightens*
What stir is this? what tumult's in the heavens?
Whence cometh this alarum and the noise?

Enter a Messenger

    Mess.   My lord, my lord, the French have gathered head;
The Dauphin, with one Joan la Pucelle joined,
A holy prophetess new risen up,
Is come with a great power to raise the siege.
            [*Here Salisbury lifteth himself up and groans*
    Tal.   Hear, hear how dying Salisbury doth groan!
It irks his heart he cannot be revenged.—
Frenchmen, I'll be a Salisbury to you;
Pucelle or puzzel, dolphin or dogfish,
Your hearts I'll stamp out with my horse's heels,
And make a quagmire of your mingled brains.—
Convey me Salisbury into his tent,
Then we'll try what these dastard Frenchmen dare.
            [*Alarum.   Exeunt*

SCENE V.—The Same

Here an alarum again; and TALBOT *pursueth the* DAUPHIN,
    and driveth him: then enter JOAN LA PUCELLE *driving
    Englishmen before her, and exit after them: then re-enter*
    TALBOT

    Tal.   Where is my strength, my valour, and my force?
Our English troops retire, I cannot stay them;
A woman clad in armour chaseth them.

Re-enter LA PUCELLE

Here, here she comes.—I'll have a bout with thee;
Devil or devil's dam, I'll conjure thee.

Blood will I draw on thee—thou art a witch—
And straightway give thy soul to him thou servest.
    Puc.   Come, come, 't is only I that must disgrace thee.
                                [Here they fight
    Tal.   Heavens, can you suffer hell so to prevail?
My breast I'll burst with straining of my courage,
And from my shoulders crack my arms asunder,
But I will chastise this high-minded strumpet.
                                [They fight again
    Puc.   Talbot, farewell; thy hour is not yet come.
I must go victual Orleans forthwith.
             [A short alarum: then enter the town with soldiers
O'ertake me, if thou canst; I scorn thy strength.
Go, go, cheer up thy hunger-starvéd men;
Help Salisbury to make his testament:
This day is ours, as many more shall be.   *[Exit*
    Tal.   My thoughts are whirléd like a potter's wheel;
I know not where I am, nor what I do.
A witch, by fear, not force, like Hannibal,
Drives back our troops and conquers as she lists;
So bees with smoke and doves with noisome stench
Are from their hives and houses driven away.
They called us for our fierceness English dogs;
Now, like to whelps, we crying run away.—
                                [A short alarum
Hark, countrymen! either renew the fight,
Or tear the lions out of England's coat;
Renounce your soil, give sheep in lions' stead:
Sheep run not half so timorous from the wolf,
Or horse or oxen from the leopard,
As you fly from your oft-subduéd slaves.
                    [Alarum.   Here another skirmish
It will not be.   Retire into your trenches;
You all consented unto Salisbury's death,
For none would strike a stroke in his revenge.—
Pucelle is entered into Orleans,
In spite of us or aught that we could do.
O, would I were to die with Salisbury!
The shame hereof will make me hide my head.
             [Exit Talbot. Alarum; retreat; flourish

Scene VI.—The Same

Enter, on the walls, La Pucelle, Charles, Reignier,
        Alençon, *and Soldiers*

    Puc.   Advance our waving colours on the walls;
Rescued is Orleans from the English:
Thus Joan la Pucelle hath performed her word.

Char. Divinest creature, Astræa's daughter,
How shall I honour thee for this success?
Thy promises are like Adonis' gardens
That one day bloomed and fruitful were the next.—
France, triumph in thy glorious prophetess!
Recovered is the town of Orleans;
More blessèd hap did ne'er befall our state.
    Reig. Why ring not out the bells throughout the town?—
Dauphin, command the citizens make bonfires,
And feast and banquet in the open streets,
To celebrate the joy that God hath given us.
    Alen. All France will be replete with mirth and joy
When they shall hear how we have played the men.
    Char. 'T is Joan, not we, by whom the day is won;
For which I will divide my crown with her,
And all the priests and friars in my realm
Shall in procession sing her endless praise.
A statelier pyramis to her I'll rear
Than Rhodope's of Memphis ever was;
In memory of her when she is dead,
Her ashes, in an urn more precious
Than the rich-jewelled coffer of Darius,
Transported shall be at high festivals
Before the kings and queens of France.
No longer on Saint Denis will we cry,
But Joan la Pucelle shall be France's saint.
Come in, and let us banquet royally,
After this golden day of victory.   [*Flourish. Exeunt*

ACT TWO

SCENE I.—Before Orleans

Enter a Sergeant of a band, with two Sentinels

    Serg. Sirs, take your places and be vigilant;
If any noise or soldier you perceive
Near to the walls, by some apparent sign
Let us have knowledge at the court of guard.
    First Sent. Sergeant, you shall.—[*Exit Sergeant*]   Thus
        are poor servitors,
When others sleep upon their quiet beds,
Constrained to watch in darkness, rain, and cold.

Enter TALBOT, BEDFORD, BURGUNDY, *and forces, with
    scaling-ladders, their drums beating a dead march*

    Tal. Lord Regent, and redoubted Burgundy,

By whose approach the regions of Artois,
Wallon, and Picardy are friends to us,
This happy night the Frenchman are secure,
Having all day caroused and banqueted.
Embrace we then this opportunity
As fitting best to quittance their deceit
Contrived by art and baleful sorcery.
    Bed. Coward of France! how much he wrongs his fame,
Despairing of his own arm's fortitude,
To join with witches and the help of hell!
    Bur. Traitors have never other company.
But what's that Pucelle whom they term so pure?
    Tal. A maid, they say.
    Bed.   A maid! and be so martial!
    Bur. Pray God she prove not masculine ere long,
If underneath the standard of the French
She carry armour as she hath begun!
    Tal. Well, let them practise and converse with spirits;
God is our fortress, in whose conquering name
Let us resolve to scale their flinty bulwarks.
    Bed. Ascend, brave Talbot; we will follow thee.
    Tal. Not all together; better far, I guess,
That we do make our entrance several ways,
That, if it chance the one of us do fail
The other yet may rise against their force.
    Bed. Agreed; I'll to yond corner.
    Bur.   And I to this.
    Tal. And here will Talbot mount, or make his grave.—
Now, Salisbury, for thee, and for the right
Of English Henry, shall this night appear
How much in duty I am bound to both.
    Sent. Arm! arm! the enemy doth make assault!
                  [*Cry:* ' *St. George,*' '*A Talbot*'

The French leap over the walls in their shirts. Enter, several
*   ways, the* BASTARD OF ORLEANS, ALENÇON, *and*
*   *REIGNIER, *half ready, and half unready*

    Alen. How now, my lords! what, all unready so?
    Bast. Unready! ay, and glad we 'scaped so well.
    Reig. 'T was time, I trow, to wake and leave our beds,
Hearing alarums at our chamber-doors.
    Alen. Of all exploits since first I followed arms,
Ne'er heard I of a warlike enterprise
More venturous or desperate than this.
    Bast. I think this Talbot be a fiend of hell.
    Reig. If not of hell, the heavens, sure, favour him.
    Alen. Here cometh Charles; I marvel how he sped.
    Bast. Tut, holy Joan was his defensive guard.

Enter CHARLES *and* LA PUCELLE

Char. Is this thy cunning, thou deceitful dame?
Didst thou at first, to flatter us withal,
Make us partakers of a little gain,
That now our loss might be ten times so much?
Puc. Wherefore is Charles impatient with his friend?
At all times will you have my power alike?
Sleeping or waking must I still prevail,
Or will you blame and lay the fault on me?—
Improvident soldiers! had your watch been good,
This sudden mischief never could have fall'n.
Char. Duke of Alençon, this was your default,
That, being captain of the watch to-night,
Did look no better to that weighty charge.
Alen. Had all your quarters been as safely kept
As that whereof I had the government,
We had not been thus shamefully surprised.
Bast. Mine was secure.
Reig.   And so was mine, my lord.
Char. And, for myself, most part of all this night,
Within her quarter and mine own precinct
I was employed in passing to and fro,
About relieving of the sentinels;
Then how or which way should they first break in?
Puc. Question, my lords, no further of the case
How or which way; 't is sure they found some place
But weakly guarded, where the breach was made.
And now there rests no other shift but this,—
To gather our soldiers, scattered and dispersed.
And lay new platforms to endamage them.

*Alarum.   Enter an English Soldier, crying 'A Talbot! a
      Talbot! ' They fly, leaving their clothes behind*

Sol. I 'll be so bold to take what they have left.
The cry of Talbot serves me for a sword;
For I have loaden me with many spoils,
Using no other weapon but his name.   [*Exit*

SCENE II.—Orleans. Within the Town

Enter TALBOT, BEDFORD, BURGUNDY, *a Captain,
                    and others*

Bed. The day begins to break, and night is fled,
Whose pitchy mantle over-veiled the earth.
Here sound retreat, and cease our hot pursuit.
                                      [*Retreat sounded*

Tal. Bring forth the body of old Salisbury,
And here advance it in the market-place,
The middle centre of this curséd town.—
Now have I paid my vow unto his soul;
For every drop of blood was drawn from him
There hath at least five Frenchmen died to-night.
And that hereafter ages may behold
What ruin happened in revenge of him,
Within their chiefest temple I'll erect
A tomb, wherein his corpse shall be interred;
Upon the which, that every one may read,
Shall be engraved the sack of Orleans,
The treacherous manner of his mournful death,
And what a terror he had been to France.
But, lords, in all our bloody massacre,
I muse we met not with the Dauphin's grace,
His new-come champion, virtuous Joan of Arc,
Nor any of his false confederates.
Bed. 'T is thought, Lord Talbot, when the fight began,
Roused on the sudden from their drowsy beds,
They did amongst the troops of arméd men
Leap o'er the walls for refuge in the field.
Bur. Myself, as far as I could well discern
For smoke and dusky vapours of the night,
Am sure I scared the Dauphin and his trull,
When arm in arm they both came swiftly running,
Like to a pair of loving turtle-doves
That could not live asunder day or night.
After that things are set in order here,
We'll follow them with all the power we have.

Enter a Messenger

Mess. All hail, my lords! Which of this princely train
Call ye the warlike Talbot, for his acts
So much applauded through the realm of France?
Tal. Here is the Talbot; who would speak with him?
Mess. The virtuous lady, Countess of Auvergne,
With modesty admiring thy renown,
By me entreats, great lord, thou wouldst vouchsafe
To visit her poor castle where she lies,
That she may boast she hath beheld the man
Whose glory fills the world with loud report.
Bur. Is it e'en so? Nay, then, I see our wars
Will turn unto a peaceful comic sport,
When ladies crave to be encountered with.—
You may not, my lord, despise her gentle suit.
Tal. Ne'er trust me then; for when a world of men
Could not prevail with all their oratory,
Yet hath a woman's kindness over-ruled.—

And therefore tell her I return great thanks,
And in submission will attend on her.—
Will not your honours bear me company?
   Bed.   No, truly; it is more than manners will:
And I have heard it said, unbidden guests
Are often welcomest when they are gone.
   Tal.   Well then, alone, since there's no remedy,
I mean to prove this lady's courtesy.—
Come hither, captain. [*Whispers*] You perceive my
      mind?
   Cap.   I do, my lord, and mean accordingly.   [*Exeunt*

SCENE III.—Auvergne. The Court of the Castle

Enter the COUNTESS *and her Porter*

   Count.   Porter, remember what I gave in charge;
And when you have done so, bring the keys to me.
   Port.   Madam, I will.   [*Exit*
   Count.   The plot is laid; if all things fall out right.
I shall as famous be by this exploit
As Scythian Tomyris by Cyrus' death.
Great is the rumour of this dreadful knight,
And his achievements of no less account;
Fain would mine eyes be witness with mine ears,
To give their censure of these rare reports.

Enter Messenger and TALBOT

   Mess.   Madam,
According as your ladyship desired,
By message craved, so is Lord Talbot come.
   Count.   And he is welcome. What! is this the man?
   Mess.   Madam, it is.
   Count.   Is this the scourge of France?
Is this the Talbot, so much feared abroad
That with his name the mothers still their babes?
I see report is fabulous and false;
I thought I should have seen some Hercules,
A second Hector, for his grim aspéct,
And large proportion of his strong-knit limbs.
Alas, this is a child, a silly dwarf!
It cannot be this weak and writhled shrimp
Should strike such terror to his enemies.
   Tal.   Madam, I have been bold to trouble you;
But since your ladyship is not at leisure,
I'll sort some other time to visit you.
   Count.   What means he now?—Go ask him whither he
      goes.

Mess. Stay, my Lord Talbot; for my lady craves
To know the cause of your abrupt departure.
Tal. Marry, for that she's in a wrong belief,
I go to certify her Talbot's here.

Re-enter Porter with keys

Count. If thou be he, then art thou prisoner.
Tal. Prisoner! to whom?
Count.   To me, blood-thirsty lord;
And for that cause I trained thee to my house.
Long time thy shadow hath been thrall to me,
For in my gallery thy picture hangs:
But now the substance shall endure the like,
And I will chain these legs and arms of thine,
That hast by tyranny these many years
Wasted our country, slain our citizens,
And sent our sons and husbands captivate.
Tal. Ha, ha, ha!
Count. Laughest thou, wretch? thy mirth shall turn
          to moan.
Tal. I laugh to see your ladyship so fond
To think that you have aught but Talbot's shadow
Whereon to practise your severity.
Count. Why, art not thou the man?
Tal.   I am indeed.
Count. Then have I substance too.
Tal. No, no, I am but shadow of myself;
You are deceived, my substance is not here,
For what you see is but the smallest part
And least proportion of humanity.
I tell you, madam, were the whole frame here.
It is of such a spacious lofty pitch,
Your roof were not sufficient to contain't.
Count. This is a riddling merchant for the nonce;
He will be here, and yet he is not here:
How can these contrarieties agree?
Tal. That will I show you presently.
          [*Winds his horn. Drums strike up: a peal of
                    ordnance. Enter soldiers*
How say you, madam? are you now persuaded
That Talbot is but shadow of himself?
These are his substance, sinews, arms, and strength,
With which he yoketh your rebellious necks,
Razeth your cities, and subverts your towns,
And in a moment makes them desolate.
Count. Victorious Talbot! pardon my abuse;
I find thou art no less than fame hath bruited,
And more than may be gathered by thy shape.
Let my presumption not provoke thy wrath;

For I am sorry that with reverence
I did not entertain thee as thou art.
    Tal. Be not dismayed, fair lady, nor misconstrue
The mind of Talbot, as you did mistake
The outward composition of his body.
What you have done hath not offended me;
Nor other satisfaction do I crave,
But only, with your patience, that we may
Taste of your wine and see what cates you have;
For soldiers' stomachs always serve them well.
    Count. With all my heart, and think me honouréd
To feast so great a warrior in my house.   [*Exeunt*

SCENE IV.—London. The Temple Garden

Enter the EARLS OF SOMERSET, SUFFOLK, *and* WARWICK;
RICHARD PLANTAGENET, VERNON, *and another Lawyer*

    Plan. Great lords and gentlemen, what means this
        silence?
Dare no man answer in a case of truth?
    Suf. Within the Temple Hall we were too loud;
The garden here is more convenient.
    Plan. Then say at once if I maintained the truth,
Or else was wrangling Somerset in the error?
    Suf. Faith, I have been a truant in the law,
And never yet could frame my will to it,
And therefore frame the law unto my will.
    Som. Judge you, my Lord of Warwick, then, between us.
    War. Between two hawks, which flies the higher pitch,
Between two dogs, which hath the deeper mouth,
Between two blades, which bears the better temper,
Between two horses, which doth bear him best,
Between two girls, which hath the merriest eye,
I have perhaps some shallow spirit of judgment;
But in these nice sharp quillets of the law,
Good faith, I am no wiser than a daw.
    Plan. Tut, tut, here is a mannerly forbearance;
The truth appears so naked on my side
That any purblind eye may find it out.
    Som. And on my side it is so well apparelled,
So clear, so shining, and so evident,
That it will glimmer through a blind man's eye.
    Plan. Since you are tongue-tied and so loath to speak,
In dumb significants proclaim your thoughts.
Let him that is a true-born gentleman
And stands upon the honour of his birth,
If he suppose that I have pleaded truth,
From off this brier pluck a white rose with me

Som.   Let him that is no coward nor no flatterer,
But dare maintain the party of the truth,
Pluck a red rose from off this thorn with me.
War.   I love no colours, and without all colour
Of base insinuating flattery
I pluck this white rose with Plantagenet.
Suf.   I pluck this red rose with young Somerset,
And say withal I think he held the right.
Ver.   Stay, lords and gentlemen, and pluck no more,
Till you conclude that he upon whose side
The fewest roses are cropped from the tree
Shall yield the other in the right opinion.
Som.   Good Master Vernon, it is well objected;
If I have fewest, I subscribe in silence.
Plan.   And I.
Ver.   Then for the truth and plainness of the case,
I pluck this pale and maiden blossom here,
Giving my verdict on the white rose side.
Som.   Prick not your finger as you pluck it off,
Lest bleeding you do paint the white rose red
And fall on my side so, against your will.
Ver.   If I, my lord, for my opinion bleed,
Opinion shall be surgeon to my hurt,
And keep me on the side where still I am.
Som.   Well, well, come on; who else?
Law.   Unless my study and my books be false,
The argument you held was wrong in you;
In sign whereof I pluck a white rose too.
Plan.   Now, Somerset, where is your argument?
Som.   Here in my scabbard, meditating that
Shall dye your white rose in a bloody red.
Plan.   Meantime your cheeks do counterfeit our roses;
For pale they look with fear, as witnessing
The truth on our side.
Som.   No, Plantagenet,
'T is not for fear but anger that thy cheeks
Blush for pure shame to counterfeit our roses,
And yet thy tongue will not confess thy error.
Plan.   Hath not thy rose a canker, Somerset?
Som.   Hath not thy rose a thorn, Plantagenet?
Plan.   Ay, sharp and piercing, to maintain his truth,
Whiles thy consuming canker eats his falsehood.
Som.   Well, I'll find friends to wear my bleeding roses,
That shall maintain what I have said is true,
Where false Plantagenet dare not be seen.
Plan.   Now, by this maiden blossom in my hand,
I scorn thee and thy faction, peevish boy.
Suf.   Turn not thy scorns this way, Plantagenet.
Plan.   Proud Pole, I will, and scorn both him and thee.
Suf.   I'll turn my part thereof into thy throat.

Som. Away, away, good William de la Pole!
We grace the yeoman by conversing with him.
War. Now, by God's will, thou wrong'st him, Somerset;
His grandfather was Lionel Duke of Clarence,
Third son to the third Edward King of England.
Spring crestless yeomen from so deep a root?
Plan. He bears him on the place's privilege,
Or durst not, for his craven heart, say thus.
Som. By him that made me, I'll maintain my words
On any plot of ground in Christendom.
Was not thy father, Richard Earl of Cambridge,
For treason executed in our late king's days?
And, by his treason, stand'st not thou attainted,
Corrupted, and exempt from ancient gentry?
His trespass yet lives guilty in thy blood;
And, till thou be restored, thou art a yeoman.
Plan. My father was attachéd, not attainted,
Condemned to die for treason, but no traitor;
And that I'll prove on better men than Somerset,
Were growing time once ripened to my will.
For your partaker Pole and you yourself,
I'll note you in my book of memory,
To scourge you for this apprehension;
Look to it well, and say you are well warned.
Som. Ah, thou shalt find us ready for thee still;
And know us by these colours for thy foes,
For these my friends in spite of thee shall wear.
Plan. And, by my soul, this pale and angry rose,
As cognisance of my blood-drinking hate,
Will I for ever and my faction wear,
Until it wither with me to my grave
Or flourish to the height of my degree.
Suf. Go forward and be choked with thy ambition!
And so farewell until I meet thee next.   [*Exit*
Som. Have with thee, Pole.—Farewell, ambitious
          Richard.   [*Exit*
Plan. How I am braved, and must perforce endure it!
War. This blot that they object against your house
Shall be wiped out in the next parliament
Called for the truce of Winchester and Gloster;
And if thou be not then created York,
I will not live to be accounted Warwick.
Meantime, in signal of my love to thee,
Against proud Somerset and William Pole,
Will I upon thy party wear this rose.
And here I prophesy: this brawl to-day,
Grown to this faction in the Temple Garden,
Shall send between the red rose and the white
A thousand souls to death and deadly night.
Plan. Good Master Vernon, I am bound to you,

That you on my behalf would pluck a flower.
  Ver. In your behalf still will I wear the same.
  Law. And so will I.
  Plan. Thanks, gentle sir.
Come, let us four to dinner; I dare say
This quarrel will drink blood another day.   [*Exeunt*

SCENE V.—The Tower of London

Enter MORTIMER, *brought in a chair, and Gaolers*

  Mor. Kind keepers of my weak decaying age,
Let dying Mortimer here rest himself.
Even like a man new haléd from the rack,
So fare my limbs with long imprisonment;
And these grey locks, the pursuivants of death,
Nestor-like agéd in an age of care,
Argue the end of Edmund Mortimer.
These eyes, like lamps whose wasting oil is spent,
Wax dim, as drawing to their exigent;
Weak shoulders, overborne with burthening grief,
And pithless arms, like a withered vine
That droops his sapless branches to the ground:
Yet are these feet, whose strengthless stay is numb,
Unable to support this lump of clay,
Swift-wingéd with desire to get a grave,
As witting I no other comfort have.—
But tell me, keeper, will my nephew come?
  First Gaol. Richard Plantagenet, my lord, will come;
We sent unto the Temple, unto his chamber,
And answer was returned that he will come.
  Mor. Enough; my soul shall then be satisfied.—
Poor gentleman! his wrong doth equal mine.
Since Henry Monmouth first began to reign,
Before whose glory I was great in arms,
This loathsome sequestration have I had;
And even since then hath Richard been obscured:
Deprived of honour and inheritance.
But now the arbitrator of despairs,
Just Death, kind umpire of men's miseries,
With sweet enlargement doth dismiss me hence.
I would his troubles likewise were expired,
That so he might recover what was lost.

Enter RICHARD PLANTAGENET

  First Gaol. My lord, your loving nephew now is come.
  Mor. Richard Plantagenet, my friend, is he come?
  Plan. Ay, noble uncle, thus ignobly used,

Your nephew, late despiséd Richard, comes.
   Mor. Direct mine arms I may embrace his neck,
And in his bosom spend my latter gasp.
O, tell me when my lips do touch his cheeks,
That I may kindly give one fainting kiss.—
And now declare, sweet stem from York's great stock,
Why didst thou say, of late thou wert despised?
   Plan. First, lean thine agéd back against mine arm;
And, in that ease, I'll tell thee my disease.
This day, in argument upon a case,
Some words there grew 'twixt Somerset and me;
Among which terms he used his lavish tongue
And did upbraid me with my father's death:
Which obloquy set bars before my tongue,
Else with the like I had requited him.
Therefore, good uncle, for my father's sake,
In honour of a true Plantagenet
And for alliance sake, declare the cause
My father, Earl of Cambridge, lost his head.
   Mor. That cause, fair nephew, that imprisoned me
And hath detained me all my flowering youth
Within a loathsome dungeon, there to pine,
Was curséd instrument at his decease.
   Plan. Discover more at large what cause that was,
For I am ignorant and cannot guess.
   Mor. I will, if that my fading breath permit,
And death approach not ere my tale be done.
Henry the Fourth, grandfather to this king,
Deposed his nephew Richard, Edward's son,
The first-begotten and the lawful heir
Of Edward king, the third of that descent,
During whose reign the Percys of the north,
Finding his usurpation most unjust,
Endeavoured my advancement to the throne.
The reason moved these warlike lords to this
Was, for that—young King Richard thus removed,
Leaving no heir begotten of his body—
I was the next by birth and parentage;
For by my mother I derivéd am
From Lionel Duke of Clarence, the third son
To King Edward the Third, whereas that he
From John of Gaunt doth bring his pedigree,
Being but fourth of that heroic line.
But mark: as in this haughty great attempt
They labouréd to plant the rightful heir,
I lost my liberty and they their lives.
Long after this, when Henry the Fifth,
Succeeding his father Bolingbroke, did reign,
Thy father, Earl of Cambridge, then derived
From famous Edmund Langley, Duke of York,

Marrying my sister that thy mother was,
Again in pity of my hard distress
Levied an army, weening to redeem
And have installed me in the diadem;
But, as the rest, so fell that noble earl
And was beheaded. Thus the Mortimers,
In whom the title rested, were suppressed.
    Plan. Of which, my lord, your honour is the last.
    Mor. True; and thou seest that I no issue have.
And that my fainting words do warrant death.
Thou art my heir; the rest I wish thee gather:
But yet be wary in thy studious care.
    Plan. Thy grave admonishments prevail with me;
But yet, methinks, my father's execution
Was nothing less than bloody tyranny.
    Mor. With silence, nephew, be thou politic;
Strong-fixéd is the house of Lancaster
And like a mountain, not to be removed.
But now thy uncle is removing hence,
As princes do their courts when they are cloyed
With long continuance in a settled place.
    Plan. O, uncle, would some part of my young years
Might but redeem the passage of your age!
    Mor. Thou dost then wrong me, as that slaughterer
        doth
Which giveth many wounds when one will kill.
Mourn not, except thou sorrow for my good;
Only give order for my funeral:
And so farewell, and fair be all thy hopes,
And prosperous be thy life in peace and war!   [*Dies*
    Plan. And peace, no war, befall thy parting soul!
In prison hast thou spent a pilgrimage
And like a hermit overpassed thy days.—
Well, I will lock his counsel in my breast;
And what I do imagine let that rest.—
Keepers, convey him hence, and I myself
Will see his burial better than his life.—
      [*Exeunt Gaolers, bearing out the body of Mortimer*
Here dies the dusky torch of Mortimer,
Choked with ambition of the meaner sort:
And for those wrongs, those bitter injuries,
Which Somerset hath offered to my house,
I doubt not but with honour to redress;
And therefore haste I to the Parliament,
Either to be restoréd to my blood,
Or make my ill the advantage of my good.   [*Exit*

262

ACT THREE

Scene I.—London. The Parliament House

Flourish. Enter King, Exeter, Gloster, Warwick,
Somerset, *and* Suffolk; *the* Bishop of Winchester,
Richard Plantagenet, *and others.* Gloster *offers to
put up a bill;* Winchester *snatches it, and tears it*

Win. Com'st thou with deep-premeditated lines,
With written pamphlets studiously devised,
Humphrey of Gloster? If thou canst accuse,
Or aught intend'st to lay unto my charge,
Do it without invention, suddenly;
As I with sudden and extemporal speech
Purpose to answer what thou canst object.
    Glo. Presumptuous priest! this place commands my
        patience,
Or thou shouldst find thou hast dishonoured me.
Think not, although in writing I preferred
The manner of thy vile outrageous crimes,
That therefore I have forged, or am not able
Verbatim to rehearse the method of my pen.
No, prelate; such is thy audacious wickedness,
Thy lewd, pestiferous, and dissentious pranks,
As very infants prattle of thy pride.
Thou art a most pernicious usurer,
Froward by nature, enemy to peace;
Lascivious, wanton, more than well beseems
A man of thy profession and degree;
And for thy treachery, what's more manifest,
In that thou laid'st a trap to take my life,
As well at London bridge as at the Tower?
Beside, I fear me, if thy thoughts were sifted,
The king, thy sovereign, is not quite exempt
From envious malice of thy swelling heart.
    Win. Gloster, I do defy thee.—Lords, vouchsafe
To give me hearing what I shall reply.
If I were covetous, ambitious, or perverse,
As he will have me, how am I so poor?
Or how haps it I seek not to advance
Or raise myself, but keep my wonted calling?
And for dissension, who preferreth peace
More than I do, except I be provoked?
No, my good lords, it is not that offends;
It is not that that hath incensed the duke:
It is because no one should sway but he;
No one but he should be about the king;
And that engenders thunder in his breast,

And makes him roar these accusations forth,
But he shall know I am as good—
   Glo.   As good!
Thou bastard of my grandfather!
   Win.   Ay, lordly sir; for what are you, I pray,
But one imperious in another's throne?
   Glo.   Am I not Protector, saucy priest?
   Win.   And am not I a prelate of the church?
   Glo.   Yes, as an outlaw in a castle keeps,
And useth it to patronage his theft.
   Win.   Unreverent Gloster!
   Glo.   Thou art reverent
Touching thy spiritual function, not thy life.
   Win.   Rome shall remedy this.
   War.   Roam thither, then.
   Som.   My lord, it were your duty to forbear.
   War.   Ay, see the bishop be not overborne.
   Som.   Methinks my lord should be religious,
And know the office that belongs to such.
   War.   Methinks his lordship should be humbler;
It fitteth not a prelate so to plead.
   Som.   Yes, when his holy state is touched so near.
   War.   State holy or unhallowed, what of that?
Is not his grace Protector to the king?
   Plan.   [*Aside*] Plantagenet, I see, must hold his tongue,
Lest it be said 'Speak, sirrah, when you should;
Must your bold verdict enter talk with lords?'
Else would I have a fling at Winchester.
   King.   Uncles of Gloster and of Winchester,
The special watchmen of our English weal,
I would prevail, if prayers might prevail,
To join your hearts in love and amity.
O, what a scandal is it to our crown,
That two such noble peers as ye should jar!
Believe me, lords, my tender years can tell
Civil dissension is a viperous worm
That gnaws the bowels of the commonwealth.—
          [*A noise within*, 'Down with the tawny coats!'
What tumult's this?
   War.   An uproar, I dare warrant,
Begun through malice of the bishop's men.
            [*A noise again*, 'Stones! stones!'

Enter MAYOR

   Mayor.   O, my good lords, and virtuous Henry,
Pity the city of London, pity us!
The bishop and the Duke of Gloster's men,
Forbidden late to carry any weapon,
Have filled their pockets full of pebble stones,

And banding themselves in contráry parts
Do pelt so fast at one another's pate
That many have their giddy brains knocked out.
Our windows are broke down in every street,
And we for fear compelled to shut our shops.

Enter Serving-men, in skirmish, with bloody pates

    King. We charge you, on allegiance to ourself,
To hold your slaughtering hands and keep the peace.—
Pray, uncle Gloster, mitigate this strife.
    First Serv. Nay, if we be forbidden stones, we'll fall to
it with our teeth.
    Sec. Serv. Do what ye dare, we are as resolute.
                               [*Skirmish again*
    Glo. You of my household, leave this peevish broil,
And set this unaccustomed fight aside.
    Third Serv. My lord, we know your grace to be a man
Just and upright, and, for your royal birth,
Inferior to none but his majesty;
And ere that we will suffer such a prince,
So kind a father of the common weal,
To be disgracéd by an inkhorn mate,
We and our wives and children all will fight,
And have our bodies slaughtered by thy foes.
    First Serv. Ay, and the very parings of our nails
Shall pitch a field when we are dead.   [*Begin again*
    Glo.   Stay, stay, I say!
And if you love me, as you say you do,
Let me persuade you to forbear awhile.
    King. O, how this discord doth afflict my soul!—
Can you, my Lord of Winchester, behold
My sighs and tears and will not once relent?
Who should be pitiful, if you be not?
Or who should study to prefer a peace,
If holy churchmen take delight in broils?
    War. Yield, my lord Protector;—yield, Winchester;
Except you mean with obstinate repulse
To slay your sovereign and destroy the realm.
You see what mischief and what murther too
Hath been enacted through your enmity;
Then be at peace, except ye thirst for blood.
    Win. He shall submit, or I will never yield.
    Glo. Compassion on the king commands me stoop,
Or I would see his heart out, ere the priest
Should ever get that privilege of me.
    War. Behold, my Lord of Winchester, the duke
Hath banished moody discontented fury,
As by his smoothéd brows it doth appear;
Why look you still so stern and tragical?

Glo. Here, Winchester, I offer thee my hand.
King. Fie, Uncle Beaufort! I have heard you preach
That malice was a great and grievous sin;
And will not you maintain the thing you teach,
But prove a chief offender in the same?
War. Sweet king!—the bishop hath a kindly gird.
For shame, my lord of Winchester, relent!
What, shall a child instruct you what to do?
Win. Well, Duke of Gloster, I will yield to thee;
Love for thy love and hand for hand I give.
Glo. [*Aside*] Ay, but, I fear me, with a hollow heart.—
See here, my friends and loving countrymen,
This token serveth for a flag of truce
Betwixt ourselves and all our followers.
So help me God, as I dissemble not.
Win. [*Aside*] So help me God, as I intend it not!
King. O loving uncle, kind Duke of Gloster,
How joyful am I made by this contract!—
Away, my masters! trouble us no more;
But join in friendship, as your lords have done.
First Serv. Content; I'll to the surgeon's.
Sec. Serv.   And so will I.
Third Serv. And I will see what physic the tavern
      affords.   [*Exeunt Serving-men, Mayor, etc.*
War. Accept this scroll, most gracious sovereign,
Which in the right of Richard Plantagenet
We do exhibit to your majesty.
Glo. Well urged, my lord of Warwick;—for, sweet
      prince,
An if your grace mark every circumstance,
You have great reason to do Richard right;
Especially for those occasions
At Eltham Place I told your majesty.
King. And those occasions, uncle, were of force;
Therefore, my loving lords, our pleasure is
That Richard be restoréd to his blood.
War. Let Richard be restoréd to his blood;
So shall his father's wrongs be recompensed.
Win. As will the rest, so willeth Winchester.
King. If Richard will be true, not that alone
But all the whole inheritance I give
That doth belong unto the house of York,
From whence you spring by lineal descent.
Plan. Thy humble servant vows obedience
And humble service till the point of death.
King. Stoop then and set your knee against my foot;
And, in reguerdon of that duty done,
I gird thee with the valiant sword of York.
Rise, Richard, like a true Plantagenet,
And rise created princely Duke of York.

Plan. And so thrive Richard as thy foes may fall!
And as my duty springs, so perish they
That grudge one thought against your majesty!
All. Welcome, high prince, the mighty Duke of York!
Som. [*Aside*] Perish, base prince, ignoble Duke of York!
Glo. Now will it best avail your majesty
To cross the seas and to be crowned in France.
The presence of a king engenders love
Amongst his subjects and his loyal friends,
As it disanimates his enemies.
King. When Gloster says the word, King Henry goes;
For friendly counsel cuts off many foes.
Glo. Your ships already are in readiness.
                [*Sennet. Fourish. Exeunt all but Exeter*
Exeter. Ay, we may march in England or in France,
Not seeing what is likely to ensue.
This late dissension grown betwixt the peers
Burns under feignéd ashes of forged love,
And will at last break out into a flame.
As festered members rot but by degree,
Till bones and flesh and sinews fall away,
So will this base and envious discord breed.
And now I fear that fatal prophecy
Which in the time of Henry named the Fifth
Was in the mouth of every sucking babe,—
That Henry born at Monmouth should win all,
And Henry born at Windsor should lose all;
Which is so plain that Exeter doth wish
His days may finish ere that helpless time.   [*Exit*

SCENE II.—France. Before Rouen

Enter LA PUCELLE *disguised, with four Soldiers with sacks
upon their backs*

Puc. These are the city gates, the gates of Rouen,
Through which our policy must make a breach.
Take heed, be wary how you place your words;
Talk like the vulgar sort of market men
That come to gather money for their corn.
If we have entrance, as I hope we shall,
And that we find the slothful watch but weak,
I'll by a sign give notice to our friends,
That Charles the Dauphin may encounter them.
First Sol. Our sacks shall be a mean to sack the city,
And we be lords and rulers over Rouen;
Therefore we'll knock.   [*Knocks*
Watch. [*Within*] Qui est là?
Puc. Paysans, pauvres gens de France;
                267

Poor market folks that come to sell their corn.
Watch. Enter, go in; the market bell is rung.
Puc. Now, Rouen, I'll shake thy bulwarks to the
    ground.   [*Exeunt*

Enter CHARLES, *the* BASTARD OF ORLEANS, ALENÇON,
    REIGNIER, *and forces*

Char. Saint Denis bless this happy stratagem,
And once again we'll sleep secure in Rouen!
Bast. Here entered Pucelle and her practisants;
Now she is there, how will she specify
Where is the best and safest passage in?
Reig. By thrusting out a torch from yonder tower;
Which, once discerned, shows that her meaning is,—
No way to that, for weakness, which she entered.

Enter LA PUCELLE *on the top, thrusting out a torch
    burning*

Puc. Behold, this is the happy wedding torch
That joineth Rouen unto her countrymen,
But burning fatal to the Talbotites!   [*Exit*
Bast. See, noble Charles, the beacon of our friend;
The burning torch in yonder turret stands.
Char. Now shine it like a comet of revenge,
A prophet to the fall of all our foes!
Reig. Defer no time, delays have dangerous ends;
Enter, and cry 'The Dauphin!' presently,
And then do execution on the watch.   [*Alarum. Exeunt*

An alarum. Enter TALBOT *in an excursion*

Tal. France, thou shalt rue this treason with thy tears,
If Talbot but survive thy treachery.
Pucelle, that witch, that damnéd sorceress,
Hath wrought this hellish mischief unawares,
That hardly we escaped the pride of France.   [*Exit*

An alarum: excursions. BEDFORD *brought in sick in a
    chair. Enter* TALBOT *and* BURGUNDY *without: within*
    LA PUCELLE, CHARLES, BASTARD, ALENÇON, *and*
    REIGNIER, *on the walls*

Puc. Good morrow, gallants! want ye corn for bread?
I think the Duke of Burgundy will fast
Before he'll buy again at such a rate.
'T was full of darnel; do you like the taste?
Bur. Scoff on, vile fiend and shameless courtesan!
I trust ere long to choke thee with thine own,

And make thee curse the harvest of that corn.
   Char.   Your grace may starve perhaps before that time.
   Bed.   O, let no words, but deeds, revenge this treason!
   Puc.   What will you do, good grey-beard? break a lance,
And run a tilt at death within a chair?
   Tal.   Foul fiend of France, and hag of all despite,
Encompassed with thy lustful paramours!
Becomes it thee to taunt his valiant age,
And twit with cowardice a man half dead?
Damsel, I'll have a bout with you again,
Or else let Talbot perish with this shame.
   Puc.   Are ye so hot, sir?—yet, Pucelle, hold thy peace;
If Talbot do but thunder, rain will follow.—
              [*The English whisper together in council*
God speed the parliament! who shall be the speaker?
   Tal.   Dare ye come forth and meet us in the field?
   Puc.   Belike your lordship takes us then for fools,
To try if that our own be ours or no.
   Tal.   I speak not to that railing Hecate,
But unto thee, Alençon, and the rest.
Will ye, like soldiers, come and fight it out?
   Alen.   Signior, no.
   Tal.   Signior, hang! base muleters of France!
Like peasant footboys do they keep the walls,
And dare not take up arms like gentlemen.
   Puc.   Away, captains! let's get us from the walls;
For Talbot means no goodness by his looks.—
God be wi' you, my lord! we came but to tell you
That we are here.   [*Exeunt from the walls*
   Tal.   And there will we be too, ere it be long,
Or else reproach be Talbot's greatest fame!—
Vow, Burgundy, by honour of thy house,
Pricked on by public wrongs sustained in France;
Either to get the town again or die;
And I, as sure as English Henry lives
And as his father here was conqueror,
As sure as in this late-betrayéd town
Great Cœur-de-lion's heart was buriéd,
So sure I swear to get the town or die.
   Bur.   My vows are equal partners with thy vows.
   Tal.   But, ere we go, regard this dying prince,
The valiant Duke of Bedford.—Come, my lord,
We will bestow you in some better place,
Fitter for sickness and for crazy age.
   Bed.   Lord Talbot, do not so dishonour me;
Here will I sit before the walls of Rouen
And will be partner of your weal or woe.
   Bur.   Courageous Bedford, let us now persuade you.
   Bed.   Not to be gone from hence; for once I read

That stout Pendragon in his litter sick
Came to the field and vanquishéd his foes.
Methinks I should revive the soldiers' hearts,
Because I ever found them as myself.
    Tal.   Undaunted spirit in a dying breast!
Then be it so.—Heavens keep old Bedford safe!—
And now no more ado, brave Burgundy,
But gather we our forces out of hand
And set upon our boasting enemy.
                [Exeunt all but Bedford and Attendants

An alarum: excursions. Enter SIR JOHN FASTOLFE *and*
a Captain

    Cap.   Whither away, Sir John Fastolfe, in such haste?
    Fast.   Whither away! to save myself by flight;
We are like to have the overthrow again.
    Cap.   What! will you fly, and leave Lord Talbot?
    Fast.   Ay,
All the Talbots in the world, to save my life.   *[Exit*
    Cap.   Cowardly knight! ill fortune follow thee! *[Exit*

Retreat; excursions. LA PUCELLE, ALENCON, *and*
CHARLES *fly*

    Bed.   Now, quiet soul, depart when heaven please,
For I have seen our enemies' overthrow.
What is the trust or strength of foolish man?
They that of late were daring with their scoffs
Are glad and fain by flight to save themselves.
        [Bedford dies, and is carried in by two in his chair

An alarum. Re-enter TALBOT, BURGUNDY, *and the rest*

    Tal.   Lost, and recovered in a day again!
This is a double honour, Burgundy;
Yet heavens have glory for this victory!
    Bur.   Warlike and martial Talbot, Burgundy
Enshrines thee in his heart, and there erects
Thy noble deeds as valour's monuments.
    Tal.   Thanks, gentle duke. But where is Pucelle now?
I think her old familiar is asleep.
Now where's the Bastard's braves, and Charles his gleeks?
What, all amort? Rouen hangs her head for grief
That such a valiant company are fled.
Now will we take some order in the town,
Placing therein some expert officers,
And then depart to Paris to the king,
For there young Henry and his nobles lie.
    Bur.   What wills Lord Talbot pleaseth Burgundy.

Tal.   But yet, before we go, let's not forget
The noble duke of Bedford late deceased,
But see his exequies fulfilled in Rouen.
A braver soldier never couchéd lance,
A gentler heart did never sway in court;
But kings and mightiest potentates must die,
For that's the end of human misery.   [*Exeunt*

SCENE III.—The Plains near Rouen

Enter CHARLES, *the* BASTARD OF ORLEANS, ALENÇON, LA
PUCELLE, *and forces*

Puc.   Dismay not, princes, at this accident,
Nor grieve that Rouen is so recoveréd;
Care is no cure, but rather córrosive,
For things that are not to be remedied.
Let frantic Talbot triumph for awhile,
And like a peacock sweep along his tail;
We'll pull his plumes and take away his train,
If Dauphin and the rest will be but ruled.
Char.   We have been guided by thee hitherto,
And of thy cunning had no diffidence;
One sudden foil shall never breed distrust.
Bast.   Search out thy wit for secret policies,
And we will make thee famous through the world.
Alen.   We'll set thy statue in some holy place,
And have thee reverenced like a blessed saint;
Employ thee then, sweet virgin, for our good.
Puc.   Then thus it must be; this doth Joan devise:
By fair persuasions mixed with sugared words
We will entice the Duke of Burgundy
To leave the Talbot and to follow us.
Char.   Ay, marry, sweeting, if we could do that,
France were no place for Henry's warriors;
Nor should that nation boast it so with us,
But be extirped from our provinces.
Alen.   For ever should they be expulsed from France,
And not have title of an earldom here.
Puc.   Your honours shall perceive how I will work
To bring this matter to the wishéd end.
                              [*Drum sounds afar off*
Hark! by the sound of drum you may perceive
Their powers are marching unto Paris-ward.

*Here sound an English march.   Enter, and pass over at a
distance,* TALBOT *and his forces*

There goes the Talbot, with his colours spread,
And all the troops of English after him.

French march.   Enter the DUKE OF BURGUNDY
and forces

Now in the rearward comes the duke and his;
Fortune in favour makes him lag behind.
Summon a parley; we will talk with him.
                              [*Trumpet sounds a parley*

Char.   A parley with the Duke of Burgundy!
Bur.   Who craves a parley with the Burgundy?
Puc.   That princely Charles of France, thy countryman.
Bur.   What say'st thou, Charles? for I am marching
    hence.
Char.   Speak, Pucelle, and enchant him with thy words.
Puc.   Brave Burgundy, undoubted hope of France!
Stay, let thy humble handmaid speak to thee.
Bur.   Speak on; but be not over-tedious.
Puc.   Look on thy country, look on fertile France,
And see the cities and the towns defaced
By wasting ruin of the cruel foe.
As looks the mother on her lovely babe
When death doth close his tender dying eyes,
See, see the pining malady of France;
Behold the wounds, the most unnatural wounds,
Which thou thyself hast given her woful breast.
O, turn thy edgéd sword another way;
Strike those that hurt, and hurt not those that help.
One drop of blood drawn from thy country's bosom
Should grieve thee more than streams of foreign gore;
Return thee therefore with a flood of tears,
And wash away thy country's stainéd spots.
Bur.   Either she hath bewitched me with her words,
Or nature makes me suddenly relent.
Puc.   Besides, all French and France exclaims on thee,
Doubting thy birth and lawful progeny.
Who join'st thou with but with a lordly nation
That will not trust thee but for profit's sake?
When Talbot hath set footing once in France
And fashioned thee that instrument of ill,
Who then but English Henry will be lord
And thou be thrust out like a fugitive?
Call we to mind, and mark but this for proof,
Was not the Duke of Orleans thy foe?
And was he not in England prisoner?
But when they heard he was thine enemy,
They set him free without his ransom paid
In spite of Burgundy and all his friends.
See, then, thou fight'st against thy countrymen,
And join'st with them will be thy slaughter-men.
Come, come, return; return, thou wandering lord.
Charles and the rest will take thee in their arms.

Bur.　I'm vanquishéd; these haughty words of hers
Have battered me like roaring cannon-shot,
And made me almost yield upon my knees.—
Forgive me, country, and sweet countrymen,
And, lords, accept this hearty kind embrace;
My forces and my power of men are yours.—
So farewell, Talbot; I'll no longer trust thee.
　　Puc.　[*Aside*]　Done like a Frenchman; turn, and turn
　　　　again!
　　Char.　Welcome, brave duke! thy friendship makes us
　　　　fresh.
　　Bast.　And doth beget new courage in our breasts.
　　Alen.　Pucelle hath bravely played her part in this,
And doth deserve a coronet of gold.
　　Char.　Now let us on, my lords, and join our powers,
And seek how we may prejudice the foe.　　　　*[Exeunt*

SCENE IV.—Paris.　The Palace

Enter the KING, GLOSTER, BISHOP OF WINCHESTER, YORK,
　　SUFFOLK, SOMERSET, WARWICK, EXETER, VERNON,
　　BASSET, *and others.　To them with his Soldiers,* TALBOT

Tal.　My gracious prince, and honourable peers,
Hearing of your arrival in this realm,
I have awhile given truce unto my wars,
To do my duty to my sovereign;
In sign whereof, this arm, that hath reclaimed
To your obedience fifty fortresses,
Twelve cities, and seven walléd towns of strength,
Beside five hundred prisoners of esteem,
Lets fall his sword before your highness' feet,
And with submissive loyalty of heart
Ascribes the glory of his conquest got
First to my God and next unto your grace.　　　　*[Kneels*
　　King.　Is this the Lord Talbot, uncle Gloster,
That hath so long been resident in France?
　　Glos.　Yes, if it please your majesty, my liege.
　　King.　Welcome, brave captain and victorious lord!
When I was young, as yet I am not old,
I do remember how my father said
A stouter champion never handled sword.
Long since we were resolvéd of your truth,
Your faithful service, and your toil in war;
Yet never have you tasted our reward,
Or been reguerdoned with so much as thanks,
Because till now we never saw your face.
Therefore, stand up; and, for these good deserts,
We here create you Earl of Shrewsbury;

And in our coronation take your place.
            [*Sennet. Flourish. Exeunt all but Vernon and Basset*
    Ver. Now, sir, to you, that were so hot at sea,
Disgracing of these colours that I wear
In honour of my noble lord of York,
Dar'st thou maintain the former words thou spakest?
    Bas. Yes, sir; as well as you dare patronage
The envious barking of your saucy tongue
Against my lord the Duke of Somerset.
    Ver. Sirrah, thy lord I honour as he is.
    Bas. Why, what is he? as good a man as York.
    Ver. Hark ye, not so; in witness, take ye that.
                                              [*Strikes him*
    Bas. Villain, thou know'st the law of arms is such
That whoso draws a sword, 't is present death,
Or else this blow should broach thy dearest blood
But I'll unto his majesty, and crave
I may have liberty to venge this wrong,
When thou shalt see I'll meet thee to thy cost.
    Ver. Well, miscreant, I'll be there as soon as you,
And, after, meet you sooner than you would.   [*Exeunt*

ACT FOUR

SCENE I.—Paris.   A Hall of State

Enter the KING, GLOSTE.., BISHOP OF WINCHESTER, YORK,
    SUFFOLK, SOMERSET, WARWICK, TALBOT, EXETER, *the*
    GOVERNOR OF PARIS, *and others*

    Glo. Lord bishop, set the crown upon his head.
    Win.   God save King Henry, of that name the Sixth!
    Glo. Now, governor of Paris, take your oath,
That you elect no other king but him,
Esteem none friends but such as are his friends,
And none your foes but such as shall pretend
Malicious practices against his state;
This shall ye do, so help you righteous God!

Enter SIR JOHN FASTOLFE

    Fast. My gracious sovereign, as I rode from Calais,
To haste unto your coronation,
A letter was delivered to my hands,
Writ to your grace from the Duke of Burgundy.
    Tal. Shame to the Duke of Burgundy and thee!
I vowed, base knight, when I did meet thee next,
To tear the garter from thy craven's leg. [*Plucking it off*

Which I have done, because unworthily
Thou wast installéd in that high degree.—
Pardon me, princely Henry, and the rest:
This dastard, at the battle of Patay,
When but in all I was six thousand strong
And that the French were almost ten to one,
Before we met or that a stroke was given,
Like to a trusty squire did run away:
In which assault we lost twelve hundred men;
Myself and divers gentlemen beside
Were there surprised and taken prisoners.
Then judge, great lords, if I have done amiss;
Or whether that such cowards ought to wear
This ornament of knighthood, yea or no.
   Glo. To say the truth, this fact was infamous·
And ill beseeming any common man,
Much more a knight, a captain, and a leader.
   Tal. When first this order was ordained, my lords,
Knights of the Garter were of noble birth,
Valiant and virtuous, full of haughty courage,
Such as were grown to credit by the wars;
Not fearing death, nor shrinking for distress,
But always resolute in most extremes.
He then that is not furnished in this sort
Doth but usurp the sacred name of knight,
Profaning this most honourable order,
And should, if I were worthy to be judge,
Be quite degraded, like a hedge-born swain
That doth presume to boast of gentle blood.
   King. Stain to thy countrymen, thou hear'st thy doom!
Be packing, therefore, thou that wast a knight;
Henceforth we banish thee, on pain of death.—
                                 [*Exit Fastolfe*
And now, my lord Protector, view the letter
Sent from our uncle Duke of Burgundy.
   Glo. What means his grace, that he hath changed his
     style?
No more but, plain and bluntly, 'To the king!'
Hath he forgot he is his sovereign?
Or doth this churlish superscription
Pretend some alteration in good will?
What's here? [*Reads*] ' *I have, upon especial cause*
Moved with compassion of my country's wrack,
Together with the pitiful complaints
Of such as your oppression feeds upon,
Forsaken your pernicious faction
And joined with Charles, the rightful King of France.'—
O monstrous treachery! can this be so,
That in alliance, amity, and oaths,
There should be found such false dissembling guile?

King.   What! doth my uncle Burgundy revolt?
Glo.   He doth, my lord, and is become your foe.
King.   Is that the worst this letter doth contain?
Glo.   It is the worst, and all, my lord, he writes.
King.   Why, then, Lord Talbot there shall talk with him,
And give him chastisement for this abuse.—
How say you, my lord? are you not content?
Tal.   Content, my liege! yes, but that I am prevented,
I should have begged I might have been employed.
King.   Then gather strength and march unto him straight;
Let him perceive how ill we brook his treason,
And what offence it is to flout his friends.
Tal.   I go, my lord, in heart desiring still
You may behold confusion of your foes.   [*Exit*

Enter VERNON *and* BASSET

Ver.   Grant me the combat, gracious sovereign.
Bas.   And me, my lord, grant me the combat too.
York.   This is my servant; hear him, noble prince.
Som.   And this is mine; sweet Henry, favour him.
King.   Be patient, lords; and give them leave to speak.—
Say, gentlemen, what makes you thus exclaim?
And wherefore crave you combat? or with whom?
Ver.   With him, my lord; for he hath done me wrong.
Bas.   And I with him; for he hath done me wrong.
King.   What is that wrong whereof you both complain?
First let me know, and then I'll answer you.
Bas.   Crossing the sea from England into France,
This fellow here, with envious carping tongue,
Upbraided me about the rose I wear;
Saying, the sanguine colour of the leaves
Did represent my master's blushing cheeks,
When stubbornly he did repugn the truth
About a certain question in the law
Argued betwixt the Duke of York and him,
With other vile and ignominious terms;
In confutation of which rude reproach
And in defence of my lord's worthiness,
I crave the benefit of law of arms.
Ver.   And that is my petition, noble lord:
For though he seem with forgéd quaint conceit
To set a gloss upon his bold intent,
Yet know, my lord, I was provoked by him;
And he first took exceptions at this badge,
Pronouncing that the paleness of this flower
Bewrayed the faintness of my master's heart.

York. Will not this malice, Somerset, be left?
Som. Your private grudge, my Lord of York, will out,
Though ne'er so cunningly you smother it.
King. Good Lord, what madness rules in brain-sick men.
When for so slight and frivolous a cause
Such factious emulations shall arise!—
Good cousins both, of York and Somerset,
Quiet yourselves, I pray, and be at peace.
York. Let this dissension first be tried by fight,
And then your highness shall command a peace.
Som. The quarrel toucheth none but us alone;
Betwixt ourselves let us decide it then.
York. There is my pledge; accept it, Somerset.
Ver. Nay, let it rest where it began at first.
Bas. Confirm it so, mine honourable lord.
Glo. Confirm it so! Confounded be your strife!
And perish ye, with your audacious prate!
Presumptuous vassals, are you not ashamed
With this immodest clamorous outrage
To trouble and disturb the king and us?—
And you, my lords, methinks you do not well
To bear with their perverse objections;
Much less to take occasion from their mouths
To raise a mutiny betwixt yourselves.
Let me persuade you take a better course.
Exe. It grieves his highness.—Good my lords, be friends.
King. Come hither, you that would be combatants.
Henceforth I charge you, as you love our favour,
Quite to forget this quarrel and the cause.—
And you, my lords, remember where we are;
In France, amongst a fickle wavering nation.
If they perceive dissension in our looks,
And that within ourselves we disagree,
How will their grudging stomachs be provoked
To wilful disobedience, and rebel!
Beside, what infamy will there arise,
When foreign princes shall be certified
That for a toy, a thing of no regard,
King Henry's peers and chief nobility
Destroyed themselves, and lost the realm of France;
O, think upon the conquest of my father,
My tender years, and let us not forego
That for a trifle that was bought with blood!
Let me be umpire in this doubtful strife.
I see no reason, if I wear this rose,   [*Putting on a red rose*
That any one should therefore be suspicious
I more incline to Somerset than York;
Both are my kinsmen, and I love them both.
As well they may upbraid me with my crown,
Because, forsooth, the king of Scots is crowned.

But your discretions better can persuade
Than I am able to instruct or teach;
And therefore, as we hither came in peace,
So let us still continue peace and love.—
Cousin of York, we institute your grace
To be our Regent in these parts of France;—
And, good my lord of Somerset, unite
Your troops of horsemen with his bands of foot:
And, like true subjects, sons of your progenitors.
Go cheerfully together and digest
Your angry choler on your enemies.
Ourself, my lord Protector, and the rest,
After some respite will return to Calais;
From thence to England; where I hope ere long
To be presented, by your victories.
With Charles, Alençon, and that traitorous rout.
       [*Flourish. Exeunt all but York, Warwick, Exeter,*
                               and Vernon

  War. My Lord of York, I promise you, the king
Prettily, methought, did play the orator.
  York. And so he did; but yet I like it not,
In that he wears the badge of Somerset.
  War. Tush, that was but his fancy, blame him not;
I dare presume, sweet prince, he thought no harm.
  York. And if I wist he did,—but let it rest;
Other affairs must now be managéd. [*Exeunt all but Exeter*
  Exe. Well didst thou, Richard, to suppress thy voice;
For, had the passions of thy heart burst out,
I fear we should have seen deciphered there
More rancorous spite, more furious raging broils
Than yet can be managed or supposed.
But howsoe'er, no simple man that sees
This jarring discord of nobility,
This shouldering of each other in the court,
This factious bandying of their favourites,
But that it doth presage some ill event.
'T is much when sceptres are in children's hands,
But more when envy breeds unkind division;
There comes the ruin, there begins confusion.   [*Exit*

SCENE II.—Before Bordeaux

Enter TALBOT, *with trump and drum*

  Tal. Go to the gates of Bordeaux, trumpeter;
Summon their general unto the wall.

    Trumpet sounds. Enter General and others, aloft

English John Talbot, captains, calls you forth,
Servant in arms to Harry King of England;

And thus he would: Open your city gates,
Be humble to us; call my sovereign yours,
And do him homage as obedient subjects,
And I 'll withdraw me and my bloody power:
But, if you frown upon this proffered peace,
You tempt the fury of my three attendants,
Lean famine, quartering steel, and climbing fire,
Who in a moment even with the earth
Shall lay your stately and air-braving towers,
If you forsake the offer of our love.
    Gen. Thou ominous and fearful owl of death,
Our nation's terror and their bloody scourge!
The period of thy tyranny approacheth.
On us thou canst not enter but by death;
For, I protest, we are well fortified
And strong enough to issue out and fight.
If thou retire, the Dauphin, well appointed,
Stands with the snares of war to tangle thee;
On either hand thee there are squadrons pitched,
To wall thee from the liberty of flight,
And no way canst thou turn thee for redress,
But death doth front thee with apparent spoil,
And pale destruction meets thee in the face.
Ten thousand French have ta'en the sacrament
To rive their dangerous artillery
Upon no Christian soul but English Talbot.
Lo, there thou stand'st, a breathing valiant man,
Of an invincible unconquered spirit!
This is the latest glory of thy praise
That I, thy enemy, due thee withal;
For ere the glass that now begins to run
Finish the process of his sandy hour,
These eyes that see thee now well colouréd,
Shall see thee withered, bloody, pale, and dead.
                        [Drum afar off
Hark! hark! the Dauphin's drum, a warning bell,
Sings heavy music to thy timorous soul;
And mine shall ring thy dire departure out.
                        [Exeunt General, etc.
    Tal. He fables not; I hear the enemy.—
Out, some light horsemen, and peruse their wings.
O negligent and heedless discipline!
How are we parked and bounded in a pale,
A little herd of England's timorous deer,
Mazed with a yelping kennel of French curs!
If we be English deer, be then in blood;
Not rascal-like, to fall down with a pinch,
But rather, moody-mad and desperate stags,
Turn on the bloody hounds with heads of steel,
And make the cowards stand aloof at bay.

Sell every man his life as dear as mine,
And they shall find dear deer of us, my friends.
God and Saint George, Talbot and England's right,
Prosper our colours in this dangerous fight!   [*Exeunt*

SCENE III.—Plains in Gascony

Enter a Messenger that meets YORK. *Enter* YORK *with trumpet and many Soldiers*

    York. Are not the speedy scouts returned again,
That dogged the mighty army of the Dauphin?
    Mess. They are returned, my lord, and give it out
That he is marched to Bourdeaux with his power,
To fight with Talbot. As he marched along,
By your espials were discovéred
Two mightier troops than that the Dauphin led,
Which joined with him and made their march for Bour-
    deaux.
    York. A plague upon that villain Somerset,
That thus delays my promiséd supply
Of horsemen, that were levied for this siege!
Renownèd Talbot doth expect my aid,
And I am louted by a traitor villain
And cannot help the noble chevalier.
God comfort him in this necessity!
If he miscarry, farewell wars in France!

Enter SIR WILLIAM LUCY

    Lucy. Thou princely leader of our English strength,
Never so needful on the earth of France,
Spur to the rescue of the noble Talbot,
Who now is girdled with a waist of iron
And hemmed about with grim destruction.
To Bordeaux, warlike duke! to Bordeaux, York!
Else, farewell Talbot, France, and England's honour.
    York. O God, that Somerset, who in proud heart
Doth stop my cornets, were in Talbot's place!
So should we save a valiant gentleman
By forfeiting a traitor and a coward.
Mad ire and wrathful fury makes me weep,
That thus we die, while remiss traitors sleep.
    Lucy. O, send some succour to the distressed lord!
    York. He dies, we lose; I break my warlike word:
We mourn, France smiles; we lose, they daily get;
All long of this vile traitor Somerset.
    Lucy. Then God take mercy on brave Talbot's soul;
And on his son young John, who two hours since

I met in travel toward his warlike father!
This seven years did not Talbot see his son,
And now they meet where both their lives are done.
    York.   Alas, what joy shall noble Talbot have
To bid his young son welcome to his grave?
Away! vexation almost stops my breath,
That sundered friends greet in the hour of death.—
Lucy, farewell; no more my fortune can,
But curse the cause I cannot aid the man.—
Maine, Blois, Poictiers, and Tours are won away,
'Long all of Somerset and his delay.
                           [Exit, with his soldiers
    Lucy.   Thus, while the vulture of sedition
Feeds in the bosom of such great commanders,
Sleeping neglection doth betray to loss
The conquest of our scarce cold conqueror,
That ever living man of memory,
Henry the Fifth.   Whiles they each other cross,
Lives, honours, lands, and all hurry to loss.   *[Exit*

SCENE IV.—Other Plains in Gascony

Enter SOMERSET, *with his army; a Captain of* TALBOT'S
with him

    Som.   It is too late; I cannot send them now.
This expedition was by York and Talbot
Too rashly plotted; all our general force
Might with a sally of the very town
Be buckled with.   The over-daring Talbot
Hath sullied all his gloss of former honour
By this unheedful, desperate, wild adventure.
York set him on to fight and die in shame,
That, Talbot dead, great York might bear the name.
    Cap.   Here is Sir William Lucy, who with me
Set from our o'ermatched forces forth for aid.

Enter SIR WILLIAM LUCY

    Som.   How now, Sir William! whither were you sent?
    Lucy.   Whither, my lord? from bought and sold Lord
        Talbot,
Who, ringed about with bold adversity,
Cries out for noble York and Somerset,
To beat assailing death from his weak legions:
And whiles the honourable captain there
Drops bloody sweat from his war-wearied limbs,
And, in advantage lingering, looks for rescue,
You, his false hopes, the trust of England's honour,

Keep off aloof with worthless emulation.
Let not your private discord keep away
The levied succours that should lend him aid,
While he, renownéd gentleman,
Yields up his life unto a world of odds.
Orleans the Bastard, Charles, Burgundy,
Alençon, Reignier, compass him about,
And Talbot perisheth by your default.
    Som.   York set him on. York should have sent him aid.
    Lucy.   And York as fast upon your grace exclaims;
Swearing that you withheld his levied host,
Collected for this expedition.
    Som.   York lies; he might have sent, and had the horse.
I owe him little duty, and less love,
And take foul scorn to fawn on him by sending.
    Lucy.   The fraud of England, not the force of France,
Hath now entrapped the noble-minded Talbot.
Never to England shall he bear his life,
But dies betrayed to fortune by your strife.
    Som.   Come, go; I will dispatch the horsemen straight:
Within six hours they will be at his aid.
    Lucy.   Too late comes rescue: he is ta'en or slain;
For fly he could not, if he would have fled.
And fly would Talbot never, though he might.
    Som.   If he be dead, brave Talbot, then adieu!
    Lucy.   His fame lives in the world, his shame in you.
                            [*Exeunt*

Scene V.—The English Camp near Bordeaux

Enter TALBOT *and* JOHN *his son*

    Tal.   O young John Talbot! I did send for thee
To tutor thee in stratagems of war,
That Talbot's name might be in thee revived
When sapless age and weak unable limbs
Should bring thy father to his drooping chair.
But, O malignant and ill-boding stars!
Now thou art come unto a feast of death,
A terrible and unavoided danger.
Therefore, dear boy, mount on my swiftest horse,
And I'll direct thee how thou shalt escape
By sudden flight; come, dally not, be gone.
    John.   Is my name Talbot? and am I your son?
And shall I fly? O, if you love my mother,
Dishonour not her honourable name,
To make a bastard and a slave of me!
The world will say he is not Talbot's blood,
That basely fled when noble Talbot stood.
    Tal.   Fly, to revenge my death, if I be slain.

John. He that flies so will ne'er return again.
Tal. If we both stay, we both are sure to die.   •
John. Then let me stay, and, father, do you fly;
Your loss is great, so your regard should be;
My worth unknown, no loss is known in me.
Upon my death the French can little boast;
In yours they will; in you all hopes are lost.
Flight cannot stain the honour you have won;
But mine it will, that no exploit have done.
You fled for vantage, every one will swear;
But, if I bow, they'll say it was for fear.
There is hope that ever I will stay,
In the first hour I shrink and run away.
Here on my knee I beg mortality,
Rather than life preserved with infamy.
Tal. Shall all thy mother's hopes lie in one tomb?
John. Ay, rather than I'll shame my mother's womb.
Tal. Upon my blessing, I command thee go.
John. To fight I will, but not to fly the foe.
Tal. Part of thy father may be saved in thee.
John. No part of him but will be shame in me.
Tal. Thou never hadst renown, nor canst not lose it.
John. Yes, your renownéd name; shall flight abuse it?
Tal. Thy father's charge shall clear thee from that stain.
John. You cannot witness for me, being slain.
If death be so apparent, then both fly.
Tal. And leave my followers here to fight and die?
My age was never tainted with such shame.
John. And shall my youth be guilty of such blame?
No more can I be severed from your side,
Than can yourself yourself in twain divide.
Stay, go, do what you will, the like do I;
For live I will not, if my father die.
Tal. Then here I take my leave of thee, fair son,
Born to eclipse thy life this afternoon.
Come, side by side together live and die,
And soul with soul from France to heaven fly.   [*Exeunt*

SCENE VI.—A Field of Battle

Alarum; excursions, wherein TALBOT'S SON *is hemmed
about, and* TALBOT *rescues him*

Tal. Saint George and victory! fight, soldiers, fight!
The Regent hath with Talbot broke his word,
And left us to the rage of France his sword.
Where is John Talbot?—Pause, and take thy breath;
I gave thee life, and rescued thee from death.
John. O, twice my father, twice am I thy son!

283

The life thou gav'st me first was lost and done,
Till with thy warlike sword, despite of fate,
To thy determined time thou gav'st new date.
    Tal.   When from the Dauphin's crest thy sword struck
        fire,
It warmed thy father's heart with proud desire
Of bold-faced victory.   Then leaden age,
Quickened with youthful spleen and warlike rage,
Beat down Alençon, Orleans, Burgundy,
And from the pride of Gallia rescued thee.
The ireful bastard Orleans, that drew blood
From thee, my boy, and had the maidenhood
Of thy first fight, I soon encounteréd;
And interchanging blows I quickly shed
Some of his bastard blood, and in disgrace
Bespoke him thus: 'Contaminated, base,
And misbegotten blood I spill of thine,
Mean and right poor, for that pure blood of mine
Which thou didst force from Talbot, my brave boy.
Here, purposing the Bastard to destroy,
Came in strong rescue. Speak, thy father's care,
Art thou not weary, John? how dost thou fare?
Wilt thou yet leave the battle, boy, and fly,
Now thou art sealed the son of chivalry?
Fly, to revenge my death when I am dead;
The help of one stands me in little stead.
O, too much folly is it, well I wot,
To hazard all our lives in one small boat!
If I to-day die not with Frenchmen's rage,
To-morrow I shall die with mickle age.
By me they nothing gain an if I stay;
'T is but the shortening of my life one day:
In thee thy mother dies, our household's name,
My death's revenge, thy youth, and England's fame.
All these and more we hazard by thy stay;
All these are saved if thou wilt fly away.
    John.   The sword of Orleans hath not made me smart:
These words of yours draw life-blood from my heart.
On that advantage, bought with such a shame,
To save a paltry life and slay bright fame,
Before young Talbot from old Talbot fly,
The coward horse that bears me fall and die!
And like me to the peasant boys of France,
To be shame's scorn and subject of mischance!
Surely, by all the glory you have won,
An if I fly, I am not Talbot's son.
Then talk no more of flight, it is no boot;
If son to Talbot, die at Talbot's foot.
    Tal.   Then follow thou thy desperate sire of Crete.
Thou Icarus! Thy life to me is sweet;

If thou wilt fight, fight by thy father's side,
And, commendable proved, let's die in pride.   [*Exeunt*

SCENE VII.—*Another Part of the Field*

Alarum; excursions.   Enter old TALBOT *led by a Servant*

Tal.   Where is my other life? mine own is gone;
O, where's young Talbot? where is valiant John?
Triumphant death, smeared with captivity,
Young Talbot's valour makes me smile at thee.
When he perceived me shrink and on my knee,
His bloody sword he brandished over me
And, like a hungry lion, did commence
Rough deeds of rage and stern impatience:
But when my angry guardant stood alone,
Tendering my ruin and assailed of none,
Dizzy-eyed fury and great rage of heart
Suddenly made him from my side to start
Into the clustering battle of the French;
And in that sea of blood my boy did drench
His over-mounting spirit, and there died,
My Icarus, my blossom, in his pride.
    Serv.   O my dear lord, lo, where your son is borne!

Enter SOLDIERS, *with the body of young* TALBOT

Tal.   Thou antic Death, which laugh'st us here to scorn,
Anon, from thy insulting tyranny,
Coupled in bonds of perpetuity,
Two Talbots wingéd through the lither sky,
In thy despite shall scape mortality.—
O thou, whose wounds become hard-favoured death,
Speak to thy father ere thou yield thy breath!
Brave death by speaking, whether he will or no;
Imagine him a Frenchman and thy foe.—
Poor boy! he smiles, methinks, as who should say,
Had Death been French, then Death had died to-day.
Come, come and lay him in his father's arms;
My spirit can no longer bear these harms.—
Soldiers, adieu! I have what I would have,
Now my old arms are young John Talbot's grave.   [*Dies*

Enter CHARLES, ALENÇON, BURGUNDY, BASTARD,
LA PUCELLE, *and forces*

Char.   Had York and Somerset brought rescue in,
We should have found a bloody day of this.
    Bast.   How the young whelp of Talbot's, raging-wood,

Did flesh his puny sword in Frenchmen's blood!
  Puc. Once I encountered him, and thus I said:
'Thou maiden youth, be vanquished by a maid;'
But, with a proud majestical high scorn,
He answered thus: 'Young Talbot was not born
To be the pillage of a giglot wench.'
So, rushing in the bowels of the French,
He left me proudly, as unworthy fight.
  Bur. Doubtless he would have made a noble knight.
See, where he lies inhearséd in the arms
Of the most bloody nurser of his harms!
  Bast. Hew them to pieces, hack their bones asunder,
Whose life was England's glory, Gallia's wonder.
  Char. O, no, forbear! for that which we have fled
During the life, let us not wrong it dead.

Enter Sir William Lucy, *attended; Herald of the
French preceding*

  Lucy. Herald, conduct me to the Dauphin's tent,
To know who hath obtained the glory of the day.
  Char. On what submissive message art thou sent?
  Lucy. Submission, Dauphin! 't is a mere French word;
We English warriors wot not what it means.
I come to know what prisoners thou hast ta'en
And to survey the bodies of the dead.
  Char. For prisoners ask'st thou! hell our prison is.
But tell me whom thou seekest.
  Lucy. But where 's the great Alcides of the field,
Valiant Lord Talbot, Earl of Shrewsbury,
Created for his rare success in arms:
Great Earl of Washford, Waterford, and Valence;
Lord Talbot of Goodrig and Urchinfield,
Lord Strange of Blackmere, Lord Verdun of Alton,
Lord Cromwell of Wingfield, Lord Furnival of Sheffield,
The thrice-victorious Lord of Falconbridge;
Knight of the noble order of Saint George,
Worthy Saint Michael, and the Golden Fleece;
Great Marshal to Henry the Sixth
Of all his wars within the realm of France?
  Puc. Here is a silly stately style indeed!
The Turk, that two and fifty kingdoms hath,
Writes not so tedious a style as this.
Him that thou magnifiest with all these titles,
Stinking and fly-blown, lies here at our feet.
  Lucy. Is Talbot slain, the Frenchmen's only scourge,
Your kingdom's terror and black Nemesis?
O, were mine eyeballs into bullets turned,
That I in rage might shoot them at your face
O, that I could but call these dead to life!

It were enough to fright the realm of France.
Were but his picture left amongst you here,
It would amaze the proudest of you all.
Give me their bodies, that I may bear them hence
And give them burial as beseems their worth.
   Puc.   I think this upstart is old Talbot's ghost,
He speaks with such a proud commanding spirit.
For God's sake, let him have 'em; to keep them here,
They would but stink, and putrefy the air.
   Char.   Go, take their bodies hence.
   Lucy.   I'll bear them hence; but from their ashes shall
     be reared
A phœnix that shall make all France afeard.
   Char.   So we be rid of them, do with them what thou
     wilt.—
And now to Paris, in this conquering vein;
All will be ours, now bloody Talbot's slain.   *[Exeunt*

ACT FIVE

Scene I.—London. The Palace

Sennet. Enter King, Gloster, *and* Exeter

   King.   Have you perused the letters from the pope,
The emperor, and the Earl of Armagnac?
   Glo.   I have, my lord, and their intent is this:
They humbly sue unto your excellence
To have a godly peace concluded of
Between the realms of England and of France.
   King.   How doth your grace affect their motion?
   Glo.   Well, my good lord; and as the only means
To stop effusion of our Christian blood
And stablish quietness on every side.
   King.   Ay, marry, uncle; for I always thought
It was both impious and unnatural
That such immanity and bloody strife
Should reign among professors of one faith.
   Glo.   Beside, my lord, the sooner to effect
And surer bind this knot of amity,
The Earl of Armagnac, near kin to Charles,
A man of great authority in France,
Proffers his only daughter to your grace
In marriage, with a large and sumptuous dowry.
   King.   Marriage, uncle? alas, my years are young!
And fitter is my study and my books
Than wanton dalliance with a paramour.
Yet call the ambassadors; and, as you please,

So let them have their answers every one,
I shall be well content with any choice
Tends to God's glory and my country's weal.

Enter WINCHESTER *in Cardinal's habit, a Legate, and two
Ambassadors*

 Exe. What! is my Lord of Winchester installed,
And called unto a cardinal's degree?
Then I perceive that will be verified
Henry the Fifth did sometime prophesy,—
' If once he come to be a cardinal,
He'll make his cap co-equal with the crown.'
 King. My lords ambassadors, your several suits
Have been considered and debated on.
Your purpose is good both and reasonable;
And therefore are we certainly resolved
To draw conditions of a friendly peace,
Which by my Lord of Winchester we mean
Shall be transported presently to France.
 Glo. And for the proffer of my lord your master,
I have informed his highness so at large
As, liking of the lady's virtuous gifts,
Her beauty, and the value of her dower,
He doth intend she shall be England's queen.
 King. In argument and proof of which contract,
Bear her this jewel, pledge of my affection.—
And so, my lord Protector, see them guarded
And safely brought to Dover, where inshipped
Commit them to the fortunes of the sea.
        [Exeunt all but Winchester and Legate
 Win. Stay, my lord legate; you shall first receive
The sum of money which I promiséd
Should be delivered to his holiness
For clothing me in these grave ornaments.
 Leg. I will attend upon your lordship's leisure.
 Win. [*Aside*] Now Winchester will not submit, I trow,
Or be inferior to the proudest peer.
Humphrey of Gloster, thou shalt well perceive
That, neither in birth or for authority,
The bishop will be overborne by thee.
I'll either make thee stoop and bend thy knee,
Or sack this country with a mutiny.   *[Exeunt*

SCENE II.—France. Plains in Anjou

Enter CHARLES, BURGUNDY, ALENÇON, BASTARD, REIGNIER,
LA PUCELLE, *and forces*

    Char.   These news, my lords, may cheer our drooping
spirits.
'T is said the stout Parisians do revolt
And turn again unto the warlike French.
    Alen.   Then march to Paris, royal Charles of France,
And keep not back your powers in dalliance.
    Puc.   Peace be amongst them, if they turn to us;
Else, ruin combat with their palaces!

Enter Scout

    Scout.   Success unto our valiant general,
And happiness to his accomplices!
    Char.   What tidings send our scouts? I prithee, speak.
    Scout.   The English army, that divided was
Into two parts, is now conjoined in one,
And means to give you battle presently.
    Char.   Somewhat too sudden, sirs, the warning is;
But we will presently provide for them.
    Bur.   I trust the ghost of Talbot is not there;
Now he is gone, my lord, you need not fear.
    Puc.   Of all base passions, fear is most accursed.—
Command the conquest, Charles, it shall be thine,
Let Henry fret and all the world repine.
    Char.   Then on, my lords; and France be fortunate!
                            [*Exeunt*

SCENE III.—Before Angiers

Alarum. Excursions. Enter LA PUCELLE

    Puc.   The Regent conquers, and the Frenchmen fly.—
Now help, ye charming spells and periapts;
And ye choice spirits that admonish me
And give me signs of future accidents.   [*Thunder*
You speedy helpers, that are substitutes
Under the lordly monarch of the north,
Appear and aid me in this enterprise.—

Enter Fiends

This speedy and quick appearance argues proof
Of your accustomed diligence to me.
Now, ye familiar spirits, that are called
Out of the powerful regions under earth,
Help me this once, that France may get the field.
                       [*They walk, and speak not*

O, hold me not with silence over-long!
Where I was wont to feed you with my blood,
I'll lop a member off and give it you
In earnest of a further benefit,
So you do condescend to help me now.—
                   [They hang their heads
No hope to have redress?—My body shall
Pay recompense, if you will grant my suit.
                   [They shake their heads
Cannot my body nor blood-sacrifice
Entreat you by your wonted furtherance?
Then take my soul, my body, soul and all,
Before that England give the French the foil.—
                         [They depart
See, they forsake me! Now the time is come
That France must vail her lofty-pluméd crest
And let her head fall into England's lap.
My ancient incantations are too weak,
And hell too strong for me to buckle with.
Now, France, thy glory droopeth to the dust.   *[Exit*

Excursions. Re-enter La Pucelle *fighting hand to hand
  with* York: La Pucelle *is taken. The French fly*

  York. Damsel of France, I think I have you fast;
Unchain your spirits now with spelling charms,
And try if they can gain your liberty.—
A goodly prize, fit for the devil's grace!
See, how the ugly wench doth bend her brows,
As if with Circe she would change my shape!
  Puc. Changed to a worser shape thou canst not be.
  York. O, Charles the Dauphin is a proper man;
No shape but his can please your dainty eye.
  Puc. A plaguing mischief light on Charles and thee!
And may ye both be suddenly surprised
By bloody hands, in sleeping on your beds!
  York. Fell banning hag, enchantress, hold thy tongue!
  Puc. I prithee, give me leave to curse awhile.
  York. Curse, miscreant, when thou comest to the stake.
                         [Exeunt

Alarum. Enter Suffolk, *with* Margaret *in his hand*

  Suf. Be what thou wilt, thou art my prisoner.
                     [Gazes on her
O fairest beauty, do not fear nor fly!
For I will touch thee but with reverent hands;
I kiss these fingers for eternal peace,
And lay them gently on thy tender side.
Who art thou? say, that I may honour thee.

Mar. Margaret my name, and daughter to a king,
The King of Naples, whosoe'er thou art.
Suf. An earl I am, and Suffolk am I called.
Be not offended, nature's miracle,
Thou art allotted to be ta'en by me;
So doth the swan her downy cygnets save,
Keeping them prisoner underneath her wings.
Yet, if this servile usage once offend,
Go and be free again as Suffolk's friend.   [*She is going*
O, stay!—I have no power to let her pass!
My hand would free her, but my heart says no.—
As plays the sun upon the glassy streams,
Twinkling another counterfeited beam,
So seems this gorgeous beauty to mine eyes.
Fain would I woo her, yet I dare not speak;
I'll call for pen and ink, and write my mind.
Fie, de la Pole! disable not thyself;
Hast not a tongue? is she not here?
Wilt thou be daunted at a woman's sight?
Ay, beauty's princely majesty is such,
Confounds the tongue and makes the senses rough.
Mar. Say, Earl of Suffolk—if thy name be so—
What ransom must I pay before I pass?
For I perceive I am thy prisoner.
Suf. How canst thou tell she will deny thy suit,
Before thou make a trial of her love?
Mar. Why speak'st thou not? what ransom must I pay?
Suf. She's beautiful and therefore to be wooed;
She is a woman, therefore to be won.
Mar. Wilt thou accept of ransom? yea, or no.
Suf. Fond man, remember that thou hast a wife;
Then how can Margaret be thy paramour?
Mar. I were best leave him, for he will not hear.
Suf. There all is marred; there lies a cooling card.
Mar. He talks at random; sure, the man is mad.
Suf. And yet a dispensation may be had.
Mar. And yet I would that you would answer me.
Suf. I'll win this lady Margaret. For whom?
Why, for my king; tush, that's a wooden thing!
Mar. He talks of wood; it is some carpenter.
Suf. Yet so my fancy may be satisfied,
And peace establishéd between these realms.
But there remains a scruple in that too;
For though her father be the King of Naples,
Duke of Anjou and Maine, yet is he poor,
And our nobility will scorn the match.
Mar. Hear ye, captain, are you not at leisure?
Suf. It shall be so, disdain they ne'er so much;
Henry is useful and will quickly yield.—
Madam, I have a secret to reveal.

Mar.   What though I be enthralled? he seems a knight,
And will not any way dishonour me.
   Suf.   Lady, vouchsafe to listen what I say.
   Mar.   Perhaps I shall be rescued by the French,
And then I need not crave courtesy.
   Suf.   Sweet madam, give me hearing in a cause—
   Mar.   Tush, women have been captivate ere now.
   Suf.   Lady, wherefore talk you so?
   Mar.   I cry you mercy, 't is but quid for quo.
   Suf.   Say, gentle princess, would you not suppose
Your bondage happy, to be made a queen?
   Mar.   To be a queen in bondage is more vile
Than is a slave in base servility,
For princes should be free.
   Suf.   And so shall you,
If happy England's royal king be free.
   Mar.   Why, what concerns his freedom unto me?
   Suf.   I'll undertake to make thee Henry's queen,
To put a golden sceptre in thy hand
If thou wilt condescend to be my—
   Mar.   What?
   Suf.   His love.
   Mar.   I am unworthy to be Henry's wife.
   Suf.   No, gentle madam; I unworthy am
To woo so fair a dame to be his wife,
And have no portion in the choice myself.
How say you madam, are ye so content?
   Mar.   An if my father please, I am content.
   Suf.   Then call our captains and our colours forth.
And, madam, at your father's castle walls
We'll crave a parley, to confer with him.—

A parley sounded.   Enter REIGNIER *on the walls*

See, Reignier, see, thy daughter prisoner!
   Reig.   To whom?
   Suf.   To me.
   Reig.   Suffolk, what remedy?
I am a soldier and unapt to weep
Or to exclaim on fortune's fickleness.
   Suf.   Yes, there is remedy enough, my lord;
Consent, and for thy honour give consent,
Thy daughter shall be wedded to my king,
Whom I with pain have wooed and won thereto,
And this her easy-held imprisonment
Hath gained thy daughter princely liberty.
   Reig.   Speaks Suffolk as he thinks?
   Suf.   Fair Margaret knows
That Suffolk doth not flatter, face, or feign.

Reig.   Upon thy princely warrant, I descend
To give thee answer of thy just demand.
                                   [*Exit from the walls*
   Suf.   And here I will expect thy coming.

Trumpets sound.   Enter REIGNIER, *below*

   Reig.   Welcome, brave earl, into our territories;
Command in Anjou what your honour pleases.
   Suf.   Thanks, Reignier, happy for so sweet a child,
Fit to be made companion with a king.
What answer makes your grace unto my suit?
   Reig.   Since thou dost deign to woo her little worth
To be the princely bride of such a lord,
Upon condition I may quietly
Enjoy mine own, the county Main and Anjou,
Free from oppression or the stroke of war,
My daughter shall be Henry's, if he please.
   Suf.   That is her ransom, I deliver her;
And those two counties I will undertake
Your grace shall well and quietly enjoy.
   Reig.   And I again, in Henry's royal name,
As deputy unto that gracious king,
Give thee her hand, for sign of plighted faith.
   Suf.   Reignier of France, I give thee kingly thanks,
Because this is in traffic of a king.——
[*Aside*]   And yet, methinks, I could be well content
To be mine own attorney in this case.
I'll over then to England with this news,
And make this marriage to be solemnised.——
So farewell, Reignier; set this diamond safe
In golden palaces, as it becomes.
   Reig.   I do embrace thee, as I would embrace
The Christian prince, King Henry, were he here.
   Mar.   Farewell, my lord; good wishes, praise, and
          prayers
Shall Suffolk ever have of Margaret.   [*Going*
   Suf.   Farewell, sweet madam; but hark you, Margaret,
No princely commendations to my king?
   Mar.   Such commendations as become a maid,
A virgin, and his servant, say to him.
   Suf.   Words sweetly placed and modestly directed.
But, madam, I must trouble you again;
No loving token to his majesty?
   Mar.   Yes, my good lord, a pure unspotted heart,
Never yet taint with love, I send the king.
   Suf.   And this withal.   [*Kisses her*
   Mar.   That for thyself; I will not so presume
To send such peevish tokens to a king.
                         [*Exeunt Reignier and Margaret*

Suf. O, wert thou for myself!—But, Suffolk, stay!
Thou mayst not wander in that labyrinth;
There Minotaurs and ugly treasons lurk.
Solicit Henry with her wondrous praise;
Bethink thee on her virtues that surmount,
And natural graces that extinguish art;
Repeat their semblance often on the seas,
That, when thou com'st to kneel at Henry's feet,
Thou may'st bereave him of his wits with wonder. [*Exit*

SCENE IV.—Camp of the DUKE of YORK in Anjou

Enter YORK, WARWICK, *and others*

York. Bring forth that sorceress condemned to burn.

Enter LA PUCELLE, *guarded, and a Shepherd*

Shep. Ah, Joan, this kills thy father's heart outright!
How I have sought every country far and near,
And, now it is my chance to find thee out,
Must I behold thy timeless cruel death?
Ah, Joan, sweet daughter Joan, I'll die with thee!
Puc. Decrepit miser! base ignoble wretch!
I am descended of a gentler blood;
Thou art no father nor no friend of mine.
Shep. Out, out!—My lords, an please you, 't is not so;
I did beget her, all the parish knows:
Her mother liveth yet, can testify
She was the first fruit of my bachelorship.
War. Graceless! wilt thou deny thy parentage?
York. This argues what her kind of life hath been,
Wicked and vile; and so her death concludes.
Shep. Fie, Joan, that thou wilt be so obstacle!
God knows thou art a collop of my flesh,
And for thy sake have I shed many a tear;
Deny me not, I prithee, gentle Joan.
Puc. Peasant, avaunt! You have suborned this man,
Of purpose to obscure my noble birth.
Shep. 'T is true, I gave a noble to the priest
The morn that I was wedded to her mother.—
Kneel down and take my blessing, good my girl.—
Wilt thou not stoop? Now cursèd be the time
Of thy nativity! I would the milk
Thy mother gave thee when thou suck'dst her breast,
Had been a little ratsbane for thy sake!
Or else when thou didst keep thy lambs afield,
I wish some ravenous wolf had eaten thee!
Dost thou deny thy father, cursèd drab?—
O, burn her, burn her! hanging is too good.   [*Exit*

York.   Take her away; for she hath lived too long,
To fill the world with vicious qualities.
Puc.   First, let me tell you whom you have condemned:
Not me begotten of a shepherd swain,
But issued from the progeny of kings;
Virtuous and holy; chosen from above,
By inspiration of celestial grace,
To work exceeding miracles on earth.
I never had to do with wicked spirits;
But you, that are polluted with your lusts,
Stained with the guiltless blood of innocents,
Corrupt and tainted with a thousand vices,
Because you want the grace that others have,
You judge it straight a thing impossible
To compass wonders but by help of devils.
No, misconceivéd! Joan of Arc hath been
A virgin from her tender infancy,
Chaste and immaculate in very thought;
Whose maiden blood, thus rigorously effused,
Will cry for vengeance at the gates of heaven.
York.   Ay, ay.—Away with her to execution!
War.   And hark ye, sirs: because she is a maid,
Spare for no faggots, let there be enow;
Place barrels of pitch upon the fatal stake,
That so her torture may be shortenéd.
Puc.   Will nothing turn your unrelenting hearts?—
Then, Joan, discover thine infirmity
That warranteth by law thy privilege.—
I am with child, ye bloody homicides;
Murther not then the fruit within my womb,
Although ye hale me to a violent death.
York.   Now heaven forfend! the holy maid with child!
War.   The greatest miracle that e'er ye wrought!
Is all your strict preciseness come to this?
York.   She and the Dauphin have been juggling;
I did imagine what would be her refuge.
War.   Well, go to; we will have no bastards live,
Especially since Charles must father it.
Puc.   You are deceived; my child is none of his;
It was Alençon that enjoyed my love.
York.   Alençon! that notorious Machiavel!
It dies, an if it had a thousand lives.
Puc.   O, give me leave, I have deluded you:
'T was neither Charles nor yet the duke I named,
But Reignier, king of Naples, that prevailed.
War.   A married man! that's most intolerable.
York.   Why, here's a girl! I think she knows not well,
There were so many, whom she may accuse.
War.   It's sign she hath been liberal and free.
York.   And yet, forsooth, she is a virgin pure.—

Strumpet, thy words condemn thy brat and thee;
Use no entreaty, for it is in vain.
    Puc.   Then lead me hence;—with whom I leave my
        curse.
May never glorious sun reflex his beams
Upon the country where you make abode,
But darkness and the gloomy shade of death
Environ you, till mischief and despair
Drive you to break your necks or hang yourselves!
                                [Exit, guarded
    York.   Break thou in pieces and consume to ashes,
Thou foul accursèd minister of hell!

    Enter CARDINAL BEAUFORT, BISHOP OF WINCHESTER,
                    attended

    Car.   Lord Regent, I do greet your excellence
With letters of commission from the king.
For know, my lords, the states of Christendom,
Moved with remorse of these outrageous broils,
Have earnestly implored a general peace
Betwixt our nation and the aspiring French;
And here at hand the Dauphin and his train
Approacheth, to confer about some matter.
    York.   Is all our travail turned to this effect?
After the slaughter of so many peers,
So many captains, gentlemen, and soldiers,
That in this quarrel have been overthrown
And sold their bodies for their country's benefit,
Shall we at last conclude effeminate peace?
Have we not lost most part of all the towns,
By treason, falsehood, and by treachery,
Our great progenitors had conquerèd?—
O, Warwick, Warwick! I foresee with grief
The utter loss of all the realm of France.
    War.   Be patient, York; if we conclude a peace,
It shall be with such strict and severe covenants
As little shall the Frenchmen gain thereby.

    Enter CHARLES, ALENÇON, BASTARD, REIGNIER, *and others*

    Char.   Since, lords of England, it is thus agreed
That peaceful truce shall be proclaimed in France,
We come to be informèd by yourselves
What the conditions of that league must be.
    York.   Speak, Winchester; for boiling choler chokes
The hollow passage of my prisoned voice,
By sight of these our baleful enemies.
    Car.   Charles, and the rest, it is enacted thus:
That, in regard King Henry gives consent,

Of mere compassion and of lenity,
To ease your country of distressful war,
And suffer you to breathe in fruitful peace,
You shall become true liegemen to his crown;
And, Charles, upon condition thou wilt swear
To pay him tribute, and submit thyself,
Thou shalt be placed as viceroy under him
And still enjoy thy regal dignity.
    Alen. Must he be then as shadow of himself?
Adorn his temples with a coronet,
And yet, in substance and authority,
Retain but privilege of a private man?
This proffer is absurd and reasonless.
    Char. 'T is known already that I am possessed
With more than half the Gallian territories,
And therein reverenced for their lawful king;
Shall I, for lucre of the rest unvanquished,
Detract so much from that prerogative,
As to be called but viceroy of the whole?
No, lord ambassador, I'll rather keep
That which I have than, coveting for more,
Be cast from possibility of all.
    York. Insulting Charles! hast thou by secret means
Used intercession to obtain a league,
And, now the matter grows to compromise,
Stand'st thou aloof upon comparison?
Either accept the title thou usurp'st,
Of benefit proceeding from our king
And not of any challenge of desert,
Or we will plague thee with incessant wars.
    Reig. [*Aside to Charles*] My lord, you do not well in
        obstinacy
To cavil in the course of this contráct:
If once it be neglected, ten to one
We shall not find like opportunity.
    Alen. [*Aside to Charles*] To say the truth, it is your
        policy
To save your subjects from such massacre
And ruthless slaughters as are daily seen
By our proceeding in hostility;
And therefore take this compact of a truce,
Although you break it when your pleasure serves.
    War. How say'st thou, Charles? shall our condition
        stand?
    Char. It shall;
Only reserved, you claim no interest
In any of our towns of garrison.
    York. Then swear allegiance to his majesty
As thou art knight, never to disobey
Nor be rebellious to the crown of England,

Thou, nor thy nobles, to the crown of England.—
> [*Charles and the rest give tokens of fealty*

So, now dismiss your army when ye please;
Hang up your ensigns, let your drums be still,
For here we entertain a solemn peace.   [*Exeunt*

SCENE V.—London. The Palace

Enter SUFFOLK *in conference with the* KING, GLOSTER *and*
EXETER *following*

King. Your wondrous rare description, noble earl,
Of beauteous Margaret hath astonished me.
Her virtues gracéd with external gifts
Do breed love's settled passions in my heart;
And like as rigour of tempestuous gusts
Provokes the mightiest hulk against the tide,
So am I driven by breath of her renown
Either to suffer shipwreck or arrive
Where I may have fruition of her love.
    Suf. Tush, my good lord, this superficial tale,
Is but a preface of her worthy praise;
The chief perfections of that lovely dame,   ᠎
Had I sufficient skill to utter them,
Would make a volume of enticing lines,
Able to ravish any dull conceit:
And, which is more, she is not so divine,
So full-replete with choice of all delights,
But with as humble lowliness of mind
She is content to be at your command,—
Command, I mean, of virtuous chaste intents,
To love and honour Henry as her lord.
    King. And otherwise will Henry ne'er presume.—
Therefore, my lord Protector, give consent
That Margaret may be England's royal queen.
    Glo. So should I give consent to flatter sin.
You know, my lord, your highness is betrothed
Unto another lady of esteem;
How shall we then dispense with that contract,
And not deface your honour with reproach?
    Suf. As doth a ruler with unlawful oaths:
Or one that, at a triumph having vowed
To try his strength, forsaketh yet the lists
By reason of his adversary's odds.
A poor earl's daughter is unequal odds,
And therefore may be broke without offence.
    Glo. Why, what, I pray, is Margaret more than that?
Her father is no better than an earl,
Although in glorious titles he excel.

Suf.   Yes, my lord, her father is a king,
The King of Naples and Jerusalem,
And of such great authority in France
As his alliance will confirm our peace
And keep the Frenchmen in allegiance.
   Glo.   And so the Earl of Armagnac may do,
Because he is near kinsman unto Charles.
   Exe.   Beside, his wealth doth warrant liberal dower,
Where Reignier sooner will receive than give.
   Suf.   A dower, my lords! disgrace not so your king,
That he should be so abject, base, and poor,
To choose for wealth and not for perfect love.
Henry is able to enrich his queen,
And not to seek a queen to make him rich;
So worthless peasants bargain for their wives,
As market-men for oxen, sheep, or horse.
Marriage is a matter of more worth
Than to be dealt in by attorneyship:
Not whom we will, but whom his grace affects,
Must be companion of his nuptial bed:
And therefore, lords, since he affects her most,
It most of all these reasons bindeth us,
In our opinions she should be preferred.
For what is wedlock forcéd but a hell,
An age of discord and continual strife?
Whereas that the contráry bringeth bliss,
And is a pattern of celestial peace.
Whom should we match with Henry, being a king,
But Margaret, that is daughter to a king?
Her peerless feature, joinéd with her birth,
Approves her fit for none but for a king.
Her valiant courage and undaunted spirit,
More than in women commonly is seen,
Will answer our hope in issue of a king;
For Henry, son unto a conqueror,
Is likely to beget more conquerors
If with a lady of so high resolve
As is fair Margaret he be linked in love.
Then yield, my lord, and here conclude with me
That Margaret shall be queen, and none but she.
   King.   Whether it be through force of your report,
My noble lord of Suffolk, or for that
My tender youth was never yet attaint
With any passion of inflaming love,
I cannot tell; but this I am assured,
I feel such sharp dissension in my breast,
Such fierce alarums both of hope and fear,
As I am sick with working of my thoughts.
Take, therefore, shipping; post, my lord, to France;
Agree to any covenants, and procure

That Lady Margaret do vouchsafe to come
To cross the seas to England and be crowned
King Henry's faithful and anointed queen.
For your expenses and sufficient charge,
Among the people gather up a tenth.
Be gone, I say; for till you do return,
I rest perplexéd with a thousand cares.—
And you, good uncle, banish all offence:
If you do censure me by what you were,
Not what you are, I know it will excuse
This sudden execution of my will.
And so, conduct me where, from company,
I may revolve and ruminate my grief.   [*Exit*
   Glos.   Ay, grief, I fear me, both at first and last.
                         [*Exeunt Gloster and Exeter*
   Suf.   Thus Suffolk hath prevailed; and thus he goes,
As did the youthful Paris once to Greece,
With hope to find the like event in love,
But prosper better than the Trojan did.
Margaret shall now be queen, and rule the king;
But I will rule both her, the king, and realm.   [*Exit*

THE PEEBLES CLASSIC LIBRARY